UNIVERSITY OF MASSACHUSETTS OCCASIONAL PAPERS 36

PAPERS IN THEORETICAL AND COMPUTATIONAL PHONOLOGY

2007

EDITED BY

MICHAEL BECKER

Published by
GLSA
(Graduate Linguistic Student Association)
Department of Linguistics
South College
University of Massachusetts
Amherst, MA 01003-7130
U.S.A.

glsa@linguist.umass.edu
http://www.umass.edu/linguist/GLSA

Cover design: Jan Anderssen

ISBN: 1-4196-7888-4

TABLE OF CONTENTS

Acknowledgements

The editor wishes to thank all the people who contributed to making this volume possible. First, to the South College contributors, who were all kind enough to deliver their papers expediently, helping make this volume see the light of day less than nine months after its conception. Special thanks go to Jason Riggle and his coauthors for their guest contribution.

The editor would also like to thank the kind GLSA officers who helped with producing this volume, Jan Anderssen, Amy Rose Deal, and Jesse Harris.

OT-Help User Guide

Michael Becker and Joe Pater

University of Massachusetts, Amherst

1. Introduction

OT-Help (Becker, Pater & Potts 2007) is a free open-source Java-based program that aids research in Optimality Theory (OT, Prince and Smolensky 1993/2004) and its cousin, Harmonic Grammar (HG, Smolensky and Legendre 2006) OT-Help will find a constraint ranking or weighting consistent with the data provided by the user, if one exists. The solution can be displayed either in a standard tableau format, or as a comparative tableau (Prince 2002a). OT-Help will also find the set of possible languages in both OT and HG, given the user's set of constraints. Typology can also be explored interactively by selecting different sets of optima.

In the following, we provide a guide to the use of OT-Help, as well as a brief introduction to the theory underlying it, especially with respect to HG, which is less well known than OT.

In both OT and in the version of HG we are working with, a language is a set of input-output pairs that are optimal under some ranking or weighting of a set of constraints. As the number of constraints, inputs, and candidates increases, it becomes increasingly difficult to find by hand a ranking for an intended set of optima, and especially to find by hand the set of possible languages. The need for an automated means of finding rankings and calculating typologies was recognized early on in the development of OT, and been met by OT-Soft (Hayes, Tesar and Zuraw 2003) and Praat (Boersma and Weenink 2007). With HG's weighted constraints, these problems are multiplied. OT-Help is the first tool that allows a user to quickly calculate the set of languages generated by a given set of weighted constraints.

2. Ranking conditions and weighting conditions

In (1), we present a tableau for an input /kata/ with two output candidates: the intended optimum, or 'winner' (káta) has a trochee, or left-headed foot, and the sub-optimal 'loser'

Michael Becker (ed.): Papers in theoretical and computational phonology. University of Massachusetts Occasional Papers in Linguistics 36, 1-12.
GLSA Amherst.

(katá) has an iambic, right-headed foot. There are two constraints: IAMB, which demands that all feet be right-headed, and TROCHEE, which demands that all feet be left-headed.

(1)

/kata/		IAMB	TROCHEE
→	a. káta	*	
	b. katá		*

We see that the constraint TROCHEE assigns no violation marks to the winner and one violation mark to the loser, or in other words, TROCHEE prefers the winner to the loser. The opposite is true of IAMB, which prefers the loser. The same information can be represented in a comparative tableau (Prince 2002a), where W means "winner-preferring" and L means "loser-preferring".

(2)

/kata/	IAMB	TROCHEE
→ káta ~ katá	L	W

A necessary property of a ranking that produces the intended result is that every loser-preferring constraint be dominated by some winner-preferring constraint (Prince and Smolensky 1993/2004, Tesar and Smolensky 1998, Prince 2002a). In our case, IAMB must be dominated by TROCHEE, so the ranking we want is TROCHEE >> IAMB.

Prince and Smolensky (1993/2004: 236) consider (and reject) an alternative formulation of OT that replaces constraint ranking with weighting, as in Harmonic Grammar (HG; Smolensky and Legendre 2006). For a review of subsequent research pursuing this alternative, and a comparison with OT, see Pater, Bhatt and Potts (2007a). We use the translation of OT to HG introduced in Legendre, Sorace and Smolensky (2006). Violation marks are translated into negative integers, and a candidate's *harmony* is calculated by multiplying its violation score on each constraint by that constraint's weight, and summing these products. The candidate with the maximal harmony is optimal. Following Prince (2002b) and Pater et al. (2007a), we restrict weights to positive reals. OT-Help also allows users to input positive constraint satisfaction scores, and to fix the minimal values of constraint weights at zero (see Keller 2006), or any other non-negative value.

Returning to our example, the harmony of *káta* is the weight of IAMB times -1, plus the weight of TROCHEE times zero, which equals the negative weight of IAMB (3). The similar calculation for *katá* is shown in (4).

(3) $H(\text{káta}) = w(\text{IAMB}) \cdot -1 + w(\text{TROCHEE}) \cdot 0 = -1 \cdot w(\text{IAMB})$

(4) $H(\text{katá}) = w(\text{IAMB}) \cdot 0 + w(\text{TROCHEE}) \cdot -1 = -1 \cdot w(\text{TROCHEE})$

(5)

/kata/			IAMB	TROCHEE
→	a.	káta	-1	
	b.	katá		-1

Since *káta* is the winner, its harmony must be higher than the harmony of *katá* (6a), which entails that the weight of IAMB must be smaller than the weight of TROCHEE (6c):

(6) a. $H(\text{káta}) > H(\text{katá})$
     b. $-1 \cdot w(\text{IAMB}) > -1 \cdot w(\text{TROCHEE})$
     c. $w(\text{IAMB}) < w(\text{TROCHEE})$

Statements of the form in (6c) are HG's weighting conditions, which are parallel to OT's Elementary Ranking Conditions (Prince 2002a). We extend the notion of comparative tableau to HG, as in (7). In an HG comparative tableau, the numerical difference between the winner and the loser is indicated by a positive score for a winner-preferring constraint and a negative score for a loser-preferring constraint. Given a weighting that correctly chooses the optima, the sum of the weighted differences will be positive.

(7)

/kata/		IAMB	TROCHEE
→	káta ~ katá	-1	+1

Of the infinitely many sets of weights that achieve the intended result, we chose to set the weight of IAMB at 1 and the weight of TROCHEE at 2. The outcome is shown below, where the Harmony of each candidate is displayed in the rightmost column:

(8)

	Weights:	1	2	
/kata/		IAMB	TROCHEE	*H*
→ a.	káta	-1		-1
b.	katá		-1	-2

The hamony of *káta* is -1, which is higher than the harmony of *katá*, so *káta* is chosen as optimal. Note that if the winner-loser difference scores in (7) are multiplied by the weights in (8) and then summed, the result is indeed positive (+1).

To illustrate a somewhat more complicated case, we add another constraint, and another input with two candidates.

(9)

/kata/			IAMB	TROCHEE	*STRESS/HI
→	a.	káta	-1		
	b.	katá		-1	
/pika/					
	a.	píka	-1		-1
→	b.	piká		-1	

*STRESS/HI assigns a violation to a stressed high vowel, such as first vowel in *píka*. The question is whether there is a weighting that will pick a trochee as optimal for /kata/, but an iamb as optimal for /pika/, as in the indicated optima in (9).

To make *káta* win over *katá*, the weight of IAMB must be smaller than the weight of TROCHEE, as we've just seen. Now we can add the weighting conditions for the next tableau, calculated in (10-12).

(10) H(píka) $= w(\text{IAMB})\bullet\text{-}1 + w(\text{TROCHEE})\bullet0 + w(\text{*STRESS/HI})\bullet\text{-}1$
                              $= \text{-}w(\text{IAMB}) \text{-}w(\text{*STRESS/HI})$

(11) H(piká) $= w(\text{IAMB})\bullet0 + w(\text{TROCHEE})\bullet\text{-}1 + w(\text{*STRESS/HI})\bullet0$
                              $= \text{-}w(\text{TROCHEE})$

(12) H(piká) $>$ H(píka)
          $\text{-}w(\text{TROCHEE}) > \text{-}w(\text{IAMB}) \text{-}w(\text{*STRESS/HI})$
          $w(\text{TROCHEE}) < w(\text{IAMB}) + w(\text{*STRESS/HI})$

Combining the weighting conditions from (6c) and (12), we arrive at two inequalities that need to be satisfied:

(13) $w(\text{IAMB}) < w(\text{TROCHEE})$
          $w(\text{TROCHEE}) < w(\text{IAMB}) + w(\text{*STRESS/HI})$

Can we assign weights that will satisfy both? While the answer is perhaps less obvious than in the last case, one weighting that works is $w(\text{IAMB}) = 1$, $w(\text{TROCHEE}) = 2$, $w(\text{*STRESS/HI}) = 2$. The tableau below shows that these weights assign the highest harmony scores to the intended winners:

(14)

Weights:		1	2	2	
/kata/		IAMB	TROCHEE	*STRESS/HI	H
→ a.	káta	-1			-1
b.	katá		-1		-2
/pika/					
a.	píka	-1		-1	-3
→ b.	piká		-1		-2

We can also examine the possibility that in some language, *píka* would win over *piká*, and *katá* over *káta*. Is there a weighting of our constraints that would produce this result? The required weighting conditions are below:

(15) H(káta) $<$ H(katá)
          $\text{-}1\bullet w(\text{IAMB}) > \text{-}1\bullet w(\text{TROCHEE})$
          $w(\text{IAMB}) < w(\text{TROCHEE})$

(16) H(piká) $<$ H(píka)

        $-w$(Trochee) $<$ $-w$(Iamb) $-w$(*Stress/Hi)

        w(Trochee) $>$ w(Iamb) $+$ w(*Stress/Hi)

Together, we get:

(17) w(Iamb) $>$ w(Trochee)

        w(Trochee) $>$ w(Iamb) $+$ w(*Stress/Hi)

There is no set of non-negative weights we could assign to these three constraints that would satisfy the two requirements above, so we can conclude that HG predicts the impossibility of the language above.

      For these small problems, finding correct constraint weightings is not much more difficult than finding rankings. For larger problems, however, finding out whether a set of candidates can be jointly optimal can be considerably more difficult in HG than in OT. To address this difficulty, Pater, Potts and Bhatt (2007) introduce an application of Linear Programming that returns a weighting if one exists, and indicates when no weighting of the constraints will yield the intended optima. A web-based implementation of this application is available as Potts, Becker, Bhatt and Pater (2007). OT-Help includes this implementation, and extends it to the calculation of HG typologies.

3.   Using OT-Help: The data file

OT-Help is designed to read files in an extension of Hayes et al.'s (2003) OT-Soft format. These files are easiest to create in a spreadsheet program, such as the free OpenOffice "Calc" or Microsoft Excel. To submit a file to OT-Help, it must be saved as a text file (tab separated), which can then be dropped into the OT-Help window. Files that are not plain-text OT-Soft files will be rejected. The text is read as HTML, so special characters should be entered as they would be in a regular HTML file. Unicode files will be read, but special characters will not display correctly.

      The table below shows what the tableaux in (14) looks like in OT-Soft format:

(18)

			Iamb	Trochee	*Stress/Hi
			Iamb	Trochee	*Stress/Hi
kata	káta	1	1		
	katá			1	
pika	píka		1		1
	piká	1		1	

The first column is the input column. Each new input defines the beginning of a new tableau. The next column is the candidate column. In the example above, we see two tableaux, each with one input and two candidates. The third column is the winner marking column. In this column, any non-zero number will serve to mark an intended optimum. The current version of OT-Help only allows a single optimum per tableau.

Note that under the definitions of optimality that we are working with, the optimum must be evaluated as better than all other candidates; a tie is not sufficient. Therefore, if an intended optimum has the same violation marks as another candidate, it cannot be made optimal, and OT-Help will fail to find a solution in either OT or HG.

The first two rows are constraint names. You will see that most OT-Help screens only display the names from the second line of your file, but following OT-Soft format, both lines are required. Finally, the space below the first two lines and to the right of the first three columns contains violation profiles. Again following OT-Soft format, these are inserted as positive integers, though they display in OT-Help HG tableaux as negative integers. If negative integers are entered into the OT-Soft file, they will display as positive integers in the OT-Help display, and be treated as satisfaction scores (see Legendre et al.'s 2006 discussion of 'positive HG'). Zeros may be left unspecified.

After the first portion of the input file, which follows the OT-Soft format exactly and is required by OT-Help, optional parameters may be added. This is marked by the addition of a new line, after the last tableau, that reads "[end of tableaux]".

Among the options that are already implemented in the current version of OT-Help is the "[minimal weight]" directive, which allows the specification of minimal HG weights. In the absence of user specification, a default value of 1 is assumed. To specify a default minimal value for all constraints, enter any number in the second column of the "[minimal weight]" row. To specify a minimal weight for some specific constraint, enter a number under its column.

In the example below, OT-Help will set 0.5 as the minimal weight for all constraints, and 3 as the minimal weight for TROCHEE.

(19)

			Iamb	Trochee	*Stress/Hi
			Iamb	Trochee	*Stress/Hi
kata	káta	1	1		
	katá			1	
pika	píka		1		1
	piká	1		1	
[end of tableaux]					
[minimal weight]	0.5			3	

Note that you may specify a minimal weight of zero, and this will be different from not specifying a minimum, since the default value in OT-Help is 1. This is one case where leaving a blank is different from specifying a zero.

The minimal weight values are irrelevant to OT calculations, and are ignored. In future versions of OT-Help, we expect to add other user-specifiable options, such as biases for particular constraints to be ranked or weighted higher or lower than other constraints.

4. OT-Help navigation

OT-Help opens with a welcome screen, onto which you are invited to drop your input file. If a valid file is received, and each tableau in the file specifies a unique winner, three options are offered:
-   Find all solvable languages (HG & OT)
-   HG Solution
-   OT Solution
If some tableaux in your file specify more than one winner, only the first option will be offered. We now cover the three options in turn.

4.1 Find all solvable languages (HG & OT)

This option will find all the solvable *languages* in your file. Recall that in OT, a language means a set of winners that can be made jointly optimal. In a solvable language, there is a weighting (and possibly also a ranking) of the constraints that picks out the winner from each tableau. OT-Help comes with two solvers:

-   A solver for Harmonic Grammar, written by Christopher Potts, which uses the linear programming translation from Pater et al. (2007b).
-   A solver for Optimality Theory, written by Michael Becker, which uses the Recursive Constraint Demotion algorithm (Tesar and Smolensky 1998, Prince 2002a).

When given a set of intended optima, a solver returns a verdict (solvable or not solvable), and if a solution is found, it is returned as well, in the form of a weighting or ranking of the constraints.

In calculating typologies, OT-Help follows a method introduced in Hayes et al.'s (2003) OT-Soft. It starts by looking just at the first tableau of the input file. Each candidate is tried out as a winner, and OT-Help attempts to find a weighting of the constraints that chooses that candidate as a winner. If no candidate can be winner, the search for solvable languages ends, since no matter what other tableaux specify, no winner can be chosen from the current tableau.

In the more likely event that a subset of the candidates in the first tableau are possible winners, each one of them is tried out with each of the candidates of the second tableau, looking for weightings that pick out the winners from each tableau. This continues with the remaining tableaux, until OT-Help finds the list of sets of winners that have a weighting.

Once all the languages that are solvable in HG are found, each one is passed on to the RCD module, to find a ranking of the constraints that picks out the same winners, if one exists. We can solve for HG first because any set of winners that can be made optimal in OT can also be made optimal in HG.[1] Following this method allows us to efficiently compare the results in the two theories. In future versions of OT-Help, we expect to make available the possibility of calculating just the OT typology, which could be useful for large problems.

When done, OT-Help will display all the languages it found, as shown in (20), starting with ones that are solvable in both HG and OT, and then displaying languages that are only solvable in HG. The list of languages is saved and will not be recomputed until OT-Help is closed or a new input file is accepted.

(20)   **Your input file contains 2 tableaux and a total of 4 candidates. These can potentially give rise to 4 different languages.**

An HG solution was found for 3 languages. An OT solution was found for all of them.

Languages that have an HG solution and an OT solution:

1. [kata -> káta, pika -> píka]   HG Solution   OT Solution
2. [kata -> káta, pika -> piká]   HG Solution   OT Solution
3. [kata -> katá, pika -> piká]   HG Solution   OT Solution

Make .Collection file (Praat)

Back to home page of the current file

At the bottom of the page is a link "Make .Collection file (Praat)". When this link is clicked, OT-Help will create a new text file in the same directory as the input file, which can be read by Praat (Boersma and Weenink 2007). It contains a grammar file that includes all of the tableaux, and data files for each of the sets of winners that could be rendered jointly optimal by some weighting of the HG constraints. The resulting file can be opened directly in Praat. One can then test the various learners implemented in Praat on their abilities to find a correct ranking or weighting for each of the languages.

We have used the current version of OT-Help to find the predicted typologies for very large tableaux sets (see the discussion of the Kager 2006 typology in Pater et al. 2007b). It does, however, seem to have limits on the size of problems that it can process, which we hope to overcome in future versions.

4.2   HG Solution

The HG Solution page can be reached either from an input file's home page, or from the list of solvable languages. This page starts with the verdict, as in (21), stating whether a solution was found by the HG solver or the OT solver. To make the verdict more salient,

---

[1] It is theoretically possible that the linear programming solver we use in our implementation could misclassify sets of winners as infeasible, due to floating point errors, for example, but we have yet to see an example of such an error.

the page's background color will be a light blue if a solution was found, and an alarming pink if no solution could be found.

(21) **RCD status: Solved.**

Click on a loser to make it into a winner.
LP status: solved

Min constraint weight was set to 1.0

Weights	1.0	3.0	1.0	
Input: kata	Iamb	Trochee	*StressHi	
--> káta	-1.0			Weighted total: -1.0
katá		-1.0		Weighted total: -3.0

Weights	1.0	3.0	1.0	
Input: pika	Iamb	Trochee	*StressHi	
--> píka	-1.0		-1.0	Weighted total: -2.0
piká		-1.0		Weighted total: -3.0

Switch to comparative view

Back to list of languages

Back to home page of the current file

To process a new OTSoft file, drop it in this window.

Next, if the HG solver returned a successful verdict, the weights that were found for the constraints are shown in each tableau. Note that if a tableau has any losers in it, you can click on a loser to make it into a winner. This will refresh the page, passing the new language to the HG solver. If an infeasible verdict was returned by the solver, the weights are set to their minimal default values.

The HG solver finds the minimal weighting, that is, the set of weights whose summed total is as small as possible. This minimization is bounded in two ways. The first is by the minimal constraint weights discussed above. The second is by a condition that difference between the winner's harmony and any loser must be at least 1. See Pater et al. (2007b) for further discussion.

In addition to the standard view, which is displayed by default, there is a comparative view, available from a link at the bottom of the page. Once clicked, winners and losers and displayed in pairs, and instead of raw violation scores, difference in violation scores are displayed (see also Goldwater & Johnson 2003). The last column displays the total weighted difference between winners and losers.

This view is useful, for instance, for easily spotting harmonically bounded candidates, which will have nothing but zeroes and positive numbers (if the harmonically bounded candidate is a loser) or zeroes and negative numbers (if the harmonically bounded candidate is a winner). The comparative view is also useful for spotting sets of winner-loser pairs with identical vectors of differences in violation scores. Since each winner-loser pair in such a set contributes the same information to learning, the analysis would be unchanged if only one pair in the set was kept and the rest were discarded.

4.3   OT Solution

The OT Solution page can be reached either from an input file's home page, or from the list of solvable languages. This page starts with the verdict (22), stating whether the RCD-based solver found a ranking. This verdict is also reflected in the page's background color, with blue for solvable systems and pink for insolvable ones.

(22)   **RCD status: Solved**

The ranking found: Trochee >> Iamb, *StressHi

Click on a loser to make it into a winner.

input	winner ~ loser	Trochee	Iamb	*StressHi
kata	káta ~ katá	W	L	
pika	píka ~ piká	W	L	L

Switch to standard view

Back to home page of the current file

If a ranking was found, it is reported. Otherwise, constraints that could not be ranked are listed. This list can help in identifying what inconsistent data prevented the solver from finding a ranking.

In standard view, the tableaux from the input files will be presented as entered, with asterisks for violation marks. Any losers will be clickable to make them into winners. In comparative view, winners and losers are displayed in pairs, and differences in violation marks are noted with W (winner-preferring), L (loser-preferring), or blank, following the convention in Prince (2002a). Such winner-loser pairs and their vector of W's, L's and blanks are also known as ERC's, for Elementary Ranking Conditions (Prince 2002a).

In unsolvable systems, ERC's that were left unaccounted for, i.e. that could not be used to make a ranking argument are shown in red. This is useful for finding any sources of inconsistent ranking arguments present in the data.

The comparative view also notes ERC's that have at least one L but no W's, pointing out that with such an ERC in the set of tableaux, no ranking could be found. Conversely, ERC's that don't have any L in them are removed from the list of ERC's for redundancy. Finally, only one from any set of identical ERC's will be kept in the list of ERC's, to avoid redundancy.

5. Conclusions

We hope that OT-Help will serve as a useful tool for the study of ranked and weighted constraint interaction. We also hope that its implementation as a set of java classes will facilitate the use of its components in future applications. We welcome correspondence from users with suggestions on how it could be improved in future versions, and also from developers who would like to expand on its capabilities themselves.

References

Boersma, Paul and David Weenink. 2007. *Praat: doing phonetics by computer*. Software version 4.6.09. Available at www.praat.org.

Hayes, Bruce, Bruce Tesar, and Kie Zuraw. 2003. OTSoft 2.1. software package, http://www.linguistics.ucla.edu/people/hayes/otsoft/

Goldwater, Sharon and Mark Johnson. 2003. Learning OT Constraint Rankings Using a Maximum Entropy Model. Proceedings of the Workshop on Variation within Optimality Theory, Stockholm University.

Kager, R.W.J. 2006. "Rhythmic licensing: An extended typology". In *Proceedings of the 3rd International Conference on Phonology*, 5-31. Seoul: The Phonology-Morphology Circle of Korea.

Keller, F. 2006. Linear Optimality Theory as a Model of Gradience in Grammar. In *Gradience in Grammar: Generative Perspectives*, ed. Gisbert Fanselow, Caroline Féry, Ralph Vogel, and Matthias Schlesewsky. Oxford University Press.

Legendre, Géraldine, Antonella Sorace, and Paul Smolensky. 2006. The Optimality Theory–Harmonic Grammar connection. In Smolensky and Legendre (2006), 903–966.

Pater, Joe, Rajesh Bhatt and Christopher Potts. 2007a. Linguistic Optimization. Ms, University of Massachusetts, Amherst.

Pater, Joe, Christopher Potts, and Rajesh Bhatt. 2007b. Harmonic Grammar with Linear Programming. Ms, University of Massachusetts, Amherst. ROA-872.

Potts, Christopher, Michael Becker, Rajesh Bhatt and Joe Pater. 2007. HaLP: Harmonic grammar with linear programming, version 2. Software available online at http://web.linguist.umass.edu/~halp/.

Prince, Alan. 2002a. Arguing Optimality. In *University of Massachusetts Occasional Papers in Linguistics: Papers in Optimality Theory II*, ed. Angela Carpenter, Andries Coetzee, Paul de Lacy, 269-304. Amherst, MA: GLSA. [ROA-562].

Prince, Alan. 2002b. Anything Goes. In New century of phonology and phonological theory, ed. Takeru Honma, Masao Okazaki, Toshiyuki Tabata, and Shin ichi Tanaka, 66–90. Tokyo: Kaitakusha. ROA-536.

Prince, Alan, and Paul Smolensky. 1993/2004. *Optimality Theory: Constraint interaction in generative grammar*. Ms, Rutgers University and University of Colorado at Boulder, 1993. Revised version published by Blackwell, 2004. [ROA-537].

Smolensky, Paul, and Geraldine Legendre. 2006. *The harmonic mind: From neural computation to Optimality-Theoretic grammar.* Cambridge, MA: MIT Press.

Tesar, Bruce and Paul Smolensky. 1998. Learnability in Optimality Theory. *Linguistic Inquiry* 29: 229-268.

Department of Linguistics
South College
University of Massachusetts
Amherst, MA 01003

{michael,pater}@linguist.umass.edu

Inducing Functionally Grounded Constraints[*]

Kathryn Flack

University of Massachusetts Amherst

1. Introduction

Phonologists have been long concerned with finding phonetic properties which allow phonological patterns to be seen as 'natural' or 'grounded' (e.g. Stampe (1973), Hooper [Bybee] (1976), Ohala (1990), Archangeli and Pulleyblank (1994)). With the advent of Optimality Theory (Prince and Smolensky, 1993/2004), this often takes the form of identifying functional grounding for specific OT constraints (e.g. Hayes (1999), Smith (2002), Steriade (1999; 2001), and papers in Hayes et al. (eds.) (2004)).

There is general agreement that 'functionally grounded' constraints prefer forms which are more perceptually or psycholinguistically salient, or less articulatorily challenging, to less prominent or more difficult forms. Beyond this, however, there is very little agreement about the nature of the connection between phonetic facts and constraints. Most work is agnostic on this matter, enthusiastically finding phonetic facts which correlate with constraint activity while remaining uncommitted to a particular relationship between the two. Prince and Smolensky (2004) originally proposed that all constraints in the universal constraint inventory are innate. If this is true, any functional factors which shape the constraint inventory must have acted at an earlier stage of evolution. Alternatively, Hayes (1999), Smith (2002), and Steriade (1999; 2001), among others, discuss various means by which individual learners could induce functionally grounded constraints directly from their linguistic experience.

This paper takes the position that functional grounding shapes individual learners' constraint inventories: each learner induces functionally grounded constraints based on their immediate linguistic experience. An argument for this view comes from cognitive economy. Assume for the moment that learners have consistent access to phonetic data

---

[*] Thanks to Michael Becker, Tim Beechey, Gaja Jarosz, Shigeto Kawahara, John Kingston, Dan Mash, Andrew McCallum, John McCarthy, Marianne McKenzie, Joe Pater, Jason Riggle, Nathan Sanders, Matt Wolf, and the UMass Phonology Group for lots of helpful discussions and suggestions. This paper is a revised version of chapter four of Flack (2007).

Michael Becker (ed.): Papers in theoretical and computational phonology. University of Massachusetts Occasional Papers in Linguistics 36, 13-44.
GLSA Amherst.

demonstrating the relative perceptual salience, articulatory difficulty, and so on of segments (or features) in particular phonetic and phonological contexts. Further assume that learners have some reliable mechanism for evaluating this experience, allowing them to induce constraints which are grounded in these functional factors.

The consistent availability of this information to learners would make innate specifications of these constraints redundant. Assuming that innate mechanisms for language acquisition should be maximally simple, learners should use as much external information as possible. Innate specifications should therefore only be posited when the information in learners' experience is insufficient to the learning task.

Ultimately, the question of whether (and how) constraints are induced from phonetic data is an empirical one. As described above, induction is only possible if learners can observe phonetic facts which could motivate particular constraints, and if there is some mechanism which could induce the attested set of constraints from this data. Much of the current work on functional grounding addresses the first point. Smith (2002) and Steriade (1999; 2001) propose mechanisms for inducing constraints from this sort of data, and Hayes' (1999) Inductive Grounding model integrates articulatory facts with such a constraint inducer. Of course, demonstrating that constraint induction is logically possible is not the same as showing that learners actually induce constraints. Any proposed induction mechanism is at best a hypothesis about learners' behavior, and must be tested against actual speakers.

The goal of this paper is to propose a mechanism for the induction of perceptually grounded constraints, and to show how a computational model can be used to test proposals about constraint induction against real phonetic data. The empirical focus of this paper is the constraint *#P, 'No word-initial unaspirated p', which is argued to be functionally grounded in learners' perceptual experience. This constraint is active in languages including Cajonos Zapotec (Nellis and Hollenbach, 1980) and Ibibio (Akinlabi and Urua, 2002; Connell, 1994; Essien, 1990), as described in section 2. Experimental data reported in section 3 show that initial p is uniquely perceptually difficult as a result of its acoustic similarity to initial b, suggesting that *#P is phonetically natural. The latter portion of this paper describes a computational model in which virtual learners induce this constraint from precisely these phonetic facts. This model achieves realistic perception of acoustically realistic segments; the relative perceptibility of these segments then forms the basis for perceptually grounded constraint induction. The 'production' and 'perception' components of the model are described in section 5, and these form the basis for a mechanism which allows learners to consistently induce *#P from these functional factors, described in section 6.

2.   Phonological restrictions on initial p

In Cajonos Zapotec (Nellis and Hollenbach, 1980) and Ibibio (Akinlabi and Urua, 2002; Connell, 1994; Essien, 1990), unaspirated p contrasts with b in non-initial positions, but only b may surface initially. These languages allow other voicing contrasts in initial position (e.g. t and d, k and g; t and k are also unaspirated).

In Cajonos Zapotec, coronal and velar stops contrast for voicing initially, medially, and finally. Labials contrast for voicing only medially and finally. All labial-initial native words begin with *b*, rather than *p*. This restriction was productive until recently. Older Spanish loans borrowed initial /p/ as [b], as in *bẽj* 'sash' (Sp. *paño*) and *bêd* (Sp. *Pedro*). Newer loans faithfully retain initial /p/, as in *pát* 'duck' (Sp. *pato*).

(1)   <u>Cajonos Zapotec</u>

*pèn		tò	'one'	kóc	'pig'
bèn	'do!'	dò	'string'	góc	'gunny sack'
gòpée	'fog'	yítà?	'the squash'	wáké	'it can'
dòbée	'feather'	yîdà?	'the leather'	wágé	'firewood'
jáp	'will care for'	yèt	'tortilla'	wák	'it can'
jáb	'will weave'	zèd	'disturbance'	wág	'firewood'

A similar restriction against word-initial *p* is found in Ibibio (data below from Essien (1990)), though the distribution of voicing and length contrasts in Ibibio stops is more complex. Intervocalic stops are typically geminates, as intervocalic singletons are typically lenited. Ibibio has no voiced velar stop, and coronals are devoiced syllable-finally and in geminates. See Essien (1990) and especially Akinlabi and Urua (2002) for further discussion of Ibibio morphophonology.

Most interestingly for the present discussion, Ibibio licenses *b* but not *p* word-initially. Medial *p* and *b* contrast in *díppé* 'lift up' versus *díbbé* 'hide oneself', and finally in *bɔ́p* 'build (something)' versus *bɔ́ɔb* 'build many things'. While there are *b*-initial words like *bàt* 'count', there are no *p*-initial words (*pàt*). Unlike labials, coronals contrast initially as in *tàppa* 'call someone's attention' and *dàppa* 'remove something from a fire'.

(2)   <u>Ibibio</u>

*pàt		tàppa	'call someone's attention	kárá	'govern'
bàt	'count'	dàppa	'remove s.t. from a fire'	*gárá	
díppé	'lift up'	sìtté	'uncork'	dàkká	'move away'
díbbé	'hide oneself'	*sìddé		*dàggá	
bɔ́p	'build (something)'	wèt	'write'	sák	'laugh'
bɔ́ɔb	'build many things'	*wèd		*ság	

The remainder of this paper will investigate the functional grounding of this restriction on word-initial *p* (*#P). Section 3 will show that in French, where initial unaspirated *p* is attested, this segment is particularly difficult for listeners to identify. Sections 5 and 6 will then propose an induction mechanism which allows learners of both French-type languages (with initial *p*) and also Cajonos Zapotec-type languages (without initial *p*) to induce *#P from the acoustic and perceptual properties of initial stops.

3.   Phonetic properties of initial *p*

Initial *p* is uniquely difficult to identify, as it is more similar to initial *b* than other
voiceless stops are to their voiced counterparts. These facts demonstrate that *#ᴘ is
phonetically natural. This section describes perceptual and acoustic experiments which
identify these properties of initial and intervocalic *p*, *b*, *t*, and *d*.

3.1   Perceptual experiment

First, participants in the perceptual experiment heard stimuli containing a target stop (*p*,
b, *t*, or *d*) and flanking vowels; these stimuli were extracted from French words produced
by a native speaker of Parisian French. Stimuli contained stops in either word-initial or
intervocalic position, e.g. [#pa] from *paragraphe*, [#bɔ] from *bordeaux*; [edi] from
comedie, [iti] from *itineraire*. 15 native speakers of French participated in the
experiment. Each heard a total of 45 unique stimuli in each of 8 conditions: 4 stops (*p*, *b*,
t, *d*) × 2 positions (initial, medial). The task was to identify stops by pressing a button as
quickly as possible after each stimulus. See Flack (2007: ch. 3) for more about the
experimental methods.

The hypothesis investigated in this experiment has three parts: (1) initial *p* is more
difficult to accurately identify than initial *b*, (2) no similar asymmetry emerges word-
medially, and (3) this is a particular property of initial *p* rather than a general property of
initial voiceless stops (that is, initial *t* is not similarly more difficult than *d*). This
perceptual difficulty could reveal itself either in inaccurate identification of initial *p* or
slow reaction times to initial *p* (Pisoni and Tash, 1974). Thus recognition of initial *p*
should be slower and/or less accurate than initial *b*, and neither initial *t* and *d* nor medial
p and *b* should differ in the same way. To test this hypothesis, preplanned two-sample
one-tailed t-tests were performed on reaction times and accuracy scores.

Participants identified initial *p* significantly more slowly than initial *b*, as shown
in Figure 1a. The average reaction time for accurate initial *p* responses was 588 ms. This
is marginally significantly greater than the average response time for initial *b* responses
(555 ms; $t(88) = 2.445$, $p = 0.016$).[1] Reaction times for medial *p* (599 ms) are not
significantly different from reaction times for medial *b* (592 ms; $t(82) = 0.485$, $p =
0.629$), so *p* is more slowly recognized than *b* only in initial position. Turning to the
coronal stops, response times for initial *t* (495 ms) were quicker than those for initial *d*
(538 ms; $t(85) = 3.742$, $p < 0.001$), indicating that slow responses are not a general
property of initial voiceless stops but rather a unique property of initial *p*. Participants'
slow reaction times do not correlate with any difference in the accuracy of responses to
initial *p* versus *b*. 93% of initial *p* stimuli were identified correctly, and 94% of initial *b*
stimuli were identified correctly, as shown in Figure 1b. This difference is not significant
($t(88) = 0.314$, $p = 0.754$).

---

[1] Because these comparisons cover four conditions (*p*, *b*, *t*, and *d* in a given context), a Bonferroni
correction is applied to $\alpha = 0.05$ such that α here is equal to 0.05/4, 0.0125, for all t-tests. While
significance is only marginal here, no other pairs of stops shows a comparable pattern with even marginal
significance. Therefore, initial *p*'s perceptual difficulty is unique and reliable.

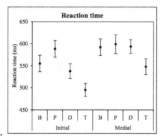 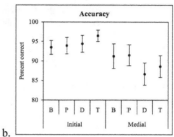

a.   b.

Figure 1. Average reaction times (a) and accuracy (b) in each condition, with 95% confidence intervals (from items analysis).

These results indicate that word-initial *p* is, as predicted, uniquely perceptually difficult. While *p* and *b* are recognized with equal accuracy in both initial and medial position, initial *p* is significantly slower than initial *b* while medial *p* and *b* are identified with equal speed. Responses to *t* and *d* follow a different pattern both initial and medial *t* are recognized more quickly than *d*, and *t* responses tend to be more accurate overall than *d* responses as well. Additional analysis in Flack (2007: ch. 3) shows that these results are not artifacts of flanking vowels or segmental frequency. The typological observation that only *p* may be banned in word-initial position correlates with these perceptual facts, supporting the hypothesis that the constraint *#P is functionally grounded.

3.2   Acoustic experiment

The perceptual difficulty of initial *p* correlates with its similarity to *b*. Initial *p* is acoustically more similar to *b* than initial *t* is to *d*, or medial *p* to *b* or *t* to *d*. Acoustic similarity was measured in terms of the stops' maximum release burst intensities and voice onset times (VOT), both of which are major cues to voicing (Lisker and Abramson, 1964; Repp, 1979). Burst intensity and VOT were calculated for the French stops used in the perceptual experiment. See Flack (2007: ch. 3) for more details about these analyses.

Looking first at the intensity measures, the maximum burst intensities of all homorganic stop pairs differ significantly, with the important exception of initial *p* and *b*, whose bursts are not significantly different. These results are shown in Figure 2a and Table 1. Initial *p–b* are therefore have more similar bursts than medial *p–b*, or initial *t–d*. The similarity between initial *p* and *b* is thus a specific fact about initial labials, rather than a general property of initial or voiceless stops.

Turning to the VOT measures, initial *p–b* are again more similar than medial *p–b* or initial or medial *t–d*. This follows from the fact that initial *p* has the shortest VOT of all four voiceless stops; initial *p* thus has the weakest VOT cue to voicelessness. In the weakness of this cue, initial *p* is the most like (or, least unlike) its voiced counterpart.[2]

---

[2] VOT was measured only for voiceless stops followed by non-high vowels. High vowels were often partially or fully devoiced after voiceless stops, giving these stops artificially long VOTs.

Initial p's 16 ms VOT is significantly shorter than that of medial p, so initial p–b are more similar than medial p–b. Initial p's VOT is also significantly shorter than initial t's, so initial p–b are also more similar than initial t–d. Further, while initial labial stops are more similar than medial labial stops, the pattern is reversed for coronals: medial t has a significantly shorter VOT than initial t. The tendency for initial p–b to have similar VOTs compared to medial p–b is thus a specific property of labials, rather than a general property of all stops. These results are summarized in Figure 2b and Table 2.

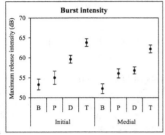 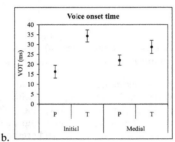

a.   b.

Figure 2.   Average maximum release burst intensity in each condition, within 5 ms of release (a); VOT of initial and medial voiceless labial and coronal stops followed by non-high vowels (b); with 95% confidence intervals.

Maximum burst intensity						
Initial				Medial		
	Mean (dB)	Difference (dB)	p value		Mean (dB)	Difference (dB)	p value
b	53	2	0.129 $t(93) =$ 1.530	b	52	4	<0.001 $t(93) =$ 4.495
p	55			p	56		
d	60	4	<0.001 $t(91) =$ 5.937	d	57	5	<0.001 $t(93) =$ 7.969
t	64			t	62		

Table 1.   Maximum release burst intensity measures for initial and medial p, b, t, and d, with differences and p values (from preplanned two-sample t-tests) for pairs of stops differing in voicing.

VOT							
Initial				Medial			
	Mean (ms)	Difference (ms)	*p* value		Mean (ms)	Difference (ms)	*p* value
p	16	18	<0.001 $t(64) =$ 7.995	*p*	22	7	0.018 $t(57) =$ 2.432
t	34			*t*	29		
Initial vs. medial *p*		6	0.008 $t(63) =$ 2.719	Initial vs. medial *t*		5	0.03 $t(56) =$ 2.432

Table 2.   VOT measures for initial and medial voiceless stops, with differences and *p* values (from preplanned two-sample t-tests).

These acoustic results have shown that initial *p* and *b* are similar. But the perceptual study indicated that these segments are not symmetrically confusable; instead, initial *p* is uniquely perceptually difficult.[3] The source of this asymmetry must be some property of *p* itself, rather than simply the similarities between *p* and *b* that have been discussed so far. A likely acoustic source of this asymmetrical difficulty lies in *p*'s greater acoustic variability. Initial *p*'s burst values have a greater standard deviation than initial *b*'s: 6.0 and 4.7 dB, respectively.[4] Similarly, while VOT was not measured for voiced stops, initial *p*'s VOT is the most variable of all voiceless stops: its standard deviation is 9.4 ms, while that of initial *t* is 8.7 ms, medial *p* 7.1 ms, and medial *t* 8.9 ms.

Because initial *p*'s burst is more variable than initial *b*'s, more initial *p* tokens have burst intensities equal to, or even less than, the mean burst intensity for initial *b* than there are initial *b* tokens with burst intensities equal to or greater than the average for initial *p*. Put more simply, there are more *b*-like initial *p*s than there are *p*-like initial *b*s, in terms of burst intensity. Initial *p*'s VOT is also more variable than, and shorter than, that of any other voiceless stop. This suggests that there are also more tokens of initial *p* with extremely short VOTs similar to that of a voiced stop than there are of other voiceless segments: there are again more *b*-like initial *p*s than *b*-like medial *p*s, or *d*-like *t*s in any position. It could thus be the case that while the general similarity between initial *p* and *b* makes them difficult to distinguish, the large variability of initial *p* makes it more *b*-like than initial *b* is *p*-like, accounting for initial *p*'s unique perceptual difficulty. Section 5.2.2 shows how a perceptual model can explore this hypothesis.

4.   Interim summary: *#P, functional grounding, and constraint induction

So far, this paper has shown that word-initial *p* is phonologically marked. Evidence of this is found in languages like Cajonos Zapotec (Nellis and Hollenbach, 1980) and Ibibio (Essien, 1990), where *p* and *b* contrast in all non-initial positions, but only *b* is licensed initially. This phonological markedness correlates with initial *p*'s acoustic and perceptual

---

[3] Nearly all misidentifications in the perceptual experiment were voicing mistakes. This suggests that slow reaction times were also caused by difficulty identifying stops' voicing. Initial *p* was identified more slowly than initial *b*, so *p* tokens apparently sounded more *b*-like than vice versa.
[4] The standard deviations of other consonants' bursts: initial *d* = 3.4; initial *t* = 3.4; medial *b* = 4.3; medial *p* = 4.0; medial *d* = 3.1; medial *t* = 3.5 (all dB).

properties. French speakers find word-initial *p* uniquely perceptually difficult. Word-initial *p* and *b* are also uniquely acoustically similar. The cross-linguistic dispreference for initial *p* is likely the result of its perceptual difficulty in this position, which in turn follows from its acoustic properties. The constraint *#P therefore appears to be functionally grounded in initial *p*'s perceptual difficulty.

For *#P to be induced by learners, they must have consistent experience of this perceptual difficulty, and must also have some mechanism for reliably deriving the attested constraint from this perceptual experience. A computational model of a learner's perceptual experience can be used to evaluate whether *#P could be induced in this way. The remainder of this paper describes such a model, in which realistic patterns of perception are based on realistic acoustic representations of initial and medial *p*, *b*, *t*, and *d*. When a constraint induction algorithm evaluates this perceptual experience, the constraint *#P can be consistently induced in languages where initial *p* is attested and also in languages where there is no initial *p*.

The model has three components. First, in the <u>production</u> component, a virtual adult speaker pronounces words with initial and medial stops whose acoustic properties are those described above. This is the input to the <u>perception</u> component, where a virtual learner develops acoustic criteria for identifying these stops in initial and medial position using a simple prototype model. At the end of phonetic learning, the learner's perceptual behavior is equivalent to that of participants in the perceptual experiment: initial *p* is uniquely difficult. Finally, in the <u>induction</u> component, the learner uses its perceptual experience to induce constraints against segments which meet 'innate' criteria for perceptual difficulty. The learner reliably induces the attested constraint *#P without inducing other, unattested constraints; this occurs whether the learner is exposed to pseudo-French, where initial *p* occurs, or pseudo-Cajonos Zapotec ('pseudo-CZ'), where it is unattested.

5.   Modelling production and perception

The production component of the model represents an adult speaker's acoustically realistic productions of initial and medial stops. The output of production is the input to perception, which represents a learner who listens to adult speech, develops acoustic prototypes of segments, and learns to identify stops based on their acoustic properties. The perception component is also realistic, as it finds word-initial *p* uniquely difficult. These properties of the perception model make it a reliable foundation for the model of constraint induction discussed in section 6.

5.1   How the model works

This section will describe the structure of first the production model and then the perception model. The following section will demonstrate that the perception model faithfully represents human perception.

5.1.1 Production and acoustic representations

In each cycle of the model, the virtual speaker produces an utterance of the form *CaCa*. Each *C* is randomly chosen from the inventory *p*, *b*, *t*, *d*, and these stops are produced with realistic acoustic properties. The virtual learner's task is to learn to identify stops based on their acoustics.

Stops in the model have four acoustic properties: maximum burst intensity (*burst*), VOT, closure voicing (*voicing*), and place. The speaker randomly chooses an appropriate numeric value for each property each time a stop is produced. These sets of acoustic values constitute the spoken utterance, as shown in (3). The learner 'hears' these sets of acoustic values and uses its developing knowledge of prototypical acoustic values for each stop to identify new stops.

```
(3)   SPOKEN: "tada!"
          Initial t:  Place = 100   Voicing = 0     VOT = 47   Burst = 61
          Medial d:   Place = 100   Voicing = 100   VOT = 18   Burst = 54[5]
```

Each acoustic value of each stop in an utterance is randomly chosen from a normal distribution with a specified mean and variance. The parameters of these normal distributions represent stops' actual acoustic properties. Each acoustic value is an integer between 0 and 100. If a normal distribution with a specified mean and variance would allow some chance for values below 0 or above 100, those values were replaced by additional 0 or 100 values, respectively.

Burst intensity and VOT values were taken from the experimental data in section 3.2. Maximum burst intensity was measured for each stop in each position, and the means and variances of the normally distributed burst values for each stop are shown in (4).

(4)

	p		*b*		*t*		*d*	
BURST	mean	variance	mean	variance	mean	variance	mean	variance
Initial	55	36	53	22	64	11	60	11
Medial	56	16	52	19	62	12	57	10

The model's 'VOT' property reflects only the positive portion of each stop's voice onset time. This is distinct from the model's 'closure voicing' property described below. This distinction reflects speakers' tendency to process the presence vs. absence of prevoicing categorically, while fine-grained distinctions among positive VOTs are interpreted gradiently (Hay, 2005). For the voiceless stops *p* and *t*, VOT means and variances were taken directly from the experimental measures. As voiced stops do not have positive voice onset times, the VOT means for *b* and *d* were set to 0, and these

---

[5] Throughout this chapter, `this font` will be used to show data from the model.

stops' variances were set to the averaged variance of all voiceless stops' VOTs.[6] Stops' possible VOT values in the model are summarized in (5).

(5)

VOT	p		b		t		d	
	mean	variance	mean	variance	mean	variance	mean	variance
Initial	16	89	0	74	34	76	0	74
Medial	22	51	0	74	29	80	0	74

In order to model the categorical nature of closure voicing perception, the possible closure voicing values of each stop are distributed such that there is a robust binary distinction between voiced and voiceless stops. Voiceless stops have closure voicing values of essentially zero (their mean is zero, and the variance is extremely small), while voiced stops have closure voicing values of essentially 100.

(6)

	Voiceless p,t		Voiced b,d	
	mean	variance	mean	variance
CLOSURE VOICING	0	2	100	2

Finally, the 'place' cue also produces a binary distinction between labial stops (with values of essentially 0) and coronal stops (with values of essentially 100). As this model is concerned with voicing distinctions within a single place rather than the perception of place distinctions themselves, these extremely simple values are placeholders for more realistic sets of detailed acoustic cues to place.

(7)

	Labial p,b		Coronal t,d	
	mean	variance	mean	variance
PLACE	0	2	100	2

The output of each round of production is a single word of the form *CaCa*, where initial and medial stops are randomly chosen. Each stop's acoustic values for place, closure voicing, VOT, and burst intensity are chosen from normal distributions with the means and variances specified above. Because the acoustic properties of these 'spoken' stops are taken from acoustic measurements of naturally produced stops, the production component of the model accurately represents a learner's acoustic experience. The result of a round of production is repeated in (8).

(8) SPOKEN: "tada!"
```
      Initial t:  Place = 100   Voicing = 0     VOT = 47  Burst = 61
      Medial d:   Place = 100   Voicing = 100   VOT = 18  Burst = 54
```

---

[6] These variances for voiced stops' VOTs are almost certainly too large. However, section 5.3 suggests that smaller, more realistic variances for these stops' VOTs would make the model behave increasingly realistically, as this change would make initial *p* even more uniquely perceptually difficult.

5.1.2 Perception: Hearing, phoneme identification, and category learning

The perception component of the model consists of three subcomponents. First, during hearing, the set of acoustic values produced by the virtual speaker is heard somewhat imperfectly. During identification, the learner guesses which stops were produced by comparing the heard values to prototypical values for each stop. Finally, during learning, the learner adjusts the stop prototypes to reflect the new acoustic information. The perception component of the model takes experimentally-determined acoustic properties as its input, and produces a pattern of perceptual accuracy consistent with experimental results. Crucially, the model finds word-initial *p* more perceptually difficult than initial *b*, without similarly finding medial *p* more difficult than medial *b*, or initial *t* more difficult than initial *d*; these results are presented in section 5.2.

Hearing: Not all spoken acoustic values are perceived accurately

In order to model imperfect perception (as in a noisy environment), transmission of the spoken acoustic values is imperfect in two ways: some acoustic values are not heard at all, and those which are heard may be perturbed slightly. The spoken properties given above can thus be heard as a subset of imperfectly-transmitted values as in (9), where the learner fails to hear the medial *d*'s closure voicing and burst cues at all and its VOT property is inaccurately transmitted. This imperfect cue transmission introduces realistic randomness into the model. Its specific details are not crucial to the model, so they are not discussed here; see Flack (2007: ch. 4) for further details.

```
(9)   SPOKEN: "tada!"
        Initial t:  Place = 100   Voicing = 0     VOT = 47  Burst = 61
        Medial d:   Place = 100   Voicing = 100   VOT = 18  Burst = 54

      HEARD:
        Initial:    Place = 100   Voicing = 0     VOT = 47  Burst = 61
        Medial:     Place = 100   Voicing =       VOT = 17  Burst =
```

Identification: Comparing heard values to prototypes

In order to identify the spoken consonant from its acoustic properties, the learner compares the set of heard acoustic properties to prototypes of each consonant. The learner guesses that the prototype most similar to the set of heard properties is the consonant produced by the speaker. A prototype is a four-dimensional vector whose coordinates represent the average value for each of a consonant's four acoustic properties, based on the tokens of that consonant heard by the learner thus far. Examples of these prototype coordinates are given in (10).

(10) Prototypes:

Initial	Place	Voicing	VOT	Burst
p:	3.9	4.3	16.5	54.1
b:	3.5	96.1	4.5	53.4
t:	94.8	7.4	30.2	65.3
d:	96.8	96.2	3.7	60.1

Medial	Place	Voicing	VOT	Burst
p:	4.1	5.6	20.9	55.4
b:	4.3	94.0	5.6	52.7
t:	95.5	5.6	22.9	63.0
d:	96.9	95.7	5.2	57.3

In order to guess which stops were heard in a particular *CaCa* word, the listener calculates the distance between the points represented by the heard acoustic values and those of each prototype. When all four cues are heard, as for the initial stop in (9), distance is calculated by the formula in (11). As the model is concerned with the details of voicing identification but not with place identification, there are three cues to voicing but only one for place. To compensate for this simplification, the single place cue is more heavily weighted in the distance calculation.

(11) *distance* =
$$\mathrm{sqrt}(\ 3*(\mathrm{place}_{\mathrm{Heard}}-\mathrm{place}_{\mathrm{C}})^2 + (\mathrm{voi}_{\mathrm{Heard}}-\mathrm{voi}_{\mathrm{C}})^2 + (\mathrm{vot}_{\mathrm{Heard}}-\mathrm{vot}_{\mathrm{C}})^2 + (\mathrm{burst}_{\mathrm{Heard}}-\mathrm{burst}_{\mathrm{C}})^2\ )$$

The distance between each prototype and the set of heard values is calculated, producing a set of distances between the heard stop and each prototype as in (12). The learner guesses that the heard stop is in the category of the nearest prototype. In this example, the learner guesses correctly that the initial stop was *t*.

(12) HEARD: Initial: Place = 100   Voicing = 0   VOT = 47   Burst = 61

Initial	DISTANCE (X~prototype)		Place	Voicing	VOT	Burst
p:	169		3.9	4.3	16.5	54.1
b:	198	Prototype	3.5	96.1	4.5	53.4
t:	**21**	coordinates:	94.8	7.4	30.2	65.3
d:	106		96.8	96.2	3.7	60.1

GUESS: Initial t (correct)

When the listener fails to hear all of the acoustic properties of some stop, as is the case for the medial stop in example (9) above, distance is calculated based on only those properties heard. For example, when the learner hears only place and VOT values, the distance between this stop and each prototype is calculated using only the prototypes' place and VOT values. The reduced distance equation for this case is given in (13).

(13) When only Place and VOT cues are heard:
$$distance\ =\ \mathrm{sqrt}(\ 3*(\mathrm{place}_{\mathrm{Heard}}-\mathrm{place}_{\mathrm{C}})^2 + (\mathrm{vot}_{\mathrm{Heard}}-\mathrm{vot}_{\mathrm{C}})^2\ )$$

Learning: Prototypes are adjusted based on new acoustic information

Finally, the learner must learn what the stops sound like. This is accomplished by updating prototype coordinates to reflect the new information acquired in each round. In this way, over time, the prototypes come to represent stops' canonical acoustic properties.

In a round where an initial *t* is produced, the learner updates the coordinates of the initial *t* prototype – even if the learner misidentifies the initial stop. Accomplishing this requires the learner to know which stops were actually produced. In assuming that the learner has this information, the model is similar to learning algorithms for OT constraint rankings where the learner compares observed surface forms to underlying representations from which they were derived (see e.g. Tesar and Smolensky (1994 et seq.), Boersma and Hayes (2001)). In giving this phonetic learner access to the 'underlying representation' of the speaker's utterance, in addition to surface acoustic values, the model focuses on learning the relationship between a given set of categories and their possible acoustic realizations. The assumption that the learner knows segments' true identities is not critical. Just as learners discover underlying representations as well as constraint rankings in elaborated models of phonological learning (Jarosz, 2006; Merchant and Tesar, to appear), this model could be enriched, allowing the learner to discover phonetic categories itself as in de Boer's model of vowel inventories (2001).

It is important to note that this knowledge about segments' identities is available only to the learning component of the model. During identification, the learner tries to identify segments based only on their acoustic properties; the learner effectively 'finds out' which segments were truly produced only after it guesses which were heard.

Learning via updating prototypes proceeds as follows. The value of a prototype coordinate for, say, initial *t*'s VOT property is the average of all VOT values for initial *t* heard by the learner. At the beginning of a simulation, each prototype's coordinates are the default values given in (14). A default value is the average of the four consonants' mean values for a particular acoustic property. For example, each word-initial stop prototype has an initial 'place' value of 50 because this is the average of the mean place values of initial *p* (0), *b* (0), *t* (100), and *d* (100). These simulation-initial default values give the model no inherent bias towards any of the four stops.

(14) Simulation-initial defaults

	Place	Voicing	VOT	Burst
Initial pbtd:	50	50	12.5	58
Medial pbtd:	50	50	12.8	56.8

After each round of identification, the learner adjusts the prototype coordinates for the actual initial and medial segments produced. For example, the initial *t* discussed above is the twelfth initial *t* heard by the model. The most recent set of acoustic values for *t* is averaged with the previous 11 sets of values to get a new set of coordinates for the initial *t* prototype. This new prototype, given in (15), represents the learner's entire experience with initial *t*, and is used in the next round of identification.[7]

(15)   Adjusted prototypes   Place   Voicing   VOT   Burst
            Initial t -->   95.2   6.6   31.8   64.8
            Medial   d -->   97.0   95.7   5.9   57.3

The learner also collects information about stops' relative perceptual difficulty. This information is the basis for perceptually grounded constraint induction. The learner calculates two aspects of perceptual difficulty: accuracy and false alarms. Accuracy measures the learner's ability to correctly identify tokens of a particular consonant: 'Of all the tokens of initial *p* the learner has heard, how many have been correctly identified?' False alarms measure the learner's ability to guess that some particular consonant was heard only when this is true: 'Of all the times the learner guessed that it heard initial *p*, how many of those guesses were wrong?' The formulas for calculating these two scores are given in (16), and sample accuracy and false alarm rates are in (17).

(16)   For some segment *x*:

$$\text{Accuracy}(x) = 100 * [\,\#\,x \text{ tokens correctly identified}\,] \div [\,\#\,x \text{ tokens heard}\,]$$

$$\text{FalseAlarm}(x) = 100 * [\,\#\,x \text{ tokens incorrectly identified}\,] \div [\,\#\,x \text{ responses}\,]$$

(17)   Initial   Accuracy   False alarm
        p: 80%   (12 of 15)   8%   (1 of 13)
        b: 88%   (15 of 17)   12%   (2 of 17)
        t: 92%   (11 of 12)   21%   (3 of 14)
        d: 94%   (17 of 18)   6%   (1 of 18)

5.2   Results and discussion

The production and perception components of the model described above provide a simple yet accurate representation of human production and perception. Section 5.2.1 shows that the model, like human listeners, finds word-initial *p* uniquely perceptually difficult. Section 5.2.2 then demonstrates that the source of this difficulty is the variability of initial *p*'s VOT values. In this way, the model can be used to generate and refine hypotheses for future perceptual experiments.

5.2.1   Initial *p* is perceptually difficult

The perceptual model behaves very much like participants in the perceptual experiment, finding word-initial *p* uniquely difficult. Initial *p* is more frequently misidentified than initial *b*, while no similar relationship holds between medial *p* and *b* or initial *t* and *d*. A difference between the model and human listeners lies in the indicator of perceptual

---

[7] As this model alternates between token identification and prototype learning, it has a similar structure to an Expectation Maximization model (Dempster et al., 1977). However, the present model doesn't implement true EM: here, learning is supervised and incremental; further, there is no explicit effort to identify prototypes which allow maximally accurate identification of all tokens heard to date. In the future, the model could be relatively straightforwardly revised to incorporate EM.

difficulty, which is measured in the model only by accuracy scores. This, like many aspects of the model, is a simplification of real behavior, where perceptual difficulty can be indicated by either accuracy or reaction times (Ashby and Maddox, 1994; Pisoni and Lazarus, 1973). The perceptual experiment found indications of initial *p*'s perceptual difficulty in participants' reaction times, but not in their overall accuracy; this is likely a consequence of the specific task. Similarly, it is a consequence of the structure of this simple model that perceptual difficulty is measured here only in terms of accuracy; these two indicators of initial *p*'s difficulty are taken to be comparable for the discussion here.

The model's overall rates of accurately identifying various segments are determined by averaging the results of many simulations, much like human listeners' overall ability to perceive segments is typically evaluated by averaging experimental results from many subjects. Each simulation represents the progress of a single learner towards stable phonetic categories which allow that learner to identify segments at stable rates of accuracy. Figure 3 represents the model's developing ability to accurately identify each initial and medial consonant, averaged over 20,000 simulations. The accuracy measure for each consonant begins at chance. As the learner acquires phonetic experience, its ability to accurately identify each segment first increases and then stabilizes over the course of a 300-round simulation.

The model's percent correct for some segment in some round is measured as follows: out of 20,000 simulations, given some segment (e.g. initial *p*) and some point in time (e.g. round 200), how many accurate identifications of that segment in that round are there, vs. the total number of times that segment was produced in that round? Here, out of 20,000 simulations, the model 'heard' initial *p* in round 200 approximately 5,000 times; initial *p* was accurately identified in 91% of those 5,000 rounds. Lines are labeled by the segments in boxes at the right of each graph, which show segments' order from most to least accurate.

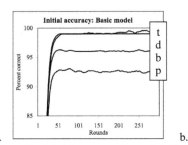 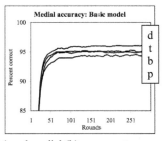

a.   b.

Figure 3.   Model accuracy for each initial (a) and medial (b) consonant, averaged across 20,000 simulations of 300 rounds each. The lines represent moving averages across 15-round windows.

Figure 3 shows that the perceptual model gives the same primary result as the perceptual experiment: initial *p* is consistently more difficult for the model to identify than initial *b*. This difference is unique to labials in initial position, as no comparable accuracy difference is seen in medial *p* and *b*. There is also no comparable difference between the accuracies of initial *t* and *d*, so initial *p* is uniquely perceptually difficult.

5.2.2   The source of initial *p*'s perceptual difficulty: VOT variances

Initial *p*'s perceptual difficulty correlates with its close acoustic similarity to initial *b*. Section 3.2 speculated that initial *p* is more difficult than initial *b* because initial *p* is more acoustically variable than initial *b*. Because the perceptual model accurately represents both the acoustics and the relative perceptibility of these segments, it can be used to investigate the acoustic source of initial *p*'s perceptual difficulty. By removing individual acoustic features (e.g. VOT and burst intensity) from the model, and by changing segments' parameters for these properties, the acoustic properties which make initial *p* difficult to perceive can be identified. These results can suggest the direction for further perceptual experiments.

First, the model can be simplified in order to examine the effects of burst and VOT on perception. The binary closure voicing cue, which provides the learner with a perfect cue to voicing, can be removed. The learner then hears all other available cues in all utterances. Under these conditions, any perceptual difficulty in the model comes from the inherent properties of VOT and burst cues. Figure 4a shows the performance of this 'place-VOT-burst' model, where the closure voicing cue is never heard and place, VOT, and burst are always heard. This is compared to the basic model in Figure 4b. The two are fundamentally similar – initial *p* is always identified much less accurately than initial *b*; both are less accurately identified than *t* and *d*, whose accuracies are fairly similar.

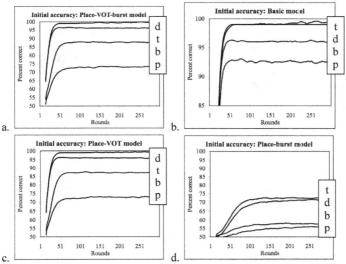

Figure 4. Model accuracy for each initial consonant when place, VOT, and burst cues are always heard, closure voicing is never heard (a); for the basic version of the model (b); when place and VOT cues are always heard, closure voicing and burst cues are never heard (c); when place and burst cues are always heard, closure voicing and VOT cues are never heard (d). Values are averaged over 20,000 300-round simulations.

Using the place-VOT-burst model as a baseline, the perceptual results of models which make voicing decisions based on only VOT or only burst cues can be explored. If one of these models similarly finds initial p uniquely perceptually difficult, the single voicing cue in that model contributes significantly to this perceptual result. If, instead, the presence of only one cue to voicing changes the perceptual results dramatically, then that cue is not responsible for the basic pattern.

Figure 4 also shows the performance of models in which only (c) place and VOT cues vs. (d) place and burst cues are heard. The place-VOT model in Figure 4c is extremely similar to the place-VOT-burst model in Figure 4a. The place-burst model in Figure 4d, though, produces a pattern of perception quite unlike the others. While initial *p* is still somewhat less accurately identified than initial *b*, this difference is comparable in size to the difference between initial *d* and *t*. Unlike the place-VOT-burst model, the place-VOT model, the basic model, and experimental results, the perceptual difficulty of initial *p* is not particularly unique. Taken together, these modified models indicate that VOT cues, rather than burst cues, are responsible for initial *p*'s perceptual difficulty.

Finally, the model can be further adjusted to show that the variances of segments' VOTs largely determine these perceptual results, (partially) confirming the hypotheses raised in section 3.2. Segments' VOT variances in the basic model are quite large, as shown in (18). When the basic model is modified such that each segment's VOT variance is 10, the resulting pattern of perception is quite different. As shown in Figure 5a, all four initial segments are now identified with very nearly equal accuracy. Crucially, the asymmetry between *p* and *b* disappears.

(18)

VOT	*p*		*b*		*t*		*d*	
	mean	variance	mean	variance	mean	variance	mean	variance
Initial	16	89	0	74	34	76	0	74

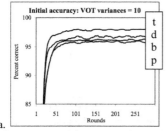
a.
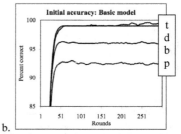
b.

Figure 5.   Model accuracy for each initial consonant where the VOT variance of each initial segment is 10 (a) and in the basic model (b). Values are averaged over 20,000 300-round simulations.

This suggests that it is in fact segments' large VOT variances – and initial *p*'s particularly large variance – which give rise to initial *p*'s perceptual difficulty. As the model typically makes voicing mistakes, this makes sense as follows. The VOT means of initial *p* and *b* are relatively similar (compared to those of initial *t–d*), so these segments have a relatively large chance of being inaccurately misidentified as each other. Initial *p* is even less accurate than initial *b* because its VOT variance is larger than that of *b*. There are more *p*s with *b*-like VOTs, so more *p*s are misidentified as *b* than vice versa. These results suggest that future perceptual experiments could manipulate stop VOTs in order to determine whether VOT variances are also the source of human listeners' perceptual difficulty with initial *p*.

5.3   Discussion and conclusion

This model is based on realistic acoustic representations of voicing cues for the initial and medial stops *p*, *b*, *t*, and *d*. From this data, the virtual learner develops criteria for identifying each stop, ultimately presenting a pattern of perception very similar to that found in the perceptual experiment. Word-initial *p* is more perceptually difficult (as indicated by the model's less accurate identification of initial *p*) than initial *b*. This is not a general property of labials: the model, like humans, finds medial *p* no more difficult than medial *b*. Neither is it a general property of initial voiceless stops: initial *t* is no more difficult than initial *d*. Within the model, initial *p*'s unique perceptual difficulty is due to both the similarity between the VOT means for initial *p* and *b* and especially to initial *p*'s greater VOT variance.

As explained in section 5.1.1, the VOT variances for voiced stops were arbitrarily set to the average of the VOT variances of initial and medial *p* and *t*. This gives the voiced stops quite large VOT variances, effectively allowing some of the model's voiced stops to have voiceless intervals following their release. This sort of brief post-release voicelessness in voiceless stops is reported by Mikuteit (2005), justifying this basic representation. However, the assumption that the variance of voiced stops' (positive) VOTs is as large as that of voiceless stops is entirely arbitrary. If anything, these post-release voiceless periods are likely shorter and rarer than assumed in this model. The variance of voiced stops' positive VOTs is thus likely smaller than assumed here. As initial *p*'s perceptual difficulty follows primarily from its large VOT variance relative to initial *b*, any revised the model in which voiced stops' VOT variance were smaller would also produce – and, in fact, enhance – this perceptual asymmetry between initial *p* and *b*.

These results about the source of initial *p*'s perceptual difficulty are, of course, necessarily true of only the model. Whether humans process these acoustic features in the same way, and thus whether humans' perceptual difficulty with initial *p* also follows primarily from its short, variable VOT, is a matter for further experimental study. The model is useful in that it allows preliminary exploration of this sort of acoustically motivated hypothesis much more rapidly than can be done with actual experimentation.

6. Modelling constraint induction

This model of learners' acoustic and perceptual experience can be used to explore the induction of functionally grounded constraints. Section 1 argued that learners induce constraints based on data from their immediate linguistic experience; section 6.1 considers the varieties of linguistic experience which play a role in constraint induction. Crucially, induction cannot refer to certain kinds of perceptual experience, e.g. infants' perception of their own speech. Further, raw linguistic experience must be evaluated in a structured way in order to give rise to phonological constraints, as Hayes (1999) argues. Towards this end, section 6.2 suggests a general schema which structures the induction of perceptually grounded constraints, and shows how a specific instantiation of this schema can consistently lead learners to induce *#P from realistic acoustic and perceptual data.

6.1 Constraint induction and linguistic experience

The general goal of constraint induction is for all learners to induce a consistent set of functionally grounded constraints from their immediate linguistic experience. A realistic model of constraint induction depends on a precise, realistic characterization of this experience. Learners' experience can vary along two dimensions. Different learners can be exposed to languages with different phonological properties, and so can have differential exposure to individual segments or structures. Each learner also has various kinds of experience with language: learners perceive adult speech, and also articulate and perceive their own babbling and early speech. This section argues that each functionally grounded constraint is consistently induced from any learner's experience with any language. However, perceptually grounded constraints can only be induced from learners' experience perceiving adult speech.

This paper has discussed two phonotactic possibilities for word-initial p. Initial p can be present in a language, in which case it is perceptually difficult as in French and the model of pseudo-French in section 5. Initial p can also be absent, as in Cajonos Zapotec and Ibibio. Learners of these two types of languages will have fundamentally different experiences of initial p; the constraint inducer discussed here is designed to consistently identify initial p as perceptually difficult in either situation, and so consistently induce *#P in either type of language.

In a language like French where initial p is licensed, its perceptual properties are readily available to learners as they induce constraints. This process can be straightforwardly implemented in a model of pseudo-French. If the inducer has a way of tracking the relative perceptual difficulty of segments in particular phonotactic positions, it will observe that p is more difficult to accurately identify than other word-initial segments. This information can trigger the induction of *#P. In a language like Cajonos Zapotec, however, this experience of initial p's acoustic properties and their perceptual consequences is unavailable to learners. If a learner of (pseudo-)Cajonos Zapotec is to consistently induce *#P from its perceptual experience like the (pseudo-)French learner, it must refer to a different aspect of perceptual experience.

It is frequently assumed that constraints like *#P, which can prevent learners of some languages from ever being exposed to perceptually difficult segments, are nonetheless universally grounded in the segment's perceptual difficulty. After all, we assume that languages like Cajonos Zapotec ultimately ban initial p is because it is perceptually difficult. This suggests that the constraint responsible for this restriction should represent each speaker's knowledge of initial p's perceptual difficulty.

This perspective is difficult to reconcile with the claim that functionally grounded constraints are induced rather than innate, as some learners lack perceptual experience of adult word-initial p. To resolve this conflict, it is often tacitly assumed that learners inducing constraints – typically through a proposed mechanism like Inductive Grounding (Hayes, 1999) or the Schema/Filter model of CON (Smith, 2002) – refer to something other than perceptual experience of adult forms of the ambient language, or their own articulations of these same forms in the case of articulatorily grounded constraints.

One possible way in which learners could experience unattested segments' articulatory and perceptual properties is through their own early productions. Hayes' discussion of Inductive Grounding focuses on learners' induction of articulatorily grounded constraints. If learners could refer to articulatory experience from babbling, they could learn about segments' articulatory properties in positions where they are not attested in an adult language (like initial p). This information could then perhaps be used to induce a complete set of typologically attested, articulatorily grounded constraints.

In the Schema/Filter model of CON, perceptually grounded constraints emerge from a mechanism similar to Inductive Grounding. Smith discusses the induction of perceptual augmentation constraints within this model; these constraints prefer perceptually salient forms to minimally different, less perceptually salient forms.[8] For example, the augmentation constraint HEAVYσ prefers more salient long vowels to less salient short vowels. In order to determine the relative perceptual salience of segments or structures unattested in learners' target languages, learners could again examine the psycholinguistic consequences of their own early productions of unattested structures.

With respect to the perceptually grounded constraint *#P, however, it is unlikely that infants' own early productions of *p*-initial forms could provide them with the same perceptual data as French-speaking adults' pronunciations. First of all, evidence of such forms would be relatively rare, and highly inconsistent across learners. While children's early babbling occasionally includes unattested segments and phonotactic structures, later stages of babbling quickly come to reflect the segmental frequency and phonotactics of the target language (Jusczyk, 1997: 177-9). Various child phonology processes such as truncation, consonant harmony, and other unfaithful mappings can also give rise to phonotactic structures unattested in adult language (Vihman, 1996: 218-21), but children vary widely in their use of these processes (as well as in the phonetic inventories and structures used in babbling). So while it is likely that many children learning languages without initial *p* could occasionally produce initial *p*, it is unlikely that this experience would be frequent enough, or consistent enough across learners, for universal induction of *#P.

A further reason why infants' early productions provide perceptual data unlike that garnered from adult speech is that infants' speech is much more articulatorily variable than adult speech (Jusczyk, 1997: 181). In fact, while young children's articulations may be impressionistically similar to various adult segments, children only very rarely produce adult-like segments before approximately 6 months, at which point the segmental content of babbling very quickly comes to resemble that of early child speech (Oller, 2000). The acoustic experiments discussed above, as well as the production component of this model, suggest that the perceptual difficulty of initial *p* follows from its relatively fine-grained acoustic properties. As infants' articulations are much more variable than those of adults, it is unlikely that an infant's own rare productions of unattested segments would be articulatorily and acoustically similar enough to those of adult speakers to trigger the same patterns of perception as adult productions. For these reasons, learners should refer only to their perceptual experience with adult speech in inducing perceptually grounded constraints.[9]

A Cajonos Zapotec learner therefore cannot induce *#P from the same knowledge of initial *p*'s perceptibility that a learner of French uses. Cajonos Zapotec and French

---

[8] Perceptual salience is a psychoacoustic measure, perhaps of neural response magnitude.

[9] Learners' articulatory experience of their own productions poses similar difficulties for constraint induction. In addition to children's articulatory inaccuracy and the scarcity of unattested segments and phonotactic structures, the size and shape of an infant's mouth (along with the initial absence of teeth) may give infants substantially different experience of articulatory difficulty than that of adult speech, which is typically assumed to shape adult phonology.

learners know fundamentally different things about initial p: a French learner knows that it is dispreferred – and so induces *#P – based on the difficulty of accurately identifying initial p. A Cajonos Zapotec learner instead knows that initial p is dispreferred simply because it is unattested in adult speech.

Reflecting this diverse knowledge about initial p, the induction mechanism proposed here refers to correspondingly diverse aspects of perceptual difficulty. In general, the constraint inducer tracks segments' perceptual properties, identifies segments which are relatively perceptually difficult in particular phonotactic positions, and generates constraints against these segments in these positions. In order to induce constraints against segments with which learners have actual perceptual experience as well as those which are absent from a particular phonotactic position, the inducer refers to two measures of perceptual difficulty: accuracy (which reflects correct identification of a segment) and false alarms (which reflect incorrect guesses that a segment was heard).

The next section describes how the mapping from perceptual data to induced constraints is governed by schemata for perceptually grounded constraints. These constraint schemata provide accuracy and false alarm criteria for labeling segments 'perceptually difficult', and for inducing constraints against these segments.

6.2   How the model works

The input to the constraint induction component of the model comes from the perception component, which hears acoustically realistic representations of initial and medial p, b, t, and d and perceives them realistically: word-initial p is uniquely perceptually difficult. The induction component induces the constraint *#P from this perceptual experience. A functionally grounded constraint schema defines the phonotactic positions which can be targeted by the induced constraints, as well as what exactly is meant by 'perceptually difficult.' Schemata are thus sets of phonotactic and perceptual (as well as articulatory, psycholinguistic, etc.) criteria for constraint induction.

Section 6.2.1 first describes the general structure of schemata for functionally grounded constraints, as well as the particular schema which governs the assessment and comparison of accuracy and false alarm scores in this model. Section 6.2.2 presents the specific criteria comparing segments' accuracy scores, allowing consistent induction of *#P in a French-type language where learners hear initial p. Induction of the same constraint from false alarm scores, as in a Cajonos Zapotec-type language where learners never hear initial p, is discussed in section 6.2.3.

6.2.1   General schemata for perceptually grounded constraint induction

The goal of the induction mechanism is to consistently induce the constraint *#P from word-initial p's unique perceptual difficulty. Hayes (1999) demonstrates that constraints cannot simply emerge from raw phonetic data; rather, learners must come know how to map phonetic information to phonological constraints. This paper proposes that four basic elements of the induction of perceptually grounded constraints must be specified. These are summarized, along with the particular parameters of the constraint induction model described here, in (19).

(19)   <u>Schemata specify four basic features of perceptual constraint induction:</u>

      (i) What kind of phonological element could be perceptually difficult.

          <u>Here:</u> Individual segments.

      (ii) Phonotactic positions where perceptual difficulty is considered.

          <u>Here:</u> Word-initial position.

      (iii) What makes a segment 'perceptually difficult'.
          (A procedure for comparing measures of perceptual difficulty.)

          How many recent tokens' accuracy/false alarm scores are considered.

            <u>Here:</u> 400 tokens of each segment.

          Properties of segments' relative accuracy and false alarm scores that trigger induction.

            <u>Here:</u> See sections 6.2.2 and 6.2.3.

      (iv) Definition of the induced constraints.

          <u>Here:</u> If a segment x is relatively perceptually difficult in $Context_Z$:

               *x/$Context_Z$ Assign one violation mark for each instance of x in $Context_Z$.

First, a constraint schema defines the type of phonological element over which perceptual difficulty is calculated. In the present model, individual segments are judged perceptually difficult. In other models, features, or sets of segments all sharing a feature or features, could be judged perceptually difficult as well.

An induction schema must also specify the phonotactic positions in which segments' perceptual difficulty will be evaluated. With no such specifications, learners would track perceptual difficulty in all logically possible phonotactic positions. This is undesirable, as some positions have no known phonological relevance: for example, no constraint targets third-syllable onsets. In this model, the inducer is further simplified in that it looks only at word-initial position, ignoring intervocalic stops. This is because stops are not typically banned intervocalically, as that is where their cues are most salient.

The third element specified by a constraint schema is the set of criteria for labelling a segment 'perceptually difficult'. In the present model, the inducer tracks two perceptibility measures: accuracy and false alarms (definitions repeated in (20)). The accuracy and false alarm scores of individual segments are compared using the criteria described in sections 6.2.2 and 6.2.3.

(20)   For some segment x:

   Accuracy(x)   =   100 * [# x tokens correctly identified] ÷ [# x tokens heard]

   FalseAlarm(x) =   100 * [# x tokens incorrectly identified] ÷ [# x responses]

Before these scores can be compared, the schema must specify both how and when they are calculated. In the early part of a simulation, before robust criteria for identifying segments have developed, a learner has low accuracy scores and high false alarm scores for all segments. For this reason, the inducer does not begin tracking accuracy or false alarm scores until phonetic categories and accuracy rates have stabilized. In the simulations reported here, induction begins after 150 rounds of production and perception. A time where prototype coordinates have stabilized (and so when induction should begin) could also be dynamically identified in each simulation in a more complex model.

A learner must also know how much of its experience to take into consideration in calculating these scores. For the sake of efficiency, learners in this model do not consider every token of every segment in their entire experience. In order to be resilient in the face of noisy data, however, learners also should not consider too little experience. Learners here consider accuracy and false alarm scores of the most recent 400 tokens of each segment, and so induce constraints only from persistent patterns of perceptual difficulty.

These scores are tracked as follows. In a given round (after round 150), each segment heard by the learner gets an accuracy score of 1 if it is correctly identified and 0 otherwise, as shown in (21). Similarly, each segment which the learner guesses it heard gets a false alarm score of 0 if the guess was correct and 1 if the guess was incorrect. Once the learner has collected 400 such accuracy or false alarm scores for a segment, they can be averaged to obtain a representative score for that segment, as in (22). Segments which are typically accurately identified have average accuracy scores close to 1, and segments for which the learner typically makes accurate guesses have false alarm scores close to 0.

(21)   HEARD: Initial p   -->   Initial p accuracy   = 0
        GUESS: Initial b   -->   Initial b false alarm = 1

(22)   ACCURACY: Initial p: 0.913   b: 0.920   t: 0.957   d: 0.970
        FALSE ALARMS: 0.080   0.093   0.027   0.040

Finally, after defining the elements that can be judged perceptually difficult, the phonotactic positions in which these elements' perceptibility is evaluated, and the criteria for finding particular segments perceptually difficult, a functionally grounded constraint schema must also define the constraints that are induced against perceptually difficult segments. Here, a positional markedness constraint of the form defined in (23) is induced. (*#P is an abbreviation for *p/#___.)

(23)   *x/Context$_z$ Assign one violation mark for each instance of x in Context$_z$.

The model described here has one additional property which is a significant simplification of any actual learners' induction processes.[10] This model is only concerned with the relative perceptibility of voiced and voiceless homorganic stop pairs. For this reason, the acoustic and perceptual differences between *p* and *b*, and *t* and *d*, are accurately modeled. Differences between other pairs of segments, however, are not. Therefore while the model can accurately assess the relative perceptual difficulty of *p* and *b* or *t* and *d*, any judgment it would make about the relative perceptibility of *b* and *d*, *p* and *t*, or other heterorganic pairs does not accurately reflect speakers' judgments about these segments' perceptibility. For this reason, the model never compares the perceptual difficulty of a segment to anything other than its homorganic counterpart.

The virtual speaker in the production component can speak either pseudo-French or pseudo-Cajonos Zapotec (pseudo-CZ); the only difference between these two languages is whether or not they allow word-initial *p*, as shown in (24). A learner of either pseudo-language compares accuracy and false alarm scores using the two methods described below. Section 6.2.2 describes the comparison of accuracy scores that allows pseudo-French learners to induce *#P, and section 6.2.3 describes the comparison of accuracy and false alarm scores that allows pseudo-CZ learners to also induce *#P.

(24)		Initial Cs	Medial Cs
	pseudo-French:	p b t d	p b t d
	pseudo-Cajonos Zapotec:	b t d	p b t d

6.2.2 Induction from accuracy scores: Pseudo-French

The virtual learner induces constraints against segments which it finds perceptually difficult. In intuitive terms, a pseudo-French learner knows that initial *p* is more perceptually difficult than initial *b* simply because initial *p* is recognized less accurately than initial *b*. In order for the learner to judge perceptual difficulty in a consistent way, it must have an explicit procedure for identifying difficulty which is persistent and significant enough to merit encoding in a constraint. This section describes the procedure which allows pseudo-French learners to consistently induce *#P.

The constraint inducer measures segments' accuracy scores against both absolute and relative criteria. A segment is perceptually difficult if its accuracy score (over the most recent 400 tokens of the segment) is lower than the absolute threshold of 0.9, and also significantly lower than that of its homorganic counterpart.

(25)   Some segment *x* is perceptually difficult in *Context$_Z$* if:

$$\text{Accuracy}(x/Context_Z) < 0.9$$

and

$$\text{Accuracy}(x/Context_Z) < \text{Accuracy}(y/Context_Z)$$

The two accuracy scores must be significantly different. ($\alpha = 0.01$)

---

[10] Restricting the model to *CaCa* words is another such simplification.

According to these criteria, initial p is perceptually difficult only if it is accurately identified less than 90% of the time, and if its accuracy score is significantly lower than that of initial b (as determined by a t-test, where $\alpha = 0.01$). The absolute difficulty measure ensures that only significant, persistent perceptual problems will be penalized by induced constraints. The relative measure further captures the inherently comparative character of markedness constraints: constraints are induced only against segments which are more difficult than others.

The results of pseudo-French simulations where constraints are induced through these accuracy criteria are summarized in Figure 6. The graph shows the sets of constraints induced in 250 pseudo-French simulations of 40,000 rounds each. Initial p's accuracy score is consistently both sufficiently low and also significantly lower than that of initial b. Therefore the inducer consistently observes that initial p is perceptually difficult, and so induces *#P in nearly every simulation; the very small number of simulations in which *#P is not induced would disappear if simulations were slightly longer. Because initial p is so much more perceptually difficult than initial b, the inducer has evidence for the opposite constraint *#B only extremely rarely.

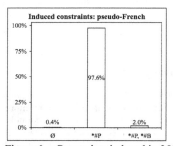

Figure 6.   Constraints induced in 250 pseudo-French simulations of 40,000 rounds each.

Unlike initial p and b, initial t and d are essentially equally perceptually difficult. While either may occasionally be significantly less accurately identified than the other, and either may very occasionally have an accuracy score below 0.9, these aspects of perceptual difficulty consistently fail to coincide. Learners therefore have no evidence for the induction of either *#T or *#D.

6.2.3   Induction from false alarm scores: Pseudo-Cajonos Zapotec

In this model of constraint induction, two segments' accuracy scores cannot be compared until a learner has collected enough accuracy scores for each segment to provide a reliable picture of the segments' overall perceptibility. This is enforced through the requirement that 400 tokens of each segment must be heard before the segments' accuracy scores can be compared. Learners who never hear any tokens of initial p never develop comparable accuracy scores for p and b, so a pseudo-CZ learner can never induce *#P via comparison of accuracy scores. It was argued above that all learners of all languages must induce the functionally grounded constraint *#p from their immediate experience with adult speech; for this reason, learners must be able to use perceptual measures in addition to accuracy score comparisons in order to identify initial *p* as perceptually difficult and induce *#p. The perceptual measure which allows pseudo-CZ learners to induce this constraint capitalizes on basic properties of the perceptual model implemented here, as follows.

The perception component of the model assumes that learners know which segments occur in the ambient language before they begin to learn segments' acoustic properties in each phonotactic position. That is, before learners undertake the perceptual learning procedure described above, they first identify an initial inventory of sounds present in their language. During perceptual learning, learners then expect to hear each of these in each phonotactic position.[11] In the case of a pseudo-CZ learner, *p* is present in pseudo-CZ, though it is never heard word-initially. But because the learner expect to hear each segment in the pseudo-CZ inventory – including initial *p* – in initial position, it occasionally misidentifies another initial stop as *p*. In this way, pseudo-CZ learners acquire false alarms for unattested initial *p*.

Learners therefore have a unique kind of perceptual experience with phonotactic gaps: segments which are missing in a particular position (e.g. word-initially) incur more false alarms than accurate identifications in that position. These false alarms are relatively rare but do consistently occur, as illustrated in Figure 7. Figure 7a shows the pseudo-CZ learner's accuracy with the three attested initial stops *b*, *t*, and *d*. This learner, like the pseudo-French learner described in section 5.1.2, identifies initial *t* and *d* with roughly comparable accuracy.

The pseudo-CZ learner is overall more accurate in its identification of initial *b* than the pseudo-French learner. This is because the pseudo-CZ learner has no knowledge of the detailed acoustic properties of initial *p* – crucially, this learner has no knowledge of the actual degree of similarity between initial *p* and *b*, and so this learner is less likely than the pseudo-French learner to misidentify initial *b* as *p*. Even without this knowledge, however, there is a small but consistent chance that the pseudo-CZ learner will make exactly this mistake, guessing that an atypical initial *b* is the expected but thus far unattested initial *p*. As the confusion matrix in Figure 7b shows, this misidentification occurs for 0.2% of initial *b* tokens.

---

[11] This initial inventory is stipulated in the present model; it could also be learned from the statistical properties of the segments that it hears, as proposed by Maye (2000) and as modelled by de Boer (2000). This initial inventory does not necessarily correspond to the language's actual phoneme inventory but instead is simply the learner's initial hypothesis space for early categorization.

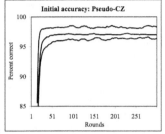

		Response			
		p	**b**	**t**	**d**
Segment	**p**				
	b	0.2%	98.4%	0.0%	1.4%
	t	0.1%	0.0%	97.1%	2.8%
	d	0.2%	1.2%	2.2%	96.4%

a.   b.

Figure 7.   Model accuracy for each initial pseudo-CZ consonant, averaged across 20,000 simulations of 300 rounds each; lines represent moving averages across 15-round windows (a). Confusion matrix for initial pseudo-CZ consonants, from the last 15 rounds of each of 20,000 simulations (b).

This property of 'gapped' segments like pseudo-CZ initial p can motivate the induction of *#P as follows. In addition to comparing different segments' accuracy scores, the model also compares each segment's false alarm score to its accuracy score. If some segment's false alarm score is not lower than its accuracy score – that is, if the false alarm score is higher than the accuracy score, or if there is a false alarm score but no accuracy score – the false-alarm-prone segment qualifies as perceptually difficult. Using this measure of perceptual difficulty, every simulated pseudo-CZ learner observes that initial p is prone to false alarms, and so induces the constraint *#P as shown in Figure 8.

(26)   Some segment x is perceptually difficult in $Context_Z$ if:

$$Accuracy(x/Context_Z) \quad \square FalseAlarm(x/Context_Z)$$

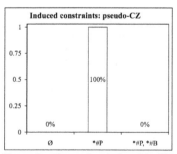

Figure 8.   Constraints induced in 250 pseudo-CZ simulations of 40,000 rounds each.

6.3   Summary of the constraint induction model

In this model, a learner of any (pseudo-)language considers accuracy and false alarm scores for recent tokens of each segment. Learners examine individual segments' accuracy scores, testing those which are below 0.9 to see whether they are significantly lower than those of their homorganic counterparts. At the same time, learners also compare individual segments' accuracy and false alarm scores. A segment is labeled perceptually difficult if either its accuracy score is below 0.9 and is significantly lower than that of some other segment, or if its false alarm score is greater than its accuracy score. These criteria are summarized in (27).

(27) Some segment x is perceptually difficult in $Context_Z$ if either:

$$\text{Accuracy}(x/Context_Z) < 0.9$$

and

$$\text{Accuracy}(x/Context_Z) < \text{Accuracy}(y/Context_Z) \rightarrow \text{Constraint } *x/Context_Z$$

This difference must be significant ($\alpha = 0.01$).

...or...

$$\text{Accuracy}(x/Context_Z) \ \square \ \text{FalseAlarm}(x/Context_Z) \rightarrow \text{Constraint } *x/Context_Z$$

Whenever a segment x is found to be perceptually difficult in some phonotactic position $Context_Z$, a positional markedness constraint of the form $*x/Context_Z$ is induced. Learners of languages like pseudo-French, where initial p is present but less perceptible than initial b, consistently induce the constraint *#P through comparison of accuracy scores. Learners of languages like pseudo-CZ, where initial p is absent, consistently induce the same constraint *#P through comparison of accuracy and false alarm scores.

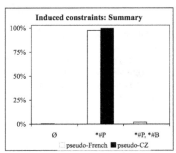

Figure 9. Constraints induced in each of 250 simulations of 40,000 rounds each.

7. General discussion and conclusion

The constraint induction component of this model has demonstrated that a perceptually grounded positional markedness constraint against word-initial p can be consistently induced from the diverse perceptual experiences of learners who hear this perceptually difficult segment, as well as those learning languages where p is banned word-initially.

This is possible because the inducer makes use of two measures of perceptual difficulty. The relative accuracy of initial p and b demonstrates p's perceptual difficulty in languages like French. In languages without initial p like Cajonos Zapotec, learners mistakenly expect to hear initial p and so occasionally misidentify initial b as p. This makes p's false alarm score higher than its accuracy score, which also indicates that initial p is difficult to accurately identify. The constraint *#P can be induced from perceptual difficulty in either case.

This case study of constraint induction illuminates the structure and role of constraint schemata in the induction of functionally grounded constraints. These schemata tell learners which positions and marked elements can be targeted by constraints. The functionally grounded schema governing the perceptual induction process described here tells the learner what how induced constraints should be defined, which kinds of phonological elements may be considered perceptually difficult, which phonotactic positions segments' perceptual difficulty should be assessed in, and how to compute and compare perceptual difficulty measures (i.e. accuracy and false alarm scores). Schemata for constraints grounded in facts of articulation, psycholinguistics, or other aspects of perception presumably make similar specifications.

While this paper has shown that the constraint *#P can be consistently induced from learners' immediate linguistic experience, it has not undertaken to show that learners actually do induce *#P in this way. The induction model demonstrated that realistic acoustic and perceptual properties of initial stops can be consistently mapped to attested constraints on initial segments; however, the question of whether real learners actually use this mechanism, or one like it, to induce *#P from the perceptual data considered here is left for future investigation. In determining that induction is possible in principle, a computational model can be used to develop hypotheses about constraint induction for further experimentation. Similarly, section 5.2.2 showed that the perceptual component of the model can also generate hypotheses about the acoustic source of initial p's perceptual difficulty, which could be tested in further perceptual experiments. In general, computational models of the sort developed here are valuable tools for showing whether constraint induction and other aspects of phonological learning are possible in principle, and also for developing further experimental investigations of these matters.

References

Akinlabi, Akinbiyi, and Eno E. Urua. 2002. Foot structure in the Ibibio verb. *Journal of African Languages and Linguistics* 23:119-160.

Archangeli, Diana, and Douglas Pulleyblank. 1994. *Grounded Phonology*. Cambridge, MA: MIT Press.

Ashby, F. Gregory, and W. Todd Maddox. 1994. A response time theory of separability and integrality in speeded classification. *Journal of Mathematical Psychology* 38:423-466.

Boersma, Paul, and Bruce Hayes. 2001. Empirical tests of the Gradual Learning Algorithm. *Linguistic Inquiry* 32:45-86.

Connell, Bruce. 1994. The Lower Cross languages: A prolegomera to the classification of the Cross River languages. *Journal of West African Linguistics* 24:3-46.

de Boer, Bart. 2001. *The Origins of Vowel Systems*. Oxford: Oxford University Press.

de Boer, Bart G. 2000. Self-organization in vowel systems. *Journal of Phonetics* 28:441-465.

Dempster, Arthur P., Nan M. Laird, and Donald B. Rubin. 1977. Maximum Likelihood from incomplete data via the EM algorithm. *Journal of Royal Statistics Society* 39:1-38.

Essien, Okon E. 1990. *A Grammar of the Ibibio Language*. Ibadan: University Press Limited.

Flack, Kathryn. 2007. The Sources of Phonological Markedness, University of Massachusetts Amherst: Doctoral dissertation.

Hay, Jessica. 2005. How Auditory Discontinuities and Linguistic Experience Affect the Perception of Speech and Non-Speech in English- and Spanish-Speaking Listeners, University of Texas Austin: Doctoral dissertation.

Hayes, Bruce, Robert Kirchner, and Donca Steriade eds. 2004. *Phonetically Based Phonology*. Cambridge: Cambridge University Press.

Hayes, Bruce P. 1999. Phonetically driven phonology: The role of Optimality Theory and inductive grounding. In *Formalism and Functionalism in Linguistics, vol. 1*, eds. M. Darness, E. A. Moravcsik, F. Newmeyer, M. Noonan and K. M. Wheatley, 243-285. Amsterdam: Benjamins.

Hooper [Bybee], Joan. 1976. *An Introduction to Natural Generative Phonology*. New York: Academic Press.

Jarosz, Gaja. 2006. Rich Lexicons and Restrictive Grammars - Maximum Likelihood Learning in Optimality Theory, Johns Hopkins University: Doctoral dissertation.

Jusczyk, Peter W. 1997. *The Discovery of Spoken Language*. Cambridge, MA: MIT Press.

Lisker, Leigh, and Arthur Abramson. 1964. A cross-language study of voicing in initial stops: Acoustical measurements. *Word* 20:384-422.

Maye, Jessica. 2000. Learning Speech Sound Categories from Statistical Information, University of Arizona: Doctoral dissertation.

Merchant, Nazzaré, and Bruce Tesar. to appear. Learning underlying forms by searching restricted subspaces. In *The Proceedings of CLS 41*. Chicago: Chicago Linguistics Society.

Mikuteit, Simone. 2006. A Cross Linguistic Inquiry on Voice, Quantity and Aspiration, Universität Konstanz: Doctoral dissertation.

Nellis, Donald G., and Barbara E. Hollenbach. 1980. Fortis versus lenis in Cajonos Zapotec phonology. *International Journal of American Linguistics* 46:92-105.

Ohala, John J. 1990. There is no interface between phonology and phonetics: A personal view. *Journal of Phonetics* 18:153-171.

Oller, D. Kimbrough. 2000. *The Emergence of the Speech Capacity*. Mahwah, N.J.: Lawrence Erlbaum Associates.

Pisoni, David B., and Joan House Lazarus. 1973. Categorical and noncategorical modes of speech perception along the voicing continuum. *Journal of the Acoustical Society of America* 55:328-333.

Pisoni, David B., and J. Tash. 1974. Reaction times to comparisons within and across phonetic categories. *Perception and Psychophysics* 15:285-290.

Prince, Alan, and Paul Smolensky. 1993/2004. *Optimality Theory: Constraint Interaction in Generative Grammar*. Malden, MA & Oxford: Blackwell.

Prince, Alan, and Paul Smolensky. 2004. *Optimality Theory: Constraint Interaction in Generative Grammar*. Malden, MA & Oxford: Blackwell.

Repp, Bruno. 1979. Relative amplitude of aspiration noise as a voicing cue for syllable-initial stop consonants. *Language and Speech* 22:173-189.

Smith, Jennifer L. 2002. Phonological Augmentation in Prominent Positions, University of Massachusetts Amherst: Doctoral dissertation.

Stampe, David. 1973. A Dissertation on Natural Phonology, University of Chicago: Doctoral dissertation.

Steriade, Donca. 1999. Alternatives to the syllabic interpretation of consonantal phonotactics. In *Proceedings of the 1998 Linguistics and Phonetics Conference*, eds. O. Fujimura, B. Joseph and B. Palek, 205-242. Prague: The Karolinum Press.

Steriade, Donca. 2001. The phonology of perceptibility effects: The P-map and its consequences for constraint organization. Ms. Los Angeles.

Tesar, Bruce, and Paul Smolensky. 1994. The learnability of Optimality Theory. In *Proceedings of the Thirteenth West Coast Conference on Formal Linguistics*, eds. Raul Aranovich, William Byrne, Susanne Preuss and Martha Senturia, 122-137. Stanford, CA: CSLI Publications.

Vihman, Marilyn May. 1996. *Phonological Development: The Origins of Language in the Child*. Oxford: Blackwell.

Department of Linguistics
South College
University of Massachusetts
Amherst, MA 01003

flack@linguist.umass.edu

Stages of Acquisition without Ranking Biases: the Roles of Frequency and Markedness in Phonological Learning[*]

Gaja Jarosz

Yale University

1.   Introduction

A growing body of literature within Optimality Theory (OT; Prince and Smolensky 1993/2004) focuses on the potential for formal computational learning algorithms to model aspects of the human acquisition process, including order of acquisition effects and intermediate stages (Boersma and Levelt 2000; Tessier 2006; Jesney and Tessier, this volume). This work characterizes learning as a gradual transition between an initial constraint ranking and the target ranking. In this and other work on acquisition and learnability within OT, initial (or persistent) explicit ranking biases are employed to structure the learner's path (Tesar 1995; Smolensky 1996; McCarthy 1998; Smith 2000; Gnanadesikan 1995/2004; Boersma and Hayes 2001; Hayes 2004; Prince and Tesar 2004; Tesar and Prince to appear). These ranking biases are used to establish an initial state from which subsequent learning of the ranking proceeds. This serves two principal functions: it aids in the identification of restrictive end-state grammars, and it enables modeling of the acquisition process as a transition from this initial state to the target grammar. In this paper, I apply MLG (Maximum Likelihood Learning of Lexicons and Grammars), the theory of phonological learning proposed in Jarosz (2006a, 2006b), to the problem of acquisition modeling. MLG models the learning of phonological grammars and lexicons of underlying forms relying on two general principals: richness of the base and likelihood maximization, but no explicit ranking biases are assumed. In related work (Jarosz to appear), I show that the first role of ranking biases is subsumed by MLG, which identifies restrictive grammar and lexicon combinations even in cases where ranking biases do not suffice.   In this paper, I show that MLG also predicts order of acquisition effects and intermediate stages without relying on ranking biases.

This paper also investigates the relative roles of markedness and frequency in phonological acquisition from both theoretical and empirical perspectives. In particular,

[*] I would like to thank Joe Pater, Karen Jesney, and Kathryn Flack for helpful comments on this paper.

Michael Becker (ed.): Papers in theoretical and computational phonology. University of Massachusetts Occasional Papers in Linguistics 36, 45-68.
GLSA Amherst.

the paper discusses the roles of markedness and frequency in MLG and presents empirical evidence of the causal connection between frequency and order of acquisition. While it is generally accepted that both markedness and frequency play some role in child acquisition, the proper characterization of the relative roles of markedness and frequency is a topic of ongoing debate (Levelt 1994; Levelt and Van de Vijver 1998; Levelt et al. 2000; Demuth 2004; Stites et al. 2004; Kirk and Demuth 2005; Zamuner et al. 2005). In MLG (see also Boersma and Levelt 2000), universal markedness is embodied in the constraint set, which defines the space of possible grammars cross-linguistically[1]. Frequency plays a secondary role, selecting the language-particular learning path based on the relative frequencies of various configurations in the ambient language. This prediction of MLG is examined in a series of case studies focusing on the acquisition of onset and coda clusters in Dutch, English, and Polish. Corpus analysis reveals that these three languages have distinct relative proportions of onset and coda clusters in adult, child-directed speech. The predictions of MLG are discussed with respect to developmental orders observed in children acquiring these languages. The observed developmental orders, evidenced by previous work on Dutch and English and novel data from Polish presented here, are consistent with the predictions of MLG.

2.   The Learning Theory

Maximum Likelihood Learning of Lexicons and Grammars (MLG) is a theory of phonological learning that accounts for the learning of phonological grammars and lexicons from unstructured overt phonological forms. This section presents an overview of the learning theory and discusses its treatment of markedness and frequency[2].

2.1.   General Structure of the Model

MLG is a generative, probabilistic model of the acquisition of a phonological grammar and lexicon of underlying forms. As such, it relies on a formal, probabilistic characterization of both the grammar and lexicon: the grammar and lexicon are both probabilistic entities. The grammar is a probability distribution over rankings of OT constraints and assigns a conditional probability to possible surface realizations of a given underlying form[3]. The lexicon is probabilistic as well and associates each morpheme with a set of possible underlying forms, each with its own likelihood. These probabilistic components can express uncertainty (as in the initial stages of learning) or variation by spreading probability over multiple rankings or underlying forms, and they can express certainty (as in the final stages of learning) by assigning to a single ranking

---

[1] Although I assume the constraint set is universal throughout this paper, I leave open the question of whether it is entirely innate. It is possible that the constraint set itself, or portions of it, can be learned from universal, shared experience; see Hayes (1999) and Flack (2007; this volume) for proposals along these lines.

[2] For a more in-depth presentation of the structure and properties of MLG see Jarosz (2006b).

[3] Various probabilistic variants of OT proposed in previous work, such as Stochastic OT, Partial Order Grammars, and Floating Constraints, are all examples of such a probabilistic grammar (Boersma 1998; Anttila 1997; Reynolds 1994).

or underlying form a probability of one. Together, the grammar and lexicon assign a likelihood, or probability, to the overt forms of the language.

Learning in MLG relies on two general principles: *richness of the base* (ROTB) and *likelihood maximization*. According to ROTB, the set of possible underlying forms is universal: there are no systematic, language-particular restrictions on underlying representations, and therefore all language-specific restrictions must be handled by the grammar (Prince and Smolensk 1993/2004). MLG incorporates a probabilistic formulation of ROTB into the learning model. The second learning principle, likelihood maximization, defines the correct grammar and lexicon combination as the one that maximizes the likelihood, or probability, of the overt forms. In other words, likelihood maximization requires that the grammar and lexicon combination generate all and only the observed forms of the target language with high probability, a standard generative perspective cast in a probabilistic setting.

These general principles form the foundation of MLG and are incorporated into a learning model with two stages of learning, phonotactic and morphophonemic learning (see also Prince and Tesar 2004; Hayes 2004):

(1)   Two Stage Learning in MLG
     a   Phonotactic Learning
        i   A fixed, universal rich base is assumed
        ii   No morphological awareness
        iii Grammar learning but no lexicon learning
     b   Morphophonemic Learning
        i   Words are analyzed into component morphemes
        ii   Learning of morpheme specific underlying forms occurs
        iii Further learning of the grammar to account for alternations

The phonotactic stage of learning occurs before morphological awareness and prior to the development of a phonological lexicon; it is during this stage that learning of a language-specific phonotactic grammar takes place. Formally, this stage consists of gradual learning of a grammar that maximizes the likelihood of the overt forms, given a (fixed) rich base. The rich base is a representation of all possible underlying forms, each with roughly equal likelihood. This base may be characterized as the expected, unbiased distribution over phonological forms given by the free combination of phonological elements. Under this characterization, phonotactic learning involves maximizing the likelihood of the observed distribution of overt forms, given the expected distribution.[4]

During morphophonemic learning, words are analyzed into component morphemes, and each morpheme is associated with its own probabilistic lexical entry. During this stage, the grammar gradually transitions between the phonotactic grammar

---

[4] A formally equivalent characterization of phonotactic learning in MLG involves an identical rich base associated with each morphologically unanalyzed overt form. Because the base is identical and unchanging, the overt forms are effectively generated from the same base.

learned in the first stage and the target grammar, while the lexicon gradually converges on the target lexicon. Formally, during morphophonemic learning the *grammar and lexicon combination* that maximizes the likelihood of the overt forms is gradually learned. Thus, the crucial difference between the two stages resides in the role of the rich base and lexical learning.

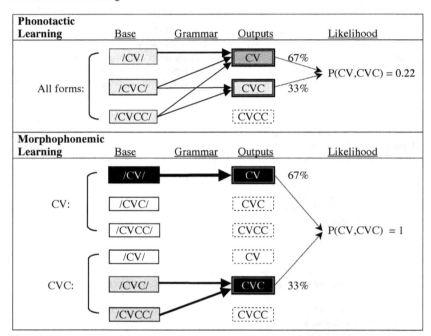

Figure 1: Outcomes of Phonotactic and Morphophonemic Learning in MLG

Figure 1 illustrates the outcomes of the two stages of learning with a simple example of a language with two overt forms, CV and CVC, the former occurring twice as often as the latter. During phonotactic learning, a single, equally-distributed rich base is held constant while the grammar that maximizes the likelihood of the overt forms is gradually learned. Phonotactic learning results in a restrictive grammar that matches the frequencies of the overt forms, given the rich base. This grammar is shown in the figure as a mapping from the rich base to the overt forms, with outputs generated in proportion to their frequency of occurrence (darker shading corresponds to higher likelihood). During morphophonemic learning, each morpheme (corresponding to each overt form in this case) is associated with its own probabilistic lexical entry. The lexical entries and grammar are gradually updated until they converge on the target lexicon and grammar shown in the lower portion of the figure. The target lexicon and grammar generate all and only the correct forms for each overt form, as indicated by the black shading of the correct output forms.

Although the division into phonotactic and morphophoremic learning in MLG follows previous work (Prince and Tesar 2004; Hayes 2004), the outcome and properties of phonotactic learning in particular are quite distinct from the earlier work. As Figure 1 illustrates, in MLG, unlike in previous work, the final phonotactic grammar is not an identity map that faithfully maps all legal configurations in the target language to themselves. The outcome of phonotactic learning in MLG is a restrictive grammar with a statistical bias against infrequent, marked configurations. This property of MLG is discussed in detail in Section 2.4.

2.2.   Linking Hypotheses to Development of Production

The division into the phonotactic and morphophonemic stages corresponds to children's phonological development. A large body of literature shows that children acquire at least some phonotactic knowledge by approximately 9 months of age (Jusczyk et al 1993; Friederici and Wessels 1993). On the other hand, learning of alternations and the lexicon occurs much later, roughly between the ages of 2 and 4.5 years, and in some cases even later (Berko 1958; Stager and Werker 1997; Pater 1997; Pater, Stager and Werker 2004; MacWhinney 1978). The two stages of MLG are based on this overall developmental progression.

Since phonotactic learning in MLG occurs prior to the development of a phonological lexicon and corresponds to development that occurs by 9 months of age, it is hypothesized that production does not occur until the morphophonemic stage. In particular, the onset of morphophonemic learning, when each form (or morpheme) is associated with an individual lexical entry, is hypothesized to correspond to the onset of production in children. In other words, the phonotactic grammar learned during the first stage serves as the initial production grammar for the model, and it is from this phonotactic grammar that further learning of the grammar proceeds. In sum, the path taken by the model between the initial production grammar and the target grammar corresponds to the predicted acquisition path. It is possible to model grammatical development in this way because phonotactic learning in MLG does not result in an identity map grammar.

This paper examines the effects of frequency and markedness on grammatical development. Since production is hypothesized to coincide with the onset of morphophonemic learning, the focus of this paper is on the grammatical progression predicted by the model during the morphophonemic stage and its correspondence to observed order of acquisition, as evidenced by production data.

2.3.   The Implementation

Given the overall structure of the MLG model, there are a number of possible implementations of the actual learning, or likelihood maximization, procedure. In the simulations described here, I employ the standard Expectation Maximization (EM) algorithm (Dempster et al. 1977). EM is a general-purpose algorithm for likelihood maximization with hidden variables, and it has some properties that make it a suitable candidate for the present task. First, EM is guaranteed to converge on a (local) maximum, and second, it adjusts the grammar and lexicon gradually. In other words, EM transitions gradually from the initial state of the grammar and lexicon to the target states, enabling an examination of the gradual learning path it predicts.

In these simulations, I make the simplifying assumption that the grammar and lexicon are lists of rankings and underlying forms, respectively, with associated probabilities. This simplifies the maximization step of the EM algorithm used here but is not an intrinsic aspect of MLG and crucially does not determine the overall, qualitative predictions of the theory. For a discussion of how more sophisticated representations of the grammar and lexicon may be implemented in MLG, see Jarosz (2006b).

2.4.   Deriving Stages in MLG: the Role of Frequency

To understand MLG's predictions for production, it is necessary to understand the final phonotactic grammar, which, as discussed above, is hypothesized to be the initial production grammar. The intermediate stages the grammar passes through on its way to the target grammar depend on the grammar's starting point and its update procedure. The central idea is that integrating a rich base into the phonotactic learning stage results in a final phonotactic grammar that is probabilistically biased against marked and infrequent forms. Essentially, the rich base results in a phonotactic grammar with a probabilistic (not absolute) Markedness » Faithfulness bias. This phonotactic grammar serves as the initial production grammar for the learner, and during the course of learning, the grammar gradually transitions from the initial Markedness » Faithfulness state to the target grammar.

To illustrate the properties of the phonotactic grammar and the predicted acquisition path, consider again the simple syllable structure example, reproduced in Figure 2 below. In this example, the target language consists of two overt forms, CV and CVC, with CV being twice as frequent as CVC. The universal rich base includes CV and CVC as well as a third form CVCC, with all three forms being equally likely.

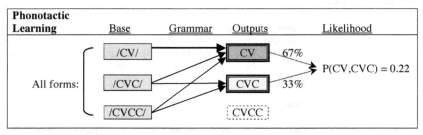

Figure 2: Derived Biases in Phonotactic Learning

Given the three constraints shown in (2)a, it is clear that the target morphophonemic grammar for this language is *COMPLEXCODA » MAX » NOCODA since complex codas are not permitted, while singleton codas are. This target grammar serves as the end-point of morphophonemic learning, while the starting point for morphophonemic learning is the final phonotactic grammar.

(2)   Phonotactic Grammar Illustration
    a   Constraint Set:
- MAX: Segments may not be deleted
- NOCODA: Syllable codas are not permitted
- *COMPLEXCODA: Complex syllable codas are not permitted

    b   Target (Morphophonemic) Grammar:
- *COMPLEXCODA » MAX » NOCODA

    c   Phonotactic Grammar:
- P(*COMPLEXCODA » NOCODA » MAX) = 50%
- P(*COMPLEXCODA » MAX » NOCODA) = 50%

As mentioned above, the phonotactic grammar exhibits a statistical bias against marked, infrequent forms. This statistical bias results from the pressure to maximize the likelihood of the overt forms *given the rich base*. In order to maximize the likelihood given the rich base in this example, the final phonotactic grammar must assign less than full probability to the mapping /CVC/ → CVC. Specifically, the maximum likelihood phonotactic grammar ranks *COMPLEXCODA highest and ranks NOCODA and MAX variably, such that the likelihood of either relative ranking is 50%, as shown in (2)c. This means that the mapping of /CVC/ → CV is just as likely as the mapping /CVC/ → CVC in the final phonotactic grammar.

To see why this is the maximum likelihood phonotactic grammar, it helps to think of the phonotactic grammar as a mapping between the distribution over underlying forms in the rich base and the distribution over overt forms in the ambient language. The maximum likelihood grammar is the mapping that does the best job of matching the frequencies of overt forms. In order to do so, the phonotactic grammar redistributes the probabilities associated with underlying forms in the base among the various overt forms. In this example, the probabilities distributed equally among /CV/, /CVC/ and /CVCC/ must be redistributed by the phonotactic grammar such that the likelihood of CV is two-thirds and the likelihood of CVC is one-third. Ranking *COMPLEXCODA highest means that the 33.3% of the probability mass associated with /CVCC/ in the rich base will be mapped to and distributed among CV and CVC. Ranking NOCODA and MAX equally means that /CVCC/ mapping to CV is equally likely as mapping to CVC, as depicted by the arrows pointing away from /CVCC/ in the figure. Under this variable ranking, /CVC/ itself will map to CV and CVC with equal likelihood, shown as arrows pointing away from /CVC/. In other words, the overt form CV gets one-third of the total, redistributed probability mass from underlying /CV/, and one-sixth of the probability mass from each of /CVC/ and /CVCC/. This redistribution is illustrated in the figure as arrows pointing to

CV. As a result, two-thirds of the probability mass ends up on CV and the remainder on CVC, matching the target distribution exactly.

The final phonotactic grammar encodes the legal and illegal phonotactics of the target language, mapping illegal configurations such as CVCC to legal ones. However, among the legal forms admitted by the grammar, there is a statistical bias, a soft preference, for unmarked and frequent configurations. In sum, in order to match the target distribution, the phonotactic grammar exhibits a bias against the marked infrequent forms by mapping some (or all, in case of illegal forms) of their input probability variably to the more frequent, less marked forms. This variable grammar serves as the starting grammar for morphophonemic learning.

At the onset of morphophonemic learning, learning of underlying representations begins: each morpheme (or overt form) is assigned its own lexical entry, which is gradually adjusted during this stage. As a result, overt forms no longer share the rich base as they do during phonotactic learning, and the maximum likelihood morphophonemic grammar generates for each overt form the correct output form(s) from their correct underlying representations[5].

In the present example, the morphophonemic stage consists of a gradual transition between the phonotactic grammar in (2)c and the adult, target grammar in (2)b. Because the phonotactic grammar maps /CVC/ to CV half the time, it displays a probabilistic Markedness » Faithfulness bias relative to the target grammar. That is, NoCoda is probabilistically higher ranked than Max in the phonotactic grammar relative to the target grammar. In this simple example, the learning path involves a gradual transition from equally ranked NoCoda and Max to a ranking with Max dominating NoCoda completely. This means the learner begins with a grammar in which codas are not reliably produced and gradually converges on the target grammar that generates codas faithfully.

This probabilistic bias against marked forms is a consequence of the target language distribution and rich base and is itself not specified anywhere in the model. The strength of the initial bias depends on a number of factors, including the target language distribution and the particular choice of rich base. In general, the lower the frequency of a marked configuration, the stronger the initial bias against it will be. For example, if the target distribution in the above example exhibited 80% CV forms, then a stronger NoCoda » Max bias would be required to match the target distribution. Thus, the strength of the bias rests in part on the presence of a statistical bias against the marked configuration in the target language relative to the rich base. However, no amount of statistical evidence in favor of a marked configuration over an unmarked configuration

---

[5] The maximum likelihood morphophonemic grammar (target grammar) does not match frequencies because the overt forms during morphophonemic learning have their own lexical entries, and probability mass is no longer shared between distinct lexical entries. In the maximum likelihood morphophonemic grammar, frequency matching only occurs among forms in free variation, forms generated from the same lexical entry.

can ever result in a bias in favor of marked forms. For instance, given the implicational universals embodied in the constraint set, no ranking characterizes a language that requires codas, and therefore no phonotactic grammar (or intermediate grammar) where codas are favored or required is possible.

The contents and distribution of the rich base also affect the strength of the bias. If a larger base consisting additionally of CVCCC were used, then a lower probability would be associated with CV in the base, and the NoCoda » Max bias would need to be stronger in order to match the high frequency associated with CV in the target distribution. In the simple example discussed above, the bias is not particularly strong, but as the simulations in the next section will show, when even marginally more complex examples are designed and applied to target distributions representative of actual languages, the biases are strong enough to predict a complex and realistic series of acquisition stages.

In sum, the morphophonemic stage in MLG models the gradual mastery in production of the various configurations in the target language. The starting point for production is a grammar that encodes the phonotactics of the target language probabilistically, assigning probability to legal configurations only and exhibiting a statistical bias against marked, infrequent configurations. The probabilistic nature of MLG enables phonotactic learning to result in a grammar that corresponds to an early stage of development in children when language-particular phonotactics have been acquired but production is unmarked relative to the target language. The predicted acquisition path corresponds to the transition between this language-particular unmarked state and the final, adult grammar.

2.5.   The Relative Roles of Markedness and Frequency in MLG

While the role of frequency in MLG is significant, its effects are secondary to that of markedness. In essence, universal markedness is embodied in the constraint set, which defines the space of possible learning paths, and language-specific frequency selects among those paths. This view of the relative roles of markedness and frequency is not new to MLG (Levelt 1994; Levelt and Van de Vijver 1998; Levelt et al. 2000; Boersma and Levelt 2000). What is new to MLG is that the initial, unmarked state of the grammar is derived from general learning principles rather than being stipulated. In MLG, as in the previous work cited above, order of acquisition is influenced, but not determined by frequency. Frequency can only influence the classes of phonological units embodied in the constraint set: the frequency of individual forms plays no direct role in grammatical learning. Each overt form contributes to the frequency of the phonological classes of which it is part, and it is the frequency of these general phonological classes that shapes learning. Phonological class membership is hierarchical and complex, however, and any attempt to calculate the effects of frequency on a single configuration must take into account the net effects of many interacting factors.

In sum, in MLG markedness and frequency both have important roles, markedness on a universal level, and frequency on a language-particular level. In particular, if any implicational relationships are entailed by universal markedness, these implications cannot be reversed in the learning path. For example, since no OT grammar can describe a language that admits complex codas but not singleton codas (complex codas entail singleton codas in universal markedness), a learning path where complex codas are learned before singleton codas is not possible. On the other hand, when markedness considerations are ambivalent or contradictory, the effects of frequency can emerge. Taking the example of coda and onset clusters that will be taken up later in the paper, since markedness does not determine a relative order for these two configurations, relative frequency is able to do so, favoring the more frequent of the two. This does not mean, however, that all types of the more frequent configuration will necessarily be acquired before all types of the less frequent configuration. It is entirely possible for other frequency and markedness factors to penalize a particularly marked subtype of the more frequent type. For example, even though complex codas may in general be acquired earlier than complex onsets, some complex codas, such as clusters with particularly difficult segments like affricates or retroflexes, may be acquired later than some complex onsets as long as there are markedness constraints against these segments.

2.6. Comparison with Explicit Ranking Biases

In general, the order of acquisition predictions of MLG and learning models with an explicit Markedness » Faithfulness ranking bias are not that different[6] (Boersma and Levelt 2000; Tessier 2006; Pater, Jesney, and Tessier to appear). One important difference between the intermediate stages predicted by MLG and theories with ranking biases is that the phonotactic grammar in MLG that serves as the initial production grammar already embodies a sort of language-specific markedness. The phonotactic grammar encodes the legal phonotactics of the target language in a way such that phonotactically illegal configurations are no longer allowed by the grammar. Therefore, the learning path will involve a gradual transition from the language-particular unmarked initial state to the language-particular target state, with only phonotactically legal productions predicted[7]. Gradual learning from a general Markedness » Faithfulness initial bias need not be so constrained.

A simple example can illustrate this point. Consider a language with intervocalic voicing, with two competing markedness constraints on voicing, *VOICE, prohibiting voicing in general, and *VTV, prohibiting voicelessness intervocalically. A general Markedness » Faithfulness may be implemented by ranking *VOICE and *VTV equally high, well above IDENTVOICE. Since *VOICE and *VTV are equally ranked, they will interact in the initial stages with some productions of phonotactically illegal voiceless intervocalic segments predicted[8]. In MLG, on the other hand, *VOICE is already

---

[6] Although I have not comprehensively explored this, the effects of other biases, such as Specific Faithfulness » General Faithfulness, should in principle be derivable as well if the ambient language supports a statistical bias in their favor relative to the rich base.

[7] It would be possible for phonotactic restrictions to be overpowered by factors that become active only in the morphophonemic stage, such as constraints that rely on morphological or lexical information.

[8] In weighted constraint systems, this prediction holds only if intervocalic voicing is an active phonological process conditioning alternations (and not a static regularity) that requires underlying voiceless intervocalic

lower ranked in the phonotactic grammar, and phonotactically illegal productions are not predicted. This seems to be a desirable prediction overall since children's non-adult-like productions in general abide by the phonotactic restrictions of the target language (Zamuner et al., in prep; though see Jesney and Tessier, this volume, for some exceptions).

3.   Case Studies: Syllable Structure Acquisition

This section describes a series of case studies that explore the role of markedness and frequency in the acquisition of syllable structure in three languages with distinct syllable type frequency profiles. The studies focus on the relationship between relative frequency and the relative order of acquisition of complex onsets and complex codas.

From a markedness perspective, there is no implicational relationship between complex onsets and complex codas. Some languages allow complex onsets but not complex codas (Spanish), while others allow complex codas but not complex onsets (Finnish). Examining the relative order of acquisition and its relationship to relative frequency in languages that permit both types of clusters can shed light on the role of frequency in phonological acquisition.

The purpose of this section is twofold. The first goal is to illustrate the capacity of MLG to predict stages of acquisition when applied to input distributions extracted from adult, child-directed speech. The input distributions in the three languages differ significantly, which provides an opportunity to examine how cross-linguistic differences in acquisition order arise in MLG.

The second goal is to examine the hypothesis that frequency plays a causal role in shaping the acquisition process by examining the relationship between relative frequency and relative acquisition orders in three languages. Previous findings are indicative of a connection between frequency and acquisition order (Ingram 1988; Levelt 1994; Levelt and Van de Vijver 1998; Levelt et al. 2000; Roark and Demuth 2000; Kirk and Demuth 2005); nonetheless; further work examining this relationship cross-linguistically for various structures is necessary before a causal connection can be established.

Previous research on acquisition of consonant clusters has examined the relative order of acquisition and relative frequencies of complex codas and onsets in English and Dutch. The predominant order attested in English-speaking children is acquisition of complex codas before complex onsets (Kirk and Demuth 2005; Templin 1957). In English, complex codas are also significantly more frequent than complex onsets in adult, child-directed speech (Kirk and Demuth 2005). Dutch-speaking children, on the other hand, show variation in the order of acquisition, with a preference for acquiring complex codas first (Levelt 1994; Levelt and Van de Vijver 1998; Levelt et al. 2000). As shown

---

segments to be mapped to voiced correspondents. Otherwise, if the voicing is underlying, lower-weighted IDENTVOICE could settle the tie between the higher-weighted constraints in favor of the phonotactically legal variant.

by Levelt et al. (2000), the relative frequencies of various syllable types in Dutch corresponds to the order of acquisition of these syllable types. The frequencies of complex onsets and codas are roughly equivalent in adult, child-directed speech (with complex codas being slightly, but not significantly, more frequent), to which the authors attribute the variation in attested acquisition orders. More precisely, the version of the frequency hypothesis under investigation in the previous work and the present study is summarized in (3).

(3)   The Frequency Hypothesis (based on Levelt and Van de Vijver (1998)):
        Universal markedness constrains possible learning paths cross-linguistically while language-particular learning paths are driven by the relative frequencies of output configurations in the ambient language.

These findings are consistent with a frequency-based explanation, but they leave open the possibility of alternative explanations as well. Overall, these two languages still show a preference for complex codas to be acquired first; therefore, an explanation in terms of universal factors, such as the structural complexity of onset clusters, or factors common to the two languages, such as articulatory difficulty, is viable as well (Kirk and Demuth 2005). In addition, in both languages word-final clusters contain more morphological information than word-initial clusters, leaving open the possibility of a morphological explanation.

To provide a more thorough test of the frequency hypothesis, an examination of the acquisition of syllable structure in a language for which the frequency hypothesis makes the opposite prediction is required. An example of such a language is Polish. As the corpus analysis presented in Section 3.1.3 reveals, complex onsets are significantly more frequent than complex codas in adult, child-directed speech in Polish. Consequently, the frequency hypothesis and the MLG simulation predict an order of acquisition favoring earlier acquisition of complex onsets. The final portion of the section presents novel data from Polish suggesting that complex onsets are indeed acquired before complex codas in child Polish.

3.1.   Syllable Structure Simulations

The three MLG simulations modeling the acquisition of syllable structure in Dutch, English and Polish are identical except for the frequencies of various syllable types that are provided to the learner. The frequencies of various syllable types are estimated from adult, child-directed speech in each language as described in the corresponding sections.

The design of the simulation is based on Boersma and Levelt (2000). All simulations model the acquisition of nine syllable types: CV, CVC, CVCC, V, VC, VCC, CCV, CCVC, and CCVCC. All simulations employ the set of five standard syllable structure constraints shown below.

(4)   Constraint Set for Syllable Structure Simulations:
        ONSET: No vowel initial syllables
        NOCODA: No consonant final syllables
        *COMPLEXONSET: No syllable-initial consonant clusters
        *COMPLEXCODA: No syllable-final consonant clusters
        MAX: No deletion

The rich base used in the simulations consists of all syllable types, each with equal likelihood, shown in (5). Since the base is assumed to be universal, the exact same base is used during phonotactic learning for all languages. As discussed in the Section 2.4, many of the precise numerical predictions of MLG depend on the exact nature of the rich base. Since this base is clearly a major simplification of the universal rich base, the predictions of the simulations should be interpreted broadly and qualitatively[9]. Nonetheless, predictions about relative order of acquisition within each language can be examined, and comparisons between languages can be made.

(5)   Rich Base Employed in All Simulations:

CV	CVC	CVCC	V	VC	VCC	CCV	CCVC	CCVCC
0.11%	0.11%	0.11%	0.11%	0.11%	0.11%	0.11%	0.11%	0.11%

As discussed in Section 2, predictions of MLG for production derive from the path taken by the grammar during the morphophonemic learning. Accordingly, the presentation of the simulations focuses on the learning path of the grammar during morphophonemic learning and the associated stages of acquisition predicted by the learning theory.

3.1.1. Dutch

As discussed above, complex onsets and complex codas in Dutch occur in roughly equal proportions. As can be seen in the distribution of syllable types in child-direct speech in Table 1 (Boersma and Levelt 2000), the combined frequency of syllables with complex onsets is 3.7%, while the combined frequency of syllables with complex codas is 4%. This difference is not statistically significant (Levelt and van de Vijver 1998). Under the frequency-based hypothesis, this results in an order of acquisition which is variable for these two syllable types. Indeed, Levelt (1994) observed two acquisition orders in a study of twelve Dutch-speaking children:

(6)   Attested Acquisition Paths in Dutch (Levelt 1994):

$$CV \rightarrow CVC \rightarrow V \rightarrow VC \rightarrow \begin{matrix} CVCC \rightarrow VCC \rightarrow CCV \rightarrow CCVC \\ CCV \rightarrow CCVC \rightarrow CVCC \rightarrow VCC \end{matrix} \rightarrow CCVCC$$

---

[9] It is worth noting that if the base were made more detailed (with distinct types of consonants for example), the Markedness » Faithfulness bias in the phonotactic grammar would become stronger overall. This is because expanding the number of segment types places more probability mass in the rich base on longer, more marked structures overall, and the phonotactic grammar must overcome this effect to match the distribution of the language.

Comparing the order of acquisition in (6) to the relative frequencies in Table 1, it is clear that there is a strong correspondence between order of acquisition and relative frequency; however, where frequency is roughly equal, variation in acquisition orders is found.

Table 1: Relative Frequencies of Syllable Types in Dutch

CV	44.8%
CVC	32.1%
CVCC	3.3%
V	3.9%
VC	12.0%
VCC	0.4%
CCV	1.4%
CCVC	2.0%
CCVCC	0.3%

This target distribution is used in the MLG simulation, and the resulting acquisition order during morphophonemic learning is depicted in the chart below. The chart shows the relative time at which three thresholds of production accuracy (95%, 85%, 75%) were reached by the learner for the various syllable types. The syllable types are ordered according to their relative learning order. As shown in the chart, the acquisition order of complex onsets and codas is predicted to be extremely close: both are produced with approximately 85% accuracy by the 150th iteration of learning.

Since the difference between the frequencies of onset and coda clusters is not significant in the sample overall, it is likely that different children are exposed to slightly different distributions, with some children hearing complex codas more frequently and others hearing complex onsets more frequently. If this simulation were repeated with slightly different relative frequencies of clusters, variation in acquisition order would be predicted over multiple trials, with earlier acquisition order corresponding to higher relative frequency in the sample. It is also possible that variation results from randomness in the learning procedure itself, as suggested by Levelt et al. (2000) and Boersma and Levelt (2000)[10]. Further work examining the effect of frequency on order of acquisition within a single language is needed to answer this question.

---

[10] The implementation adopted here employs the EM algorithm, which, in its standard form, is a deterministic algorithm. Noise could be introduced into the algorithm in any number of ways, however, and this would result in variable order of acquisition of syllable types whose acquisition orders are very close in the standard version of the algorithm.

Chart 1: Predicted Order of Acquisition for Dutch

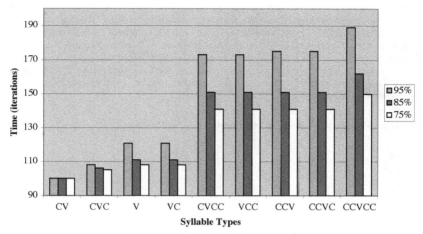

The order of acquisition of the other syllable types is consistent with the attested acquisition orders. As discussed in the previous section, frequency guides the order of acquisition in the learning model, but it does not directly translate into acquisition order. For example, the relative frequencies of V and VC, 3.9% and 12%, respectively, do not translate into a relative acquisition order with VC being learned earlier. In this constraint system, V and VC are treated as a class due to their violation of ONSET, while NOCODA can no longer distinguish between the two types because it has been ranked well below MAX and plays no active role in the grammar. This appears to coincide with children's development: children do not acquire VC earlier, despite its dramatically higher frequency[11]. This illustrates the primary role of markedness in MLG: frequency cannot drive the earlier acquisition of a more marked configuration.

3.1.2. English

Previous research has established that complex codas are significantly more frequent than complex codas in child-directed English and shown that complex codas tend to be acquired earlier (Kirk and Demuth 2005; Templin 1957). In order to set up an MLG simulation for English comparable to the above Dutch simulation, however, the relative

---

[11] The observation that VC is actually acquired later than V by children who have already acquired CVC, as reported in Levelt (1994), appears to be a kind of cumulativity effect that is problematic for all OT models. However, interestingly, the very same simulation shows that cumulativity of a sort is possible in OT. The acquisition order for the syllable type with violations of both *COMPLEXONSET and *COMPLEXCODA, CCVCC, is later than the acquisition of syllable types with only one of these violations. This is because acquisition order is defined in terms of reaching a threshold of accuracy, which may be reached later for forms that are subject to more unfaithful mappings in the developing grammar.

frequencies of all syllable types in English are required. To get an estimate of the relative token frequencies of the various syllable types in English child-directed speech, the primary stressed monosyllabic words were extracted from the CHILDES Parental Corpus (MacWhinney 2000; Li and Shirai 2000). The CHILDES Parental Corpus consists of 2.6 million word tokens and 24,156 word types of which 67% were monosyllabic, primary stressed words used in this analysis. The syllables were phonemicized using the CMU Pronouncing Dictionary (Weide 1994), and the relative frequencies of the various syllable types were tallied. This estimate of the distribution of the various syllable types in English is shown in Table 2[12].

Table 2: Relative Frequencies of Syllable Types in English

CV	24.4%
CVC	40.5%
CVCC	10.1%
V	4.7%
VC	13.0%
VCC	3.5%
CCV	0.9%
CCVC	2.2%
CCVCC	0.6%

As can be seen from these data, the overall frequency of complex codas is 14.2% while the frequency of complex onsets is 3.7%. In the MLG simulation, this difference in relative frequencies results in a predicted acquisition order with complex codas acquired much earlier than complex onsets. Given the input distribution in Table 2, no reasonable amount of noise is likely to allow variation in the order of acquisition. In other words, MLG predicts that complex codas should be acquired before complex onsets by English-speaking children.

Overall, the predicted order for English is very similar to the order in Dutch, except for the added restriction that complex codas be acquired before complex onsets. In both languages, onsetless syllables are acquired before complex margins. This is not terribly surprising as the English and Dutch distributions are very similar, and the two languages are closely related. The next simulation looks at a more distantly related language: Polish.

---

[12] This estimate could certainly be improved by including all stressed syllables, but what is crucial for present purposes is that the relative proportion of complex codas is notably higher than the proportion of complex onsets, consistent with previous findings. Kirk and Demuth (2005) find the overall proportion of complex codas to complex onsets in child-directed speech to be 2:1, suggesting that the difference in frequencies estimated here may be somewhat overestimated.

Chart 2: Predicted Order of Acquisition for English[13]

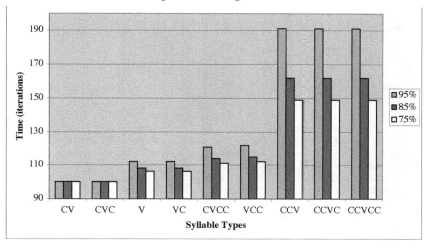

3.1.3. Polish

A corpus analysis of parental speech found in the Szuman corpus of Polish, available in CHILDES (Smoczynska 1985; MacWhinney 2000), reveals that complex onsets are more frequent than complex codas in Polish child-directed speech. Monosyllabic words were extracted from the corpus and automatically phonemicized based on the orthography (which reliably corresponds to pronunciation), resulting in a corpus of 118,701 syllables. The proportions of various syllable types are shown in Table 3. In this estimate of syllable proportions, the relative frequency of complex onsets is 10.1%, while the relative frequency of complex codas is 6%[14].

---

[13] Though this is not the focus of this study, careful readers may note that according to this simulation, CV and CVC syllable types should be acquired at roughly the same time. This prediction results from the simplifying assumptions about the rich base made in this simulation, and should not be taken as a prediction of MLG in general.

[14] To confirm the robustness of the difference between the relative frequencies of coda and onset clusters, two other corpora analyses were performed. One estimated the relative proportions of the various syllable types from the proportions of word-final and word-initial clusters in parental speech. Another analysis estimated the proportions of syllable types from monosyllabic words extracted from the IPI PAN corpus of written Polish. Both analyses revealed an even stronger difference between the two cluster types than found in the analysis used above.

Table 3: Relative Frequencies of Syllable Types in Polish

CV	54.7%
CVC	19.0%
CVCC	5.3%
V	9.0%
VC	1.6%
VCC	0.3%
CCV	4.4%
CCVC	5.3%
CCVCC	0.4%

These frequencies were submitted to the MLG learner, and the predicted order of acquisition is shown below. The difference in relative frequencies between the two cluster types results in a clear difference in the predicted order of acquisition. Unlike the Germanic languages in the previous two simulations, Polish exhibits a higher proportion of complex onsets, which in turn corresponds to the earlier acquisition of complex onsets. Another notable difference between the Germanic languages and Polish is the relative proportion of onsetless syllables to complex margins of either kind. As noted above, in English and Dutch, onsetless syllables are predicted to be acquired prior to either complex margin type. On the other hand, onsetless syllables are relatively infrequent in Polish and are therefore predicted to be acquired late relative to the other languages.

Chart 3: Predicted Order of Acquisition for Polish

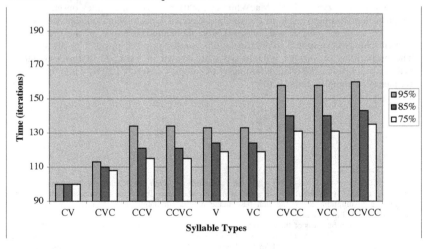

The remaining question is, of course, whether the prediction of the frequency hypothesis concerning the relative order of acquisition of cluster types corresponds to actual acquisition orders exhibited by children acquiring Polish. Previous research addressing this question is limited although one brief description of the acquisition of clusters by three Polish children suggests these children acquired initial clusters before final clusters (Dziubalska-Kołaczyk 1998). Providing a comprehensive answer to this question is beyond the scope of this paper; however, Section 3.2 discusses the results of a preliminary analysis that suggests the predicted order may be preferred in Polish.

3.2.   Developmental Order in Child Polish

This section describes a study investigating the relative order of acquisition of coda and onset clusters in child Polish.

3.2.1. Method

The data are from spontaneous productions of three Polish-speaking children from the Weist corpus of child Polish, available as part of the CHILDES corpus (Weist and Witkowska-Stadnik 1986; Weist et al. 1984; MacWhinney 2000). The digitized recordings were phonologically transcribed using the ChildPhon program (Rose 2003). The ages of the children range from 1;7 to 2;1.

For each child, target word-final and word-initial CC clusters were identified and coded as either correct or incorrect. Focusing on word edge clusters avoids the complication of the inherent ambiguity in word-medial syllabification in Polish, especially since syllabification may not be adult-like. Target clusters were coded as correct if they were produced as clusters, and coded as incorrect otherwise. Consonant-to-consonant substitutions were not counted as errors; however, less than 2% of the clusters coded as correct involved substitutions that involved a change in sonority level. In other words, when the clusters were produced, they were very close to the adult targets. The vast majority of errors (about 90%) involved deletion, although coalescence (for stop-fricative sequences to affricates) and epenthesis were also observed.

3.2.2. Results

The percent correct production for each child and each cluster type is shown in Table 4. As shown in the table, the percent correct production on initial clusters ranges from 47.7% to 71.4% while the percent correct production on final clusters ranges from 0% to 40.5%. Even with this small sample of productions, the results are significant: each of the children has a significantly higher proportion of correct complex onsets than correct complex codas (as measured by Fisher's Exact Test).

While complex onsets have a significantly higher proportion for all the children, the highest accuracy on complex codas relative to complex onsets is found in Bartosz's productions. In other words, the accuracy in production of complex onsets and codas is closest in this data. Intriguingly, the relative proportions of complex onsets to complex codas extracted just from Bartosz's parental input differ from the proportions found in parental speech sample from the three children grouped together. The relative frequencies of complex onsets and complex codas in Bartosz's parental input are 10.3% and 9.5%, respectively, which is a significant difference (Fisher's Exact Test, $p < 0.01$) from the more distinct relative frequencies found in the sample overall.

Table 4: Children's Production Accuracy on Onset and Coda Clusters in Polish

	Age	#CC Targets	#CC % Correct	CC# Targets	CC# % Correct	Fisher's Exact Test
Marta	1;7	86	47.7%	11	0%	$p < 0.01$
Bartosz	1;11	99	61.6%	42	40.5%	$p < 0.05$
Kubus	2;1	56	71.4%	14	21.4%	$p < 0.01$

3.2.3. Discussion

While these results are certainly not definitive, they suggest that children acquiring Polish do in fact show a tendency to acquire complex onsets before complex codas. The higher accuracy in production of complex onsets in the data above suggests that mastery (as defined by some threshold of accuracy) will be achieved earlier for complex onsets than for complex codas in subsequent stages. However, to fully understand the developmental progression, a longitudinal analysis examining the development of clusters in a larger sample of children is required. One potential issue with the present study is that the child productions in the corpus are spontaneous, not controlled in any way. As a result, many of the targets are represented by a small number of lexical items produced multiple times. For example, a majority of the complex coda targets are tokens of the word [jɛst] – "is" (3rd person, singular). As a result, it is not clear how representative the results are of coda clusters in general. Further work testing the accuracy of cluster production in an experimental setting will likely be required to overcome the limitations of this methodology.

Nonetheless, the results do support the frequency hypothesis and the predicted order of acquisition in the simulation, especially when considered together with the predictive success of the frequency hypothesis in English and Dutch. Since the results of this study suggest a different relative order of acquisition of complex onsets and codas in different languages, the explanations that appeal to universal factors such as structural complexity are not supported. The data presented here do not speak to an articulatory explanation. A finer-grained analysis, looking at order of acquisition of various clusters relative to their relative articulatory difficulty in the three languages, is needed to examine the articulatory explanation.

The results may also support the morphological explanation. This is because while Dutch and English final clusters contain more morphological information than initial clusters, the reverse is true in Polish. Indeed, a study examining the acquisition of clusters morpheme-internally and across morpheme boundaries in Polish found a tendency for clusters that cross morpheme boundaries to be produced more accurately earlier (Zydorowicz 2007). On the other hand, a comparable analysis for English found no effect of morphological complexity (Kirk and Demuth 2005). These mixed findings indicate that further work exploring the morphological explanation is needed as well.

An interesting possibility is raised by the apparent individual differences in the present study. The correspondence between Bartosz's input distribution and his relatively high coda cluster accuracy may be accidental. However, if there are in fact significant differences between the input distributions for different children within a single language, then the frequency hypothesis predicts that individual differences in acquisition order could arise as a result. Whether significant individual differences in input distribution exist between children acquiring the same language and, if so, whether these differences correspond to differences in acquisition order, are questions for further research. An advantage of examining the frequency hypothesis within a single language is that other factors corresponding to alternative explanations (such as the morphological, articulatory, and structural explanations) are constant.

4.   Conclusion

In conclusion, this paper has examined the relative roles of frequency and markedness from the perspectives of computational modeling and child acquisition. MLG, a theory that relies on two general principles to solve a number of learnability problems, is shown to be capable of modeling acquisition order without relying on built-in ranking biases. A strength of MLG is that productions are predicted to abide by language-particular phonotactic restrictions. The predicted acquisition orders in MLG are sensitive to markedness and frequency, with markedness constraining possible acquisition paths on a universal level and frequency constraining acquisition paths on a language-particular level.

The predictions of MLG for the acquisition order of syllable structure are examined in three languages with distinct distributions of syllable types. The distributions of syllable types in the three languages, estimated from adult, child-directed speech, are found to be predictive of the relative order of acquisition in these languages, as evidenced by previous work on Dutch and English and a study on Polish cluster acquisition presented here. These findings provide support for the causal role of frequency in acquisition, and in particular, for a learning theory in which markedness and frequency interact as they do in MLG.

References

Anttila, Arto. 1997. *Variation in Finnish Phonology and Morphology*. Ph.D. thesis, Stanford Univ.

Berko, Jean. 1958. The child's learning of English morphology. *Word* 14, 150-177.

Boersma, Paul. 1998. *Functional Phonology*. Doctoral Dissertation, University of Amsterdam. The Hague: Holland Academic Graphics.

Boersma, Paul and Bruce Hayes. 2001. Empirical tests of the Gradual Learning Algorithm. *Linguistic Inquiry* 32(1):45-86.

Boersma, Paul and Clara C. Levelt. 2000. Gradual constraint-ranking learning algorithm predicts acquisition order. In *The proceedings of the thirtieth annual child language research forum*, ed. Eve V. Clark. Stanford: CSLI.

Dempster, Arthur P., Nan M. Laird, and Donald B. Rubin. 1977. Maximum Likelihood from incomplete data via the EM Algorithm. *Journal of Royal Statistics Society.* 39(B):1-38.

Dziubalska-Kołaczyk, Katarzyna (1999): "Early L1 clusters and how they relate to universal phonotactic constraints" in Proceedings of the 14th International Congress of Phonetic Sciences, San Francisco. San Fransisco: University of Berkeley, 317-320.

Flack, Kathryn. 2007. *Sources of Phonological Markedness.* Ph.D. dissertation, University of Massachusetts, Amherst.

Flack, Kathryn. to appear. Inducing functionally grounded constraints. In M. Becker (ed.), *UMass Occasional Papers in Linguistics* 36.

Friederici, Angela D. and Jeanine E. Wessels. 1993. Phonotactic knowledge of word boundaries and its use in infant speech perception. *Perception and Psychophysics* 54, 287-295.

Gnanadesikan, Amahlia. 1995/2004. Markedness and faithfulness constraints in child phonology. In R. Kager, W. Zonneveld, J. Pater, eds., *Fixing Priorities: Constraints in Phonological Acquisition*, Cambridge, Cambridge University Press.

Hayes, Bruce. 2004. Phonological acquisition in Optimality Theory: the early stages. Appeared in Kager, Rene, Pater, Joe, and Zonneveld, Wim, (eds.), *Fixing Priorities: Constraints in Phonological Acquisition.* Cambridge University Press.

Ingram, David. 1988. The Acquisition of Word-Initial [v]. *Language and Speech.* 31(1). 77-85.

Jarosz, Gaja. 2006a. Richness of the Base and Probabilistic Unsupervised Learning in Optimality Theory. *Association for Computational Linguistics: Proceedings of the Eighth Meeting of the ACL Special Interest Group in Computational Phonology.*

Jarosz, Gaja. 2006b. *Rich Lexicons and Restrictive Grammars - Maximum Likelihood Learning in Optimality Theory.* Ph.D. dissertation, Johns Hopkins University..

Jarosz, Gaja. to appear. Restrictiveness in Phonological Grammar and Lexicon Learning. *43rd Annual Meeting of the Chicago Linguistics Society*, Chicago, Illinois.

Jesney, Karen and Anne-Michelle Tessier. to appear. ???. In M. Becker (ed.), *UMass Occasional Papers in Linguistics* 36.

Jusczyk, Peter W., Angela D. Friederici, Jeanine M.I. Wessels, Vigdis Y. Svenkerud, and Ann Marie Jusczyk. 1993. "Infants' sensitivity to the sound patterns of native language words," *Journal of Memory and Language* 32, 402-420.

Kirk, Cecilia, and Katherine Demuth. 2005. Asymmetries in the Acquisition of Word-initial and Word-final Consonant Clusters. *Journal of Child Language* 32: 709-734.

Levelt, Clara. 1994. On the Acquisition of Place. Doctoral Dissertation Leiden University, HIL Dissertation Series 8.

Levelt, C., N. Schiller, and W. Levelt. 2000. The Acquisition of Syllable Types. *Language Acquisition* 8(3), 237-264.

Levelt, Clara and Ruben Van de Vijver. 1998. Syllable Types in Cross-Linguistic and Developmental Grammars. Rutgers Optimality Archive 265.

Li, P., and Shirai, Y. 2000. *The acquisition of lexical and grammatical aspect.* Berlin & New York: Mouton de Gruyter.

MacWhinney, B. 1978. The acquisition of morphophonology. *Monographs of the Society for Research in Child Development,* 43, Whole no. 1.

MacWhinney, B. 2000. *The CHILDES project (3rd Edition).* Mahwah, NJ: Lawrence Erlbaum.

McCarthy, John J. 1998. Morpheme structure constraints and paradigm occultation. Appeared in M. Catherine Gruber, Derrick Higgins, Kenneth Olson, and Tamra Wysocki, eds., *Proceedings of the Chicago Linguistic Society 5,* Vol. II: The Panels, Chicago, CLS.

Pater, Joe, Karen Jesney and Anne-Michelle Tessier. 2007. Phonological acquisition as weighted constraint interaction. In Alyona Belikova, Luisa Meroni and Mari Umeda (eds.), *Proceedings of the Conference on Generative Approaches to Language Acquisition - North America (GALANA 2).* Somerville, MA: Cascadilla Proceedings Project.

Pater, J., C. Stager, and J. Werker. 2004. The Perceptual Acquisition of Phonological Contrasts. *Language* 80.3.

Prince, Alan, and Paul Smolensky. 1993/2004. Optimality Theory: Constraint interaction in generative grammar. Technical Report, Rutgers University and University of Colorado at Boulder, 1993. Revised version published by Blackwell, 2004.

Prince, Alan and Bruce Tesar. 2004. Learning Phonotactic Distributions. Appeared in Kager, Rene, Pater, Joe, and Zonneveld, Wim, (eds.), *Fixing Priorities: Constraints in Phonological Acquisition. Cambridge University Press.*

Reynolds, Bill. 1994. *Variation and phonological theory.* Doctoral Dissertation, University of Pennsylvania.

Roark, B. and Katherine Demuth. 2000. Prosodic constraints and the learner's environment: A corpus study. *Proceedings of the Boston University Conference on Language Development,* 24, 597-608.

Rose, Yvan. 2003. ChildPhon: A Database Solution for the Study of Child Phonology. *Proceedings of the 26th Annual Boston University Conference on Language Development.* Somerville, MA: Cascadilla Press.

Smith, Jennifer L. 2000. "Positional faithfulness and learnability in Optimality Theory," in Rebecca Daly and A. Rehl, eds., *Proceedings of ESCOL99,* Ithaca, CLC Publications.

Smoczynska, M. (1985). *The acquisition of Polish. The crosslinguistic study of language acquisition.* D. I. Slobin. Hillsdale, N. J., Erlbaum: 595-686.

Smolensky, Paul. 1996. The Initial State and 'Richness of the Base'. Technical Report JHU-CogSci-96-4.

Stager, Christine, and Janet Werker. 1997. Infants listen for more phonetic detail in speech perception than in word-learning tasks. *Nature* 388. 381-382.

Stites, Jessica, Katherine Demuth, and Cecilia Kirk. 2004. Markedness vs. Frequency Effect in Coda Acquisition. In Alejna Brugos, Linnea Micciulla, & Christine E. Smith (eds.), *Proceedings of the 28th Annual Boston University Conference on Language Development,* pp. 565-576.

Templin, Mildred. 1957. *Certain Language Skills in Children: Their Development and Interrelationship* (Monograph Series No. 26). Minneapolis: University of Minnesota, The Institute of Child Welfare.

Tesar, Bruce. 1995. *Computational Optimality Theory.* Ph.D. dissertation, University of Colorado, Boulder.

Tesar, Bruce, and Alan Prince. to appear. Using phonotactics to learn phonological alternations. Revised version will appear in *The Proceedings of CLS 39*, Vol. II: The Panels. ROA-620.

Tessier, Anne-Michelle. 2006. *Biases and stages in phonological acquisition.* Ph.D. dissertation, University of Massachusetts, Amherst.

Weide, Robert L. 1994. CMU Pronouncing Dictionary. http://www.speech.cs.cmu.edu/cgi-bin/cmudict.

Weist, R., & Witkowska-Stadnik, K. (1986). Basic relations in child language and the word order myth. *International Journal of Psychology*, 21, 363–381.

Weist, R., Wysocka, H., Witkowska-Stadnik, K., Buczowska, E., & Konieczna, E. (1984). The defective tense hypothesis: On the emergence of tense and aspect in child Polish. *Journal of Child Language,* 11, 347–374.

Zamuner, T.S., Gerken, L.A., and M. Hammond. 2005. The acquisition of phonology based on input: A closer look at the relation of cross-linguistic and child language data. *Lingua*, 10, 1403-1426.

Zamuner, T.S., Kerkhoff, A., & Fikkert, P. (in prep.). Children's knowledge of how phonotactics and morphology interact.

Zydorowicz, Paulina. 2007. Polish Morphonotactics in First Language Acquisition. In Menz, Florian and Marcus Rheindorf (eds.), *Weiner Linguistische Gazette* 74, 24-44.

Department of Linguistics
Yale University
370 Temple St.
New Haven, CT 06511

gaja.jarosz@yale.edu

Re-evaluating learning biases in Harmonic Grammar[*]

Karen Jesney[1] & Anne-Michelle Tessier[2]

[1]University of Massachusetts Amherst & [2]University of Alberta

1.   Introduction

In the Optimality Theoretic learnability and acquisition literature it has been frequently argued that certain classes of constraints must be biased toward high ranking. These biases have two primary motivations: allowing the restrictive intermediate stages attested in acquisition to emerge, and ensuring that restrictive final-state grammars can be successfully reached. Three main biases have been proposed; these are listed in (1).

(1)   *Biases required for restrictive learning with ranked constraints*
   a.   MARKEDNESS >> FAITHFULNESS (e.g., Demuth 1995, Granadesikan 2004, Pater 1997, Smolensky 1996)
   b.   SPECIFIC FAITHFULNESS >> GENERAL FAITHFULNESS (e.g., Hayes 2004, Prince & Tesar 2004, Smith 2000, Tessier 2007)
   c.   OUTPUT-OUTPUT FAITHFULNESS >> MARKEDNESS (e.g., Hayes 2004, McCarthy 1998, Tessier 2006b, 2007)

While intuitively simple, biases of this sort have proven challenging to implement using on-line learning algorithms like the Gradual Learning Algorithm (GLA; Boersma 1998, Boersma & Hayes 2001). In this paper we show that altering the mode of constraint interaction from strict ranking as in Optimality Theory (OT; Prince & Smolensky 1993/2004, McCarthy & Prince 1995) to additive weighting as in Harmonic Grammar (HG; Legendre, Miyata & Smolensky 1990, Smolensky & Legendre 2006) substantially reduces the number of biases needed in order to ensure restrictive learning. Using weighted constraints and a simple GLA-style learning algorithm allows the three biases in (1) to be reduced to the single bias in (2).

---

[*]   For comments, suggestions and criticisms that have affected this work directly or indirectly, we would like to thank Joe Pater, Michael Becker, Paul Boersma, Gaja Jarosz, John McCarthy, Pat Pratt, Bruce Tesar and Matt Wolf.

Michael Becker (ed.): Papers in theoretical and computational phonology. University of Massachusetts Occasional Papers in Linguistics 36, 69-110.
GLSA Amherst.

(2) *Single bias required for restrictive learning with weighted constraints*
     wOUTPUT-BASED CONSTRAINTS > wINPUT-OUTPUT-BASED CONSTRAINTS

This bias is incorporated into the initial state by assigning substantially greater importance (i.e., higher values) to MARKEDNESS and OUTPUT-OUTPUT FAITHFULNESS constraints than to INPUT-OUTPUT FAITHFULNESS constraints, and by requiring that the weights of Output-based constraints be adjusted more quickly than those of Input-Output-based constraints. This is sufficient to ensure that the attested range of restrictiveness effects emerges through learning based on positive evidence from the target language. No additional biases are necessary.

     Section 2 begins by reviewing the specific assumptions about weighted constraint interaction and learning that are made here. Section 3 demonstrates the need for distinct treatments of Output-based constraints and Input-Output-based constraints in this framework with particular reference to Markedness and IO-Faithfulness constraints. Section 4 illustrates how restrictive intermediate stages involving Specific Faithfulness and OO-Faithfulness constraints emerge naturally within this framework without the need for biases beyond that in (2), and section 5 demonstrates how these results extend to restrictive final-state grammars. Finally, section 6 compares the present model to previous proposals in the Optimality Theoretic learnability and acquisition literature.

2.   Grammar and Learning Assumptions
2.1   Harmonic Grammar

Like classical Optimality Theoretic grammars, Harmonic Grammars have three components: GEN, a function that takes an input form and returns a series of output candidates, CON, the set of constraints (these are normally taken to be universal), and EVAL, the means of constraint interaction that serves to select an optimal output candidate from among the set provided by GEN. The first two components – GEN and CON – are the same in OT and HG; it is only the mode of constraint interaction – EVAL – that differs crucially between the two theories.

     In OT, constraints are strictly ranked with respect to one another. Candidates are assessed based on this hierarchy in a manner such that violations of lower-ranking constraints are relevant only when higher-ranking constraints alone cannot select a single optimum.

(3) *Strict domination*

			C1	C2	C3
i.		[A]	*!		
ii.	☞	[B]		*	*
iii.		[C]		**!	

In the OT tableau in (3) the highest-ranked constraint – C1 – rules out candidate (3i), which performs worse on this constraint than both of the other candidates. The decision between candidates (3ii) and (3iii) is then passed down to the next constraint – C2. These two candidates both violate C2, but (3ii) does so to a lesser extent than (3iii), incurring one violation rather than two. Candidate (3ii) is thus deemed optimal (the 'winner'). According to the strict domination logic of OT, the fact that (3i) does not violate C2 at all does not matter; (3i) is ruled out by C1, the highest-ranking constraint, and no virtues it may display with respect to lower-ranking constraints can redeem it. (See McCarthy 2002 for thorough discussion of OT's strict-domination approach to candidate evaluation.)

In Harmonic Grammar, constraints are weighted rather than ranked, and EVAL operates by selecting the candidate with the highest Harmony value. A candidate *R*'s Harmony (*H*) is determined by multiplying its score on each constraint {C1, C2, C3, ..., C*n*} by that constraint's weight {w1, w2, w3, ..., w*n*}, and then summing. Constraint violations are treated as penalties, ensuring that the highest possible harmony value for any candidate is 0.[1]

(4) $H(R) = C1(R)*w1 + C2(R)*w2 + C3(R)*w3 + ... + Cn(R)*wn$

In many cases, the result of this additive mode of EVAL is the same as with strict domination.

(5) *Basic additive interaction*

		C1 w=4	C2 w=2	C3 w=1	H
i.	[A]	-1			-1(4)= **-4**
ii. ☞	[B]		-1	-1	-1(2)+-1(1)= **-3**
iii.	[C]		-2		-2(2)= **-4**

In (5) C1 has a weight of 4, C2 has a weight of 2, and C3 has a weight of 1. The winning candidate is the one whose violations are the least weighty – i.e., the one that has the highest score. In (5), then, it is candidate (5ii) that wins with a summed weight of -3, violating C2 once and C3 once; both of the losing candidates have summed weights of -4. (The right-most column shows the Harmony value of each candidate.)

While the result in (5) is very similar to what would occur within a ranked constraint system where C1 >> C2 >> C3 (see (3) above), this need not be the case. With weighted constraints, multiple lower-valued constraints can *gang up* to overcome a higher-valued constraint. Indeed, most of the situations discussed in the rest of this paper rely upon multiple lower-valued constraints ganging up in such a way that their combined weight is greater than the weight of single higher-valued constraint. This has the effect of allowing lower-valued constraints to impact the selection of the winner in ways not possible in ranked-constraint OT. The basic type of situation of interest here is

[1] Following Prince (2002) and Pater, Potts & Bhatt (2006), we limit constraint weights here to positive real numbers. We argue in section 3, however, that constraint weights of 0 are also necessary for learning restrictiveness purposes (see also Keller 2000, 2006).

schematized in (6), where all that has been altered from (5) are the weights of C1 (now 3 rather than 4) and C3 (now 2 rather than 1).

(6)   *Additive interaction with gang effect*

	C1 w=3	C2 w=2	C3 w=2	H
i. ☞ [A]	-1			-1(3)= **-3**
ii. [B]		-1	-1	-1(2)+-1(2)= **-4**
iii. [C]		-2		-2(2)= **-4**

Candidate (6i) violates only C1, and so incurs a summed weight of -3. Candidate (6ii) violates C2 and C3, incurring a summed weight of -4, while candidate (6iii) violates C2 twice, also incurring a summed weight of -4. The Harmony value of (6i) is thus *greater than* the Harmony value of either (6ii) or (6iii), and so (6i) is selected as optimal. This occurs despite the fact that (6i) violates C1, the highest-weighted constraint, and neither of the other candidates do. The additive mode of interaction and evaluation in HG allows *all* constraint violations to affect the selection of an optimal output form. This is the primary difference between HG and OT modes of EVAL, and plays a crucial role in reducing the number of biases necessary for restrictive learning.

2.2   Gradual Learning

Given a weighted constraint system like that described above, it is natural to consider a learning algorithm that will gradually adjust the numerical values (i.e., the weights) of the constraints on the basis of the language to which the learner is exposed. A number of such algorithms exist specifically for weighted systems, but for comparative purposes we begin with the Gradual Learning Algorithm (Boersma 1998, Boersma & Hayes 2001), which is normally applied to ranked OT grammars.

The GLA treats constraints as arrayed along a continuum like that in (7) below.

(7)

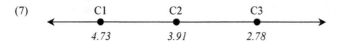

In a strict domination OT system, these numerical values are converted to a ranking with each application of EVAL, with higher-valued constraints being accorded higher positions in the hierarchy. The continuum in (7) would thus be transformed into the ranking in (8).[2]

---

²   Constraint values are typically perturbed by noise in Stochastic OT systems so that with each iteration of EVAL a specific value for each constraint is selected from a normal distribution around the mean value of that constraint. This serves to reverse rankings on occasion, allowing variation to be modeled (see especially Boersma & Hayes 2001). This same approach to variation can be applied to HG systems (Boersma & Pater 2007, Jesney 2007b, Pater 2007, to appear); all of the HG-GLA simulations presented here use a noise value of 2.0 (the standard value in Praat – Boersma & Weenink 2007).

(8)   C1 >> C2 >> C3

In a weighted constraint system, *no conversion* to a ranking like that in (8) is necessary. Instead, the numerical values associated with the constraints are simply taken as their weights and evaluation occurs as discussed in section 2.2.

Given input data from which to learn and a set of initial constraint values, the Gradual Learning Algorithm adjusts constraint values along the continuum using the procedure summarized in (9).

(9)   *GLA procedure*
   a.   Given an input-output pair from the ambient language, the learner takes the input and feeds it to his grammar (GEN, EVAL) to determine which output candidate his current grammar deems optimal.
   b.   If the output candidate selected by his grammar matches the observed output, the grammar remains unchanged.
   c.   If the output candidate selected by his grammar does not match the observed output, the observed output is identified as the *winner* and the output selected by the grammar is identified as the *loser*. The grammar is then adjusted by:
      • Increasing the numerical value of winner-favouring constraints by some small amount x,
      • Decreasing the numerical value of loser-favouring constraints by some small amount x.

There are two necessary differences between weighted and ranked constraint systems with respect to the implementation of the GLA. The first comes in step a, where the appropriate mode of EVAL (additive vs. strict domination) must be selected. The second comes in step c, where the adjustment of constraint values in the case of HG must be sensitive to the extent of violation of each constraint. This is made necessary by the fact that in HG multiple violations of a single lower-weighted constraint can gang up to overcome a single violation of a higher-valued constraint. The result of the formula in (10) is thus used to determine the extent to which each constraint's value is adjusted (i.e., the value of x) when the GLA is applied to weighted constraint grammars (see also Jäger to appear). Relativizing the adjustment of constraint values in this way makes the GLA update procedure for weighted constraints essentially the same as the Perceptron update rule of Rosenblatt (1958).

(10) $x = n(vL - vW)$, where $0 < n < 1$, and vL is the number of violations of the constraint incurred by the loser and vW is the number of violations of the constraint incurred by the winner.

The calculation in (10) is undesirable with ranked constraints. There, x can be simply set at a constant value, reflecting the fact that in a strict domination system there is no possibility for multiple violations of a lower-valued constraint to gang up and

Jesney & Tessier

overcome the weight of a higher-valued constraint (see Boersma & Pater 2007 for discussion).

For the sake of simplicity, we will use the term "GLA" throughout this paper for both versions of this general learning procedure. Application of the GLA to weighted constraint systems is greatly facilitated by the availability in Praat (Boersma & Weenink 2007) of a weighted mode of evaluation that limits constraints to values greater than or equal to zero. Following Keller (2000, 2006), this decision mode is termed 'LinearOT.'[3] The 'symmetric all' learning procedure corresponds to the procedure in (9), with appropriate adjustments for ranked vs. weighted modes of EVAL.

All versions of the GLA are error driven, with learning triggered whenever there is a mismatch between the forms found in the ambient language and those produced by the learner's current grammar. Learning occurs only in this type of mismatch scenario; no negative evidence, implicit or explicit, is used. By way of example, consider a child acquiring a language like English that allows complex onsets. This target requires that the child eventually attain a grammar where wMAX $>$ w*COMPLEX (or MAX $\gg$ *COMPLEX in ranking terms) so that forms like *black* are consistently rendered faithfully. If his current grammar assigns a greater value to *COMPLEX than to MAX, however, the simplified form will instead be selected as optimal.[4]

(11) *Grammar with non-target-like output selected*

	/black/	*COMPLEX $w=100$	MAX $w=50$	H
i.	black	-1 L ●➡		-1(100) = **-100**
ii.	☜* back		⬅●-1 W	-1(50) = **-50**

Upon noting this inconsistency between the target form and the output of his grammar, the learner identifies the intended output *black* as the 'winner' and the grammar's selected output form *back* as the 'loser.' The values of all constraints favouring the winner are then increased by x and the values of all constraints favouring the loser are decreased by x. In this case the value of x is the same for both constraints because the difference in number of violations between the winner and the loser is $|1|$ in both instances.

(12) *Adjusted grammar with non-target-like output (still) selected*

	/black/	*COMPLEX $w=99$	MAX $w=51$	H
i.	black	-1 L ●➡		-1(99) = **-99**
ii.	☜* back		⬅●-1 W	-1(51) = **-51**

---

[3]   The 'Positive HG' decision mode limits constraints to values greater than or equal to one, while the 'HarmonicGrammar' decision mode allows constraints with both positive and negative values.

[4]   The symbol ☜* is used to indicate selection of a non-target-like form – i.e., an error from which learning can occur.

Adjustment of constraint values according to this procedure continues until the value of MAX surpasses that of *COMPLEX and no further errors are made – in other words, until the grammar converges.

As Boersma & Levelt (2000) demonstrate with ranked constraints, this error-driven learning procedure is sensitive to the frequency of different types of input-output pairs and can replicate the stage-like development seen in child language. It also has the benefit of being on-line and, unlike implementations of the Biased Constraint Demotion Algorithm (BCDA; Prince & Tesar 2004), does not require storage of mark-data pairs. At the same time, however, the GLA with ranked constraints fails to learn restrictive grammars in some cases (Tessier 2007, see also section 6.1), and fails to converge entirely in others (Pater to appear).

The combination of Harmonic Grammar and the GLA retains the on-line learning benefits identified in earlier work, and also converges in cases that are problematic with ranked constraints (Boersma & Pater 2007, Pater to appear; see also Pater, Jesney & Tessier 2007). Furthermore, as we show in the following sections, the HG-GLA combination allows for restrictive learning in cases that prove problematic for OT-GLA, and does this with fewer biases than are required with off-line algorithms like the BCDA.

3.   Markedness and IO-Faithfulness Constraints

In order to ensure restrictiveness of learning, a single initial bias must be retained in the HG-GLA system. This bias, which specifies an initial high value for Output-based constraints and an initial value of zero for Input-Output-based constraints, ensures both that final-state grammars are restrictive and that the learner passes through restrictive intermediate stages in acquiring the language. This section expands upon the motivation for both aspects of this initial bias, beginning with the high initial value of Output-based (Markedness) constraints in section 3.1 and then moving on in section 3.2 to the initial value of zero for Input-Output-based (IO-Faithfulness) constraints. We return to OO-Faithfulness constraints in sections 4 and 5.

3.1   Markedness Starts High

Structures produced as part of child language are typically less marked than those found in the adult target (see, among many others, Demuth 1995, Gnanadesikan 2004, Kehoe & Stoel-Gammon 1997, Pater 1997, Stampe 1973). In Harmonic Grammar, this can be attributed to a relatively higher weighting of Markedness constraints in the child grammar than in the adult target. In particular, the value of Markedness must be greater than that of IO-Faithfulness in the child's system even if the value of IO-Faithfulness is greater than that of Markedness in the adult language.

(13)   a.   Child language: wMARKEDNESS > wIO-FAITHFULNESS
        b.   Adult target: wIO-FAITHFULNESS > wMARKEDNESS

This difference in the weighting of the relevant constraints can only be ensured in the HG-GLA system if it is built in as a bias in the initial state. Consider, for example, a target language that includes the palatal fricative [ç] within its inventory. This is a relatively uncommon segment cross-linguistically (Ladefoged & Maddieson 1994), and so it is highly unlikely that a child acquiring such a language would include it within his or her initial inventory. Ideally, then, the child's grammar should consistently display the wMarkedness $> w$IO-Faithfulness pattern in (14a) in the initial state.

(14)   a.   Child language: $w*Ç > w$IDENTPALATAL
      b.   Adult target: wIDENTPALATAL $> w*Ç$

Guaranteeing this inequality requires that the markedness constraint $*Ç$ be biased toward a higher initial value than the conflicting IO-Faithfulness constraint. As the tableau in (15) demonstrates, if Markedness and IO-Faithfulness constraints have the same initial value, the faithful output candidate [ç] will potentially be selected as optimal even at the very earliest stages of language acquisition.

(15)   *Markedness and IO-Faithfulness at the same level*

	/ç/	IDENTPAL $w=100$	$*Ç$ $w=100$	H
i.	☞ ç		-1	$-1(100) = -100$
ii.	☞ s	-1		$-1(100) = -100$

With the two constraints having the same initial value, the noise within the system is sufficient to place the selection point for $*Ç$ above that for IDENTPALATAL on a regular basis. Any time this happens, the faithful output candidate [ç] will emerge.

(16)   *Markedness and IO-Faithfulness at the same level with added noise*

	/ç/	IDENTPAL $w=101.1$	$*Ç$ $w=99.9$	H
i.	☞ ç		-1	$-1(99.9) = -99.9$
ii.	s	-1		$-1(101.1) = -101.1$

Crucially, this selection of the marked output form takes place *before any learning has occurred.*[5] In other words, the child's grammar includes the marked, faithful output at the very earliest stage. Any learning will push the weight of IDENTPALATAL further up, consolidating the admissibility of [ç]. At no point will the child pass through a stage

---

[5]   Hale & Reiss (1998) argue that IO-Faithfulness constraints must outrank Markedness constraints in the initial state of OT grammar learning. Under these assumptions, errors in children's early productions are attributed to performance factors rather than to the grammar *per se*. While it is true that young infants are very often able to perceive contrasts that are absent from the adult target, these abilities are generally held to be phonetic rather than phonemic in nature (Barton 1976, 1980). Research into children's early *phonological* systems indicates that contrasts are acquired gradually, with complexity increasing over time and with exposure to the target language (see Pater et al. 2004 for discussion and a recent review). It is this phonological development that we aim to model here.

where the marked output is strictly disallowed; even the initial state grammar of the child is unrestrictive.

As alluded to above, the solution to this problem of non-restrictiveness is quite simple. All that needs to be done is to impose a condition on the initial constraint values so that Output-based constraints (like Markedness constraints) have a greater weight than Input-Output-based constraints (like IO-Faithfulness constraints).

(17) *Bias required for restrictiveness in HG-GLA*
      *w*OUTPUT-BASED CONSTRAINTS > *w*INPUT-OUTPUT-BASED CONSTRAINTS

With this initial bias in place, child grammars will consistently disfavour marked structures like [ç] in the initial state, as can be seen in (18) below.[5]

(18) *The restrictive bias: Markedness **higher than** Faithfulness*

/ç/		*Ç $w=100$	IDENTPAL $w=0$	H
i.	ç	-1 L ●→		-1(100) = **-100**
ii.	☞ s		←● -1 W	-1(0) = **0**

For a child acquiring a language that includes palatal fricatives, selection of the unmarked output [s] as in (18) will be considered an error and will trigger learning. The winner-favouring constraint IDENTPAL will thus be promoted and the loser-favouring constraint *Ç will be demoted until eventually *w*IDENTPAL > *w**Ç and the target adult grammar is reached.

The lack of restrictiveness associated with initial equal weightings of Markedness and IO-Faithfulness constraints is also a problem for final state grammars. Consider, for example, an adult who has acquired an L1 like English whose inventory lacks palatal fricatives. Assuming, as is usual, that in acquisition the input form to the child's grammar is the adult surface form (e.g., Smith 1973, Gnanadesikan 2004, Pater 1997), this native speaker of English will never have been exposed to evidence to trigger either the promotion *Ç or the demotion of IDENTPALATAL. In the adult grammar, then, both constraints will retain their initial value of 100, leading to a tableau like (15). As a result, palatal fricatives will be optionally produced as such when non-native inputs like /ç/ are submitted to the adult grammar. Without an initial bias that distinguishes between Markedness and IO-Faithfulness constraints, the adult grammar is unrestrictive – a clearly undesirable result.

Imposing the initial bias in (17) solves the restrictiveness problem for adult grammars. Without evidence for the promotion or demotion of either the Markedness or IO-Faithfulness constraint in the target language, the final state grammar of the English learner will retain the *w***Ç > *w*IDENTPALATAL inequality, ensuring that input instances of

---

[6]   The motivation for assigning an initial value of 0 to Input-Output-based constraints is discussed in section 3.2.

the marked segment /ç/ are mapped to some other structure in the output. The bias in (17) thus helps to restrict the final state grammar so that it admits just those marked structures for which evidence is available in the ambient language.   In sum, restrictiveness in both child and adult Harmonic Grammars requires that Output-based constraints be initially valued more highly than Input-Output-based constraints.

3.2   IO-Faithfulness Starts at Zero

On the simplest interpretation of the wOUTPUT-BASED > wINPUT-OUTPUT-BASED bias, any set of weights corresponding to the inequality should be adequate. This, however, is not sufficient to ensure restrictiveness in every case. While Output-based constraints can start at any high point (e.g., 100), Input-Output-based constraints need to start very low – at zero – for restrictiveness to be guaranteed.

The necessity of this initial zero value for IO-based constraints is best illustrated by considering cases where the target language has a pattern of strict complementary distribution between two segments. In such cases, the distribution is determined solely by markedness considerations, with the input specification of the segments playing no role in selecting the optimal output form. An example of such a system is the Greek palatal-velar pattern illustrated in (19).

(19)   *Greek velar-palatal alternations in the imperfect present tense* (Kazazis 1969:384)

	"Have"	"Leave"
1sg	[éxo]	[févɣo]
2sg	[éçis]	[févjis]
3sg	[éçi]	[févji]
1pl	[éxume]	[févɣume]
2pl	[éçete]	[févjete]
3pl	[éxune]	[févɣune]

In Modern Greek, the marked palatal segments [ç] and [j] are in complementary distribution with the velars [x] and [ɣ]; the palatals appear just before front vowels, while the velars appear in all other contexts. As with other patterns of complementary distribution, two Markedness constraints are necessary to capture this pattern – a Specific Markedness constraint militating against velars before front vowels (*XI) and a General Markedness constraint disfavouring palatal segments (the same *Ç constraint as in section 3.1). In order to capture the target adult distribution, the weight of the Specific Markedness constraint must be greater than that of the General Markedness constraint (20a).   Furthermore, in order to ensure that the preferences imposed by the two Markedness constraints are not undercut by the input specification of the segments, adding the weight of IO-IDENT to that of the General Markedness constraint *Ç must not reverse the basic inequality (20b).

(20)   *Necessary inequalities for Modern Greek*
   a. w*XI > w*Ç
   b. w*XI > w*Ç + wIO-IDENT

In order for this set of target inequalities to be acquired, errors must arise in the child's language that favour the promotion of the Specific Markedness constraint *XI and/or the demotion of the General Markedness constraint *Ç so that w*XI > w*Ç. The necessary errors can only exist if the faithful mapping is not always preferred. Assigning a starting value of zero to IO-Faithfulness constraints ensures that this will be the case.

As illustration, the tableau in (21) shows the selection of a non-target-like form based on input /éçete/. Noise has perturbed the values of the Markedness constraints from their starting points so that w*Ç=101.1 and w*XI=99.9.

(21) *Selection of non-target-like form with wIDENTPAL=0 – Error prompts learning*

	/éçete/	*Ç *w=101.1*	*XI *w=99.9*	IDENTPAL *w=0*	*H*
i.	éçete	L -1●▶			-1(101.1) = **-101.1**
ii.	●※ éxete		◀●W -1	◀●W -1	-1(99.9) + -1(0) = **-99.9**

This error triggers promotion of the winner-favouring constraints *XI and IDENTPAL and demotion of the loser-favouring constraint *Ç. Constraint values are adjusted in this manner until errors cease and a consistent phonotactic grammar showing the inequalities in (20) is reached. Over a series of simulations in Praat, this convergence normally occurs when w*XI≈105, w*Ç≈95 and wIDENTPAL≈5.

(22) *Adult grammar based on initial wIDENTPAL=0 – No further errors*

	/éçete/	*XI *w=105*	*Ç *w=95*	IDENTPAL *w=5*	*H*
i.	☞ éçete		-1		-1(95) = **-95**
ii.	éxete	-1		-1	-1(105) + -1(5) = **-110**

Such patterns of complementary distribution are easily learned in the HG-GLA system when the initial weight assigned to IO-Faithfulness is zero. If a higher initial weight is given to IO-based constraints, however, no errors arise and so no learning occurs. This is illustrated with the tableaux in (23) and (24) below where the initial weight of the IO-Faithfulness constraint IDENTPAL is set at 30. Values of the Markedness constraints are again perturbed from their starting points by noise.

(23) *Selection of target-like form with initial wIDENTPAL=30 – No error*

	/éçete/	*Ç *w=101.1*	*XI *w=99.9*	IDENTPAL *w=30*	*H*
i.	☞ éçete	-1			-1(101.1) = **-101.1**
ii.	éxete		-1	-1	-1(99.9) + -1(30) = **-129.9**

(24) *Selection of target-like form with initial wIDENTPAL=30 – No error*

	/éxo/	*Ç w=101.1	*XI w=99.9	IDENTPAL w=30	H
i.	éço	-1			-1(101.1) = **-101.1**
ii. ☞	éxo				**0**

In (23) the summed weight of IDENTPAL and *XI is greater than that of *Ç alone. This ganging up effect ensures that the faithful target form [éçete] is selected as the optimal output even when w*Ç > w*XI. Without a very substantial amount of noise – far beyond the standard 2.0 used in Praat – this effect will never be reversed and no errors will arise. Similarly, in (24), the faithful, target-like candidate [éxo] violates no constraints and so is consistently selected as optimal. Again, no errors arise.

In the absence of errors, the weights of the constraints remain unchanged from their beginning values of 100 for the Markedness constraints *XI and *Ç and of 30 for the IO-Faithfulness constraint IDENTPAL. No learning occurs, making the resulting adult grammar unrestrictive. Thus, when an input form that does not correspond to the phonotactic patterns of the target language is submitted to the final grammar, it is incorrectly faithfully realized as in (25).

(25) *Adult selection of non-target form with initial wIDENTPAL=30 – Non-restrictive*

	/éxete/	*Ç w=100	*XI w=100	IDENTPAL w=30	H
i.	éçete	-1		-1	-1(100) + -1(30) = **-130**
ii. ☞*	éxete		-1		-1(100) = **-100**

This is clearly an undesirable result, and one that does not arise in the adult language if the initial value of IO-Faithfulness is set at 0. There, with the values of the two Markedness constraints adjusted using the GLA procedure so that w*XI > w*Ç and the weight of IDENTPAL remaining low, any input form that disobeys the target language's phonotactics will map unfaithfully to an output consistent with the pattern of complementary distribution. The final state grammar is appropriately restrictive.

(26) *Adult selection of target form with initial wIDENTPAL=0 – Restrictive*

	/éxete/	*XI w=105	*Ç w=95	IDENTPAL w=5	H
i. ☞	éçete		-1	-1	-1(95) + -1(5) = **-100**
ii.	éxete	-1			-1(105) = **-105**

It is clear that an initial bias for Output-based constraints (Markedness) over Input-Output-based constraints (IO-Faithfulness) must be retained in the HG-GLA approach in order to ensure restrictiveness. Output-based constraints can be assigned any high initial value, while IO-Faithfulness constraints must be initially valued at zero. What is of interest here is that this is the *only* bias that is needed within this system. As the following sections demonstrate, restrictiveness effects that require SPECIFIC

FAITHFULNESS >> GENERAL FAITHFULNESS or OO-FAITHFULNESS >> MARKEDNESS
biases in ranked-constraint OT systems can be captured in HG-GLA through additive
interaction and the single bias discussed in this section. This has the significant benefit of
reducing the complexity of both the initial state grammar and learning process. The
following sections elaborate upon the crucial interactions, beginning in section 4 with
discussion of restrictive intermediate stages, and continuing in section 5 with discussion
of restrictive final state grammars.

4.   Restrictive Emergent Stages: Interactions with IO- and OO-Faithfulness

A range of recent literature has discussed the OT learning consequences of faithfulness
constraints that reference specific positions and structural relations. With respect to Input-
Output faithfulness, several authors have either assumed or explicitly argued that OT
learners must have a ranking bias that favours the placement of more specific faithfulness
constraints above more general ones (Smith 2000, Hayes 2004, Hayes & Londe 2006,
Tessier 2006a, 2007, see also esp. Prince & Tesar 2004, but cf. Boersma 2006). This bias
has been shown to be necessary in ranked-constraint OT both for learning target
grammars where marked structures are admitted only in privileged contexts (see
especially Smith 2000, Hayes 2004, Hayes & Londe 2006) and for allowing the
emergence of intermediate developmental stages where children's grammars allow
marked structures only in privileged contexts (Tessier 2007, to appear, see also
Revithiadou & Tzakosta 2004). With respect to faithfulness relations between surface
forms – encoded through Output-Output faithfulness constraints – it has been argued that
OO-Faith constraints must be biased toward a very high ranking, above not only IO-Faith
constraints but above Markedness constraints as well. Again, support for these claims has
come from the need to learn restrictive end-state grammars (McCarthy 1998) and from
evidence that emergent grammars impose OO-faithfulness restrictions beyond the target
(Kazazis 1969, Dinnsen & McGarrity 2004, Hayes 2004, Jesney 2005, Tessier 2006b,
2007).

As already alluded to, adopting a grammar where constraint interaction is based
on additive interaction rather than on strict ranking eliminates the need for any biases
within the class of IO-Faith constraints (i.e. Specific >> General), and for any bias that
ranks OO-Faith above Markedness. In our HG-GLA model, all IO-Faith constraints have
an initial weight of 0, and OO-Faith constraints start at 100 along with the other output-
oriented (Markedness) constraints. In this section, we demonstrate that this initial state is
sufficient to model three different emergent patterns, all of which have previously been
used to argue for IO- or OO-Faithfulness ranking biases in OT learning.

Before moving on, a methodological and ideological waiver may be in order.
While the emergent stages discussed in this paper are taken from the reported productions
of real children with real perceptual and articulatory devices (ears and mouths), this paper
is primarily a learnability study, and as such it abstracts away from a series of potential
confounds in this data.   Most importantly, we set aside the possibility that the
intermediate stages discussed here may be the result of extragrammatical articulatory or

perceptual difficulties rather than the structure of the grammar *per se*.[7] Nonetheless, we take these data as a good starting point for the investigation of potential developmental paths in constraint-based error-driven learning and for the testing of predictions made by various models.

4.1   Specific IO-Faith Stages

The first type of emergent stage of interest here is what Tessier (to appear) dubs an Intermediate Faith (IF) stage. IF stages arise when the target language allows a given marked structure in all contexts, but child's developing grammar restricts that structure to a privileged position. As we demonstrate, such stages emerge in Harmonic Grammars when the *combined* weight of the relevant General and Specific IO-Faithfulness constraints is sufficient to overcome Markedness, but the weight of the General IO-Faithfulness constraint alone is not.

(27)   *Weighting conditions of the target grammar*
  *w*GeneralFaith > *w*Markedness   … Marked structures are
                     allowed in all contexts

(28)   *Weighting conditions of the child's IF stage*
  *w*Markedness > *w*GeneralFaith   … Marked structures are
                     disallowed
  *w*GeneralFaith + *w*SpecificFaith > *w*Markedness   … Except as faithful
                     mappings in privileged
                     positions

In the HG-GLA model, this set of inequalities naturally arises as the child gradually adjusts the weights of constraints based on positive evidence from the target language. No *w*SpecificFaith > *w*GeneralFaith bias is required.

As an example, we consider the production of complex onset clusters by two children learning Québécois French. (The data and pattern come from Rose (2000); see Tessier (2007) for discussion of the associated OT learnability issues.) French allows complex onsets in both stressed and unstressed syllables; Rose (2000) documents an emergent stage, however, where the two children produce complex onsets only in stressed syllables.

(29)   a.   *French IF stage*
    stressed complex onsets retained: /CV.'**CCV**/ → [CV.'**CCV**]
    unstressed complex onsets reduced: /**CCV**.'CV / → [**CV**.'CV],
                       *[**CCV**.'CV]

---

[7]   In the case of Amahl discussed in section 4.2.2, there is strong evidence that articulatory difficulty cannot be responsible for this emergent particular pattern, although perceptual errors may remain a possibility (for discussion, see Dinnsen, O'Connor & Gierut 2001, Dinnsen & McGarrity 2004, Jesney 2005, 2007a, Macken 1980).

b. *Data from IF stage: Théo at 2;05.29 - 2;11.29*

stressed syllables: retained			unstressed syllables: reduced		
/ˈgʁo/	[ˈgʁo]	'big'	/tʁak.ˈtœʁ/	[ta ˈtœº]	'tractor'
/ˈtʁɛ̃/	[ˈkʁɛ̃]	'train'	/gʁy.ˈjo/	[kʰœ.ˈjɔ]	'oatmeal'
/ˈkle/	[ˈkxe]	'key'	/tʁu.ˈve/	[kʊ.ˈβi]	'found'
/ˈplœʁ/	[ˈplœº]	's/he cries'	/ˌkʁɛm.gla.ˈse/	/ˌkʁa.ˈna.ˈse/	'ice cream'

Tessier (2007) analyzes this emergent stage using a markedness constraint *COMPLEXONSET, and two faithfulness constraints militating against deletion – one general (MAX) and one specific to stressed syllables (MAX-σ')[8]. Given our initial stage assumptions, our learner of French begins with *COMPLEXONSET valued at 100, and both MAX constraints valued at zero. With these weights, a clear pattern of cluster reduction across environments is predicted in the initial state. (Differences between target and child outputs beyond the number of onset segments are ignored here.)

(30) *French onset clusters – errors made in the initial state*
  a. *Stressed syllable*

/tʁɛ̃/ 'train'	*COMPLEX w=100	MAX w=0	MAX-σ' w=0	H
i. ˈkʁɛ̃	L -1 ●➡			-1(100) = **-100**
ii. ●⃰ ˈkɛ̃		⬅●W -1	⬅●W -1	-1(0) + -1(0) = **0**

  b. *Unstressed syllable*

/tʁu.ve/ 'find'	*COMPLEX w=100	MAX w=0	MAX-σ' w=0	H
i. kʁʊ.ˈβi	L -1 ●➡			-1(100) = **-100**
ii. ●⃰ kʊ.ˈβi		⬅●W -1		-1(0) = **0**

As indicated by the arrows in the tableaux above, these initial state errors trigger promotion of the faithfulness constraints MAX and MAX-σ' and demotion of the markedness constraint *COMPLEX. The general MAX constraint moves faster than the specific MAX-σ' constraint, because it is implicated in both errors (30a,b) whereas MAX-σ' is implicated only in (30a).

GLA learning based on these errors was simulated over multiple trials in Praat using the 'LinearOT' decision mode mentioned in section 2. Under the conditions of our simulation[9], the first change from the initial pattern of errors consistently occurred after

---

[8]   The constraint Max-σ' has a somewhat unusual character, requiring that *input segments syllabified as onsets* have output correspondents. Such reference to prominent input positions is likely needed in order to capture phenomena seen in adult language as well (see especially Wilson 2000 and the discussion of chain shifts in McCarthy 2007), but is particularly common in discussions of child language (e.g., Chambless 2006, Goad & Rose 2004, Jesney 2005, 2007a, Rose 2000).

[9]   Details of this simulation and all others discussed in this paper: 'Symmetric All' re-ranking strategy, 'LinearOT' decision mode, 1.0 initial plasticity, 0.1 plasticity decrement, 2.0 evaluation noise. This corresponds to the weighted GLA procedure discussed in section 2.2.

approximately 50 learning trials, with only minimal variation in constraint values at this stage. A representative example of the weights is given in (31), along with the effects of these weights in the privileged and non-privileged environments.

(31)   *French IF stage – cluster simplification in unstressed syllables only*
        a. *Stressed syllable*

	/tχɛ̃/	*COMPLEX w=54	MAX w=46	MAX-σ' w=23	H
i.	☞ 'kχɛ̃	-1			-1(54) = **-54**
ii.	'kɛ̃		-1	-1	-1(46) + -1(23) = **-69**

        b. *Unstressed syllable*

	/tχu.ve/	*COMPLEX w=54	MAX w=46	MAX-σ' w=23	H
i.	kχʊ.'βi	L -1●➡			-1(54) = **-54**
ii.	☛ kʊ.'βi		⬅●W -1		-1(46) = **-46**

This emergent pattern is precisely the one displayed by Théo in table (29) above. Onset clusters are preserved in stressed syllables (a privileged position), but continue to be reduced elsewhere. The crucial relations between the constraint weights that create this IF pattern are summarized in (32).

(32)   *Weighting conditions for Théo's IF stage*
        w*COMPLEX > wMAX   i.e., wMarkedness > wGenFaith
        wMAX + wMAX-σ' > w*COMPLEX   i.e., wGenFaith + wSpecFaith > wMarkedness

Learning continues from this stage as the remaining error in (31b) triggers further promotion of MAX and demotion of *COMPLEX. The final stage is reached once the selection value of MAX is consistently greater than that of *COMPLEX (i.e., wGenFaith > wMarkedness) so that marked onset clusters are retained even in unstressed syllables and errors cease. As in other simulations, this normally occurs when the two crucial constraints' weights differ by approximately 10 points, i.e. when wMAX≈55 and w*COMPLEX≈45.

(33)   *French onset clusters – the final state*
        a. *Stressed syllable*

	/tχɛ̃/	MAX w=55	*COMPLEX w=45	MAX-σ' w=23	H
i.	☞ 'kχɛ̃		-1		-1(45) = **-45**
ii.	'kɛ̃	-1		-1	-1(55) + -1(23) = **-78**

b. *Unstressed syllable*

	/tχu.ve/	MAX *w=55*	*COMPLEX *w=45*	MAX-σ' *w=23*	*H*
i.	☞ kχʊ.'βi		-1		-1(45) = **-45**
ii.	kʊ.'βi	-1			-1(55) = **-55**

Since no onset cluster reduction occurs at this stage, no further errors are being made (on this dimension), and no further learning takes place.

The crucial point to be gleaned from this simple example is that by using an additive mode of constraint interaction the IF stage emerges in the course of development despite the lack of evidence for such a stage in the target language. Observing target onset clusters in both stressed and unstressed syllables and adjusting constraint values accordingly is sufficient to produce an emergent stage where clusters are protected only in the privileged position. Even though this stage relies on the specific faithfulness constraint MAX-σ', the specific-to-general relationship between MAX-σ' and MAX does not need to be known in advance or calculated and stored by the HG-GLA learner (cf. Hayes 2004, Tessier 2007, to appear). In the HG-GLA model, IF stages are simply a natural consequence of the constraint set, the additive mode of constraint interaction, and the positive target-language evidence directly available to the learner.

4.2 OO-Faith Stages

This section addresses emergent stages driven by Output-Output faithfulness – i.e., stages where some markedness-driven process or restriction is circumvented just when failure to do so would cause morphologically-derived forms to differ phonologically from their bases. As with the IF stages discussed in section 4.1, these stages are said to be emergent because they arise despite the fact that the target language provides no evidence for any crucial activity of the OO-Faith constraints in question. Section 4.2.1 presents an OO-Faith stage in Marina's acquisition of Greek (Kazazis 1969). As discussed in section 3.2, palatal vs. velar place of articulation in adult Greek is determined solely by Markedness considerations – *not* by OO-Faith. Despite this, Marina passes through a stage where the distribution of palatals and velars in her productions is shaped by morphological concerns. Section 4.2.2 discusses a rather different OO-Faith stage from Amahl's acquisition of English (Smith 1973, Dinnsen & McGarrity 2004, Jesney 2005). In this case it is a child-specific process, rather than one found in the target language, that is subverted by OO-Faithfulness pressures. Within the present HG-GLA system, both types of OO-Faith stage emerge through additive constraint interaction as OO-Faith gangs up with supporting Markedness or IO-Faith constraints. OO-Faithfulness constraints share the same high initial value as other Output-based constraints, and their weights are adjusted according to the GLA procedure. No special OO-Faith bias is necessary.

4.2.1 Marina

Marina's emergent OO-Faith stage involves the Greek alternation discussed in section 3.2 and illustrated with the data in (19). The target language here has a strict pattern of complementary distribution, with palatal continuants appearing before front vowels and velars appearing elsewhere, regardless of morphological environment. Section 3.2 showed how a HG-GLA learner can easily learn this pattern of allophony, assuming an initial state where the Output-based Markedness constraints are weighted high and the Input-Output-based IO-Faithfulness constraints are weighted at zero.

Adding OO-Faithfulness to our constraint typology with the same high initial value as Markedness does not change this basic learning result, provided that learners begin by acquiring the purely phonological restrictions of their language in the absence of morphological knowledge (on this point, see esp. Hayes 2004, Jarosz 2006, Tessier 2007). If the learner does not yet know that two forms are morphologically related, a constraint like OO-IDENTPAL has no base against which to assess violation marks, and so it cannot affect the selection of optima or have its initial weight adjusted by the GLA. Without a basis for assessment during this early stage, OO-Faith constraints are neither winner favouring nor loser favouring.

This situation is illustrated in (34) below. Here, at the end of phonotactic learning the value of *XI has been increased to 105, the value of *Ç has been decreased to 95, and the value of IO-IDENT has been increased to 5 (see (22)). OO-Faith is consistently vacuously satisfied and so retains its initial weight of 100 and has no effect upon the selection of optima. Hypothetical inputs – i.e., inputs that disobey the pattern of the target language – are used in these tableaux to demonstrate how the phonotactic grammar selects the correct allophone *regardless* of input, in accordance with the principle of Richness of the Base (Prince & Smolensky 1993/2004).

(34)   *Final state of pure phonotactic learning: wOO-IDENT = 100, but irrelevant*
        a. *Palatal allophone before front vowels ...*

	/éxete/	*XI $w=105$	OO-IDENT $w=100$	*Ç $w=95$	IO-IDENT $w=5$	H
i.	☞ éçete			-1	-1	$-1(95) + -1(5) = \mathbf{-100}$
ii.	éxete	-1				$-1(105) = \mathbf{-105}$

        b. *... velar allophone elsewhere*

	/éço/	*XI $w=105$	OO-IDENT $w=100$	*Ç $w=95$	IO-IDENT $w=5$	H
i.	éço			-1		$-1(95) = \mathbf{-95}$
ii.	☞ éxo				-1	$-1(5) = \mathbf{-5}$

At this stage, the phonotactic pattern of Greek has been mastered, and the learner will make no more errors. In the case of Marina, Kazazis (1969) reports that she reached the stage in (34) at some point before age 4;7, with all of her fricative productions being target-like. Then for a few weeks beginning at 4;7, Marina began to produce a different pattern with velar fricatives appearing across the board in some verbal paradigms.

(35) *Marina at 4:7*

		Target	Child
2pl.	'to have'	[éçete]	[éxete]
2pl.	'to leave'	[févjete]	[févɣete]

Kazazis (1969) describes this pattern as morphologically-specific under-application of a phonological rule: a rule of Greek that turns underlying velar fricatives into palatals.

Within our HG-GLA learner, the emergence of Marina's pattern in (35) is equated with the onset of morphological awareness. Once the learner acquires enough information about the morphological relationship between the forms of the verbs in question, it becomes possible for OO-IDENTPAL to be assessed, penalizing derived forms that differ in palatal place of articulation with respect to their bases. The resulting violations of OO-IDENTPAL contribute to the harmony scores of the candidates.

Assessment of OO-IDENTPAL is dependent upon the identification of a morphological base. This is a non-trivial problem, not least of all because in the current case there is no uninflected member of the paradigm (cf. Benua 1998). While this is an interesting issue for further exploration, for present purposes it is sufficient to state that the learner selects the unmarked first person singular (velar) form of the stem (see Alderete 1999).[10] As illustrated in (36), once the velar fricative is chosen as the base segment against which OO-IDENTPAL is assessed, the grammar in (34) automatically produces Marina's emergent OO-Faith stage.

(36) *Emergent Greek OO-Faith stage, at onset of morphological awareness*

  a. *Target verb-final palatals mapped to velars under pressure of OO-Faith*

	/éx+ete/ base: /éx/	*XI $w=105$	OO-IDENT $w=100$	*Ç $w=95$	IO-IDENT $w=5$	H
i.	éçete		-1 ●→	-1 ●→	-1 ●→	-1(100)+-1(95)+-1(5)= **-200**
ii.	☞ éxete	←●-1				-1(105) = **-105**

  b. *...but target palatals still correctly produced in underived words*

	/xéri/ 'hand' (underived)	*XI $w=105$	OO-IDENT $w=100$	*Ç $w=95$	IO-IDENT $w=5$	H
i.	☞ çéri			-1	-1	-1(95) + -1(5) = **-100**
ii.	xéri	-1				-1(105) = **-105**

---

[10]   A consistent means of selecting a base that remains within the spirit of Benua's (1998) original proposal would be to select the stem allomorph that, context-independently, is most harmonic. In the present case, [éç] violates *Ç, while [éx] violates no markedness constraints; the velar allomorph would thus be deemed the optimal base form against which OO-IDENTPAL is assessed. For alternative means of determining bases in inflectional paradigms, see Albright (2004, 2005).

The existence of the general markedness constraint *Ç is central to this result. At the point when OO-IDENTPAL begins to assert itself, phonotactic learning has already raised the value of *XI above the value of *Ç. In underived contexts the w*XI > w*Ç inequality holds sway and the target allophonic pattern results (36b). In derived contexts, however, OO-IDENTPAL is able to gang up with *Ç and force paradigm leveling (36a). Because the value of *XI has surpassed that of OO-IDENTPAL during phonotactic learning, the markedness constraint *Ç is crucial to the equation; the weight of OO-IDENTPAL alone is insufficient to overcome the weight of *XI.

(37)   *Necessary inequalities for OO-Faith stage overcoming target allophony*
      a. w*XI > w*Ç   i.e., wSpecM > wGenM
      b. wOO-IDENTPAL + w*Ç > w*XI   i.e., wOOFaith + wGenM > wSpecM

The need for a general markedness constraint that OO-Faith can gang up with in order to force paradigm leveling is a key characteristic of this type of stage. Emergent OO-Faith stages where a target-language pattern of complementary distribution is disobeyed are possible only when there is a general markedness constraint that shares same favouring relations as OO-Faith. This places an important restriction upon the types of emergent OO-Faith stages that are possible, strictly ruling out leveling toward a contextually-marked allophone in cases where the alternative is not also disfavoured by some constraint (see section 6.2 for further discussion).

It is interesting to note that Marina's OO-Faith stage does not arise from the promotion of OO-Faith, as was the case with the Specific and General IO-Faith constraints in Théo's IF stage. Instead, the intermediate stage in (35) emerges as soon as OO-Faith begins to assess violations using the values already established during phonotactic learning. It should also be noted that this stage is in no way dependent upon the input form selected for the morpheme in question; IO-IDENTPAL is too low weighted to affect selection of the optimum in either derived (36a) or underived (36b) words.

Progression out of the OO-Faith stage comes about via errors like that in (36a). This error demonstrates to the learner that OO-Faith is, in fact, not decisive in the target language and must therefore be demoted; it also serves to push the two markedness constraints further apart, although this does not have any crucial consequences. In simulations, errors like (36a) cease once values approximate those in (38) below. At this stage, the weights of the constraints have been adjusted to the point that OO-IDENTPAL and *Ç can no longer gang up to overcome *XI. The correct phonotactic pattern thus re-emerges.

(38)   *Final stage: OO-IDENT ignored in favour of target language allophony pattern*
      a. *Target palatals mapped to palatals in derived contexts*

	/éx+ete/ base: /éx/	*XI $w=140$	OO-IDENT $w=65$	*Ç $w=60$	IO-IDENT $w=0$	H
i.	☞ éçete		-1	-1	-1	-1(65)+-1(60)+-1(0)= **-125**
ii.	éxete	-1				-1(140) = **-140**

b. *...and in underived words*

/xéri/ 'hand' (underived)	*XI $w=140$	OO-IDENT $w=65$	*Ç $w=60$	IO-IDENT $w=0$	H
i. ☞ çéri			-1	-1	$-1(60) + -1(0) = -60$
ii. xéri	-1				$-1(140) = -140$

We have now seen how innovative OO-Faithfulness stages like Marina's can emerge within an HG-GLA learner without the need for any bias specific to OO-Faith constraints and despite the lack of evidence for activity of the crucial OO-Faith constraint in the target language. As we have already hinted, deriving such restrictive stages via this type of additive constraint interaction, rather than by way of an OO-Faithfulness >> Markedness ranking bias, predicts a somewhat tighter range of such stages; we return to this point in section 6.2. First, though, we consider a different type of emergent OO-Faith stage.

4.2.2 Amahl

This section presents an emergent OO-Faith stage found in Amahl's acquisition of English (Smith 1973). As illustrated in (39) below, Amahl passes through a lengthy stage that includes a regular process of pre-lateral velarization where non-strident coronal stops are realized as velars before target laterals.

(39)   *Amahl's pre-lateral velarization: applies in all simple words*
        puddle   pʌgəl
        butler   bʌklə
        sandal   tæŋgəl
        gentle   dɛŋkəl

This child-specific process in Amahl's grammar can be understood as the effect of a markedness constraint that prohibits sequences of non-continuant coronal segments, *TL (Jesney 2005, 2007a, see also Dinnsen & McGarrity 2004). Since we assume that wMarkedness > wIO-Faith in the initial state, this pattern of Amahl's is simply one reflex of these initial values, with *TL outweighing faithfulness to coronal place (40).

(40)   *The initial state of Amahl's grammar – pre-lateral velarization*

/pʌdəl/	OO-IDENTCOR $w =100$	*TL $w=100$	IO-IDENTCOR $w =0$	H
i. pʌdəl		L -1●➔		$-1(100) = -100$
ii. ☞* pʌgəl			◄-●W -1	$-1(0) = 0$

As phonotactic learning progresses, errors cause the value of Markedness to decrease and the value of IO-Faithfulness to increase, though the output of the grammar does not immediately change. Morphological awareness has not yet arisen, leaving OO-IDENTCORONAL unassessed and at its original value (41).

(41) *Amahl's grammar, partway through phonotactic learning – pre-lateral velarization*

	/pʌdəl/	OO-IDENTCOR $w = 100$	*TL $w=70$	IO-IDENTCOR $w = 30$	H
i.	pʌdəl		L -1●→		-1(70) = -70
ii.	☞ pʌgəl			←●W -1	-1(30) = -30

The innovative OO-Faith twist to Amahl's pattern is illustrated in (42) below. At the same time as pre-lateral velarization holds in simple words like 'puddle', it fails to apply in complex words like those in (42a) – words where the target coronal segment is part of the base and the target lateral is part of an affix. Evidence that this blocking effect is crucially tied to the segment's realization in the base comes from examples like (42b); when the target coronal is velarized in the base, this velarization persists in the derived form.

(42) *Amahl's pre-lateral velarization in complex words:*
    a. *... blocked across base-affix boundary*
        hard ~ hardly   [ha:**d**]   [ha:**dli:**]   *[ha:**gli**]
        soft ~ softly   [sɔf**t**]   [sɔf**tli:**]   *[sɔf**kli:**]
        tight ~ tightly   [tai**t**]   [tai**tli:**]   *[tai**kli:**]
    b. *... but not if velarization also occurs in the root*
        gentle ~ gently   [dɛŋ**k**əl]   [dɛŋ**kli:**]

Having established a set of constraint values like those in (41), this pattern of morphological blocking is predicted to arise at the onset of morphological awareness. As soon as Amahl becomes aware of the affix –*ly* and its role in grouping pairs of words like 'hard' and 'hardly' into the same paradigm, OO-IDENTCORONAL can be assessed. The added weight of its violations is sufficient to ensure that the OO-Faith pattern emerges.

(43) *Amahl's OO-Faith stage: (41), plus morphological knowledge*

	/ha:d+li:/ base: [ha:d]	OO-IDENTCOR $w = 100$	*TL $w=70$	IO-IDENTCOR $w = 30$	H
i.	☞ ha:dli:		-1		-1(70) = -70
ii.	ha:gli:	-1		-1	-1(100) + -1(30) = -130

Since *TL is demoted during pure phonotactic learning but OO-IDENTCORONAL is not, this grammar levels paradigms towards the faithful (but marked) form in derived words. At the same time, phonotactic learning remains incomplete and so *TL forces unfaithfulness in simple words where OO-Faith is not assessed. The relevant inequalities are summarized in (44).

(44) *Inequalities for OO-Faith overcoming child-specific process*
    a. wOO-IDENTCOR + wIO-IDENTCOR > w*TL   i.e., wOO-Faith + wIO-Faith >
                                         wMarkedness
    b. w*TL > wIO-IDENTCOR   i.e., wMarkedness > wIO-Faith

Unlike the emergent stages of Théo and Marina, our analysis of Amahl's OO-Faith stage does not strictly rely on additive interaction. Examination of the intermediate stage tableau in (43) reveals that the weight of OO-IDENTCOR alone (*w*=100) is sufficient to overcome the weight of *TL (*w*=70); the gang effect between IO-IDENTCOR and OO-IDENTCOR is essentially incidental.

During the OO-Faith stage, Amahl's grammar allows TL sequences in derived words, but continues to make errors like (41) in simple words. These errors force further demotion of *TL and promotion of IO-IDENTCOR, until *w*IO-IDENTCOR > *w**TL, and the final state is reached. In simulations, this typically occurs when *w*IO-IDENTCOR ≈ 55 and *w**TL ≈ 45.

(45) *Final state: TL sequences tolerated in all contexts*

	/pʌdəl/	OO-IDENTCOR *w* =100	IO-IDENTCOR *w* =55	*TL *w* =45	*H*
i.	☞ pʌdəl			-1	-1(45) = **-45**
ii.	pʌgəl		-1		-1(55) = **-55**

Note that because OO-Faith is not associated with any errors, it is never demoted. This means that the final state grammar does, in fact, impose paradigm leveling, but vacuously so. Both OO-IDENTCOR and IO-IDENTCOR require that coronal stop + lateral sequences be preserved; the final value of IO-IDENTCOR is sufficiently high, however, for it to overcome the weight of *TL independently.

(46) *Final state of Amahl's grammar – no errors*
  a. *Faithful mapping due to IO-IDENTCOR in underived words*

	/dʒentəl/	OO-IDENTCOR *w* =100	IO-IDENTCOR *w* =55	*TL *w* =45	*H*
i.	☞ dɛntəl			-1	-1(45) = **-45**
ii.	dɛŋkəl		-2		-2(55) = **-110**

  b. *Faithful mapping due to IO-IDENTCOR and OO-IDENTCOR in derived words*

	/dʒent+liː/ **base: [dɛntəl]**	OO-IDENTCOR *w* =100	IO-IDENTCOR *w* =55	*TL *w* =45	*H*
i.	☞ dɛntliː			-1	-1(45) = **-45**
ii.	dɛŋkliː	-2	-2		-2 (100)+ -2(55) = **-310**

This example raises two points of general relevance. First, in order for leveling of a child-specific process to occur, it is necessary for IO-Faith and OO-Faith to share the same favouring relation with respect to the conflicting markedness constraint – or at least for IO-Faith and Markedness to not both conflict with OO-Faith. If an OO-Faith stage is to emerge, it is crucial that IO-Faith and Markedness not be able to gang up together to overcome the pressures of OO-Faith. Second, when the process in question is specific to the child's phonology, the markedness constraint responsible will undergo demotion (*w*<100) and the conflicting IO-Faith constraint will undergo promotion (*w*>0). The

OO-Faith stage can be avoided, then, if morphological awareness arises after the value of the markedness constraint has decreased and the value of the IO-Faith constraint has increased to the point that initial state inequality is reversed – i.e., to the point where wIO-Faith $>$ wMarkedness. Once this stage is reached, the child-specific process disappears from the child's grammar in all contexts, precluding the type of OO-Faith stage displayed by Amahl.

The key point here is simply this: given our limited assumptions about initial constraint values, restrictive intermediate OO-Faith stages emerge naturally in a HG-GLA system. In cases like Marina's that involve blocking of a target language process, additive interaction is crucial. In cases like Amahl's that involve blocking of a child-specific process, the unchanged high value of OO-Faith in conjunction with the demotion of the conflicting markedness constraint is sufficient. In all cases, these restrictive stages emerge despite the fact that there is no evidence of paradigm leveling in the target language. Within the HG-GLA model advanced here, the available evidence is sufficient to derive the attested effects.

5.   Restrictive Final States

The primary goal of this paper is to demonstrate the success of a HG-GLA learner with a minimal number of *a priori* constraint value biases. To this point we have primarily been concerned with capturing attested intermediate stages in child language development. However, arguments for biases in the grammar-learning literature have usually come from observations related to the *final* state of learning, and the need to learn a grammar that is as restrictive as possible but still consistent with the attested forms (e.g., Berwick 1985, Dresher 1999, Dresher & Kaye 1990, Hayes 2004, Jarosz 2006, Prince & Tesar 2004, Pulleyblank & Turkel 1998, Tesar & Smolensky 1998, 2000 *interalia*). We now turn, therefore, to the HG-GLA system's ability to reach restrictive end state grammars – in other words, its ability to avoid 'superset' languages.

5.1   Reaching a Specific Faithfulness End State Through Errors

In order to determine whether the final output of learning is restrictive, it is necessary to test the grammar on forms that never appear in the target language and ensure that the learned grammar properly rejects them. Through error-based learning and the Output-based constraints over Input-Output-based constraints bias proposed here, the HG-GLA system learns precisely this type of grammar. This occurs without any need for negative evidence.

As we have already seen, children regularly pass through stages during the course of acquisition where their linguistic system is more restrictive than that of the target language. From evidence of a more permissive language, children first learn a more restrictive one using the HG-GLA procedure. This provides the key to understanding the mechanism by which restrictive end state grammars are reached in this system. In short, if the restrictive grammar is the target, errors and learning cease once the restrictive IF stage is reached; no further adjustments are then needed.

By way of example, consider what would occur if, rather than acquiring French, Théo had been acquiring a language that was just like French but admitted consonant clusters only in stressed syllables (Goad & Rose 2004 report that Brazilian Portuguese is precisely such a language). As before, in the initial state Markedness is valued well above the general and specific IO-Faithfulness constraints, ensuring that all input clusters are simplified in the output.

(47) *French' onset clusters – errors made in the initial state*

/tχɛ̃/	*COMPLEX w=100	MAX w=0	MAX-σ' w=0	H
i.	'kχɛ̃	L -1 ●▶			-1(100) = -100
ii. ☞*	'kɛ̃		◀●W -1	◀● W -1	-1(0) + -1(0) = 0

These errors prompt an increase in the values of the winner-favouring constraints MAX-σ' and MAX, and a decrease in the value of the loser-favouring constraint *COMPLEX. Learning proceeds in this manner until the summed weight of the general and specific IO-Faithfulness constraints is greater than that of the markedness constraint and errors cease.

(48) *Weighting conditions for restrictive final state grammar of French'*
  w*COMPLEX > wMAX   i.e., wMarkedness > wGenFaith
  wMAX + wMAX-σ' > w*COMPLEX i.e., wGenFaith + wSpecFaith > wMarkedness

Unlike the French learner who continues to make errors in words containing clusters outside of stressed syllables, the French' learner's grammar converges at a stage that mirrors Théo's IF pattern (compare (48) and (32)). There are no input forms to the French' learner that contain clusters outside of the stressed syllable, and so the inequalities in (48) are sufficient to capture the range of attested forms. Unlike in actual French, at no point does the weight of MAX alone surpass that of *COMPLEX in French'. This is a positive result; if forms containing clusters in unstressed syllables are submitted to the final state grammar of French', they are appropriately rejected. The restrictive final state emerges from the constraint values learned by the child on the basis of positive target-language evidence.

This procedure works in a straightforward and uncomplicated manner in cases where end-state restrictiveness is driven by Specific Faithfulness constraints. Errors based on mismappings of input forms force adjustment of the constraint values just until the target grammar is matched and no further errors occur. Within the HG-GLA system, this restrictive final state relies on additive interaction, just as the restrictive IF stages discussed in section 4.1 do. As we see in the next section, however, the case of OO-Faithful end states can be rather more complicated.

5.2.   Reaching an OO-Faithful End State Without Errors

Within OT, McCarthy (1998) argues that a bias for high-ranking OO-Faith is necessary in order to keep morphological paradigms restrictive and without errors. A high OO-Faith bias can help to reproduce the effects of MSCs by filtering out relevant parts of a rich base. From the present perspective, the kind of target grammar that he considers and that is of interest here is one where OO-Faithfulness alone is responsible for restrictiveness in the final state – a grammar where wOO-Faith > wIO-Faith + wMarkedness, and there is no supporting constraint with which OO-Faith can gang up.

As we illustrate below, getting OO-Faith alone to ensure restrictiveness in the end state requires an addition to our model. Here we explore the idea that Output-based constraints (Markedness) and Input-Output-based constraints (IO-Faithfulness) are re-weighted at *different speeds* during phonotactic learning. This small adjustment allows McCarthy's OT result to be retained in the HG-GLA system, avoiding the need for a bias specific to OO-Faithfulness constraints.

5.2.1   Learning the Kansai B grammar

The example put forth by McCarthy (1998) involves the extent of Minimal Word restrictions (e.g., Prince 1980, Broselow 1982, McCarthy & Prince 1993) in a Kansai dialect of Japanese. The two important characteristics of the Kansai B dialect are (a) that words are minimally bimoraic (49a), and (b) that derived words never surface with a monomoraic root exponent (49b).

(49)   *Uniform paradigms in Kansai B dialect of Japanese* (McCarthy 1998)
          a.   *roots:*   i.   [kaa]   'mosquito'
                                       ii.   *[ka]
          b.   *paradigms, e.g. with -ga suffixes:*
                                       i.   [kaa] ~ [kaaga]
                                       ii.   *[kaa]~ [kaga]

The question that McCarthy (1998) raises is this: how do learners of Kansai B learn to reject paradigms like (49bii) where both members satisfy the word minimality requirement? To understand the nature of the problem we first show what our established HG-GLA learner can acquire from errors in Kansai B. We begin with phonotactic learning as it occurs prior to morphological awareness.

To capture the bimoraicity restriction on words shown in (49a), we use a simple 'MINWORD' constraint that is violated by any monomoraic word.[11] In words composed of a single open syllable this constraint conflicts directly with *LONGVOWEL, which penalizes bimoraic vowels. At the initial state, this conflict results in variation; the two markedness constraints have the same weight and IO-Faith's initial value of 0 prevents it from contributing to the selection process.

---

[11]   McCarthy (1998) derives the MINWORD restriction using FT-BIN and the Prosodic Hierarchy.

(50) *Kansai B initial state: vowel length variation in monosyllables - error*

	/kaa/	MINWD w=100	*LONGV w=100	OO-ID-VLENGTH w=100	IO-ID-VLENGTH w=0	H
i.	☞ kaa		L -1●→			-1(100) = **-100**
ii.	☜ ka	←●W -1			←● W -1	-1(100)+-1(0) = **-100**

In words with two or more syllables, each of which contributes at least one mora, MINWORD exerts no pressure, allowing longer words to contain only short vowels. OO-ID-VLENGTH cannot be assessed in the absence of morphological awareness and so it is unable to favour the attested output form [kaaga].

(51) *Kansai B initial state: short vowels in polysyllabic words - error*

	/kaaga/	MINWD w=100	*LONGV w=100	OO-ID-VLENGTH w=100	IO-ID-VLENGTH w=0	H
i.	kaaga		L -1●→			-1(100) = **-100**
ii.	☜ kaga				←●W -1	-1(0) = **0**

In the initial state, there are thus two types of error: /kaa/→[ka] (variably) and /kaaga/→[kaga] (all of the time). As shown by the arrows in the tableaux, these errors trigger promotion of MINWD and IO-ID-VLENGTH, and demotion of *LONGVOWEL.

Simulations of phonotactic learning using these three constraints (and leaving OO-ID-VLENGTH at its original value) show that the variation in monosyllables between [kaa] and [ka] is resolved very quickly. Looking at the tableau in (50), we can see that the attested winner [kaa] is preferred as soon as wMINWD + wIO-ID-VLENGTH > w*LONGV – and that this occurs as soon as either (or both) winner-preferring constraints increase even slightly in value and/or the loser-preferring constraint decreases in value by a comparably small amount. Feeding the GLA the two errors in (50) and (51) for only 20 learning trials under the present simulation conditions results in a grammar where monosyllables are always correctly realized with long vowels.

(52) *Kansai B after 20 trials*

    a. *monosyllables correctly surface with long vowels – target-like*

	/kaa/	MINWD w=101	OO-ID-VLENGTH w=100	*LONGV w=91	IO-ID-VLENGTH w=9	H
i.	☞ kaa			-1		-1(91) = **-91**
ii.	ka	-1			-1	-1(101)+-1(9) = **-110**

b. *vowels in longer words are still shortened – error*

	/kaaga/	MɪɴWᴅ w=101	OO-Iᴅ-VLᴇɴɢᴛʜ w=100	*LᴏɴɢV w=91	IO-Iᴅ-VLᴇɴɢᴛʜ w=9	H
i.	kaaga			L -1●➡		-1(91) = **-91**
ii.	☞ kaga				⬅●W -1	-1(9) = **-9**

From this point on, phonotactic learning continues to demote *LᴏɴɢV and promote IO-Iᴅ-VLᴇɴɢᴛʜ until the error in (52b) is resolved. The phonotactic end state thus stabilizes with the by-now-familiar values in (53) – *w*IO-Faith ≈ 55 and *w*Markedness ≈ 45.

(53) *End-state of Kansai B phonotactic learning – no more errors*

	/kaaga/	MɪɴWᴅ w=101	OO-Iᴅ-VLᴇɴɢᴛʜ w=100	IO-Iᴅ-VLᴇɴɢᴛʜ w=55	*LᴏɴɢV w=45	H
i.	☞ kaaga				-1	-1(45) = **-45**
ii.	kaga			-1		-1(55) = **-55**

5.2.2 The Problem of Restrictiveness and the Kansai B Grammar

With the constraint weights in (53), phonotactic learning is finished. What happens, then, at the onset of morphological awareness, when the learner recognizes the existence of paradigms like {[kaa], [kaaga]}, allowing OO-Iᴅ-VLᴇɴɢᴛʜ to be assessed? As it stands, OO-Faith cannot prompt errors in underived forms like [kaa], and, as (54) shows, OO-Faith only provides a further reason to maintain a long vowel in the derived form when the input selected is the attested /kaa+ga/.

(54) *Kansai B with morphological knowledge and attested input /kaa/ – restrictive*

	/kaa+ga/ base: [kaa]	MɪɴWᴅ w=101	OO-Iᴅ-LᴇɴɢᴛH w=100	IO-Iᴅ-LᴇɴɢᴛH w=55	*LᴏɴɢV w=45	H
i.	☞ kaaga				-1	-1(45) = **-45**
ii.	kaga		-1	-1		-1(100)+-1(55) = **-155**

This is a positive result, but in order to address the question of restrictiveness we must return to the kinds of unattested paradigms that McCarthy (1998) uses OO-Faithfulness to rule out. The crucial case is one with hypothetical input /ka/, which in the Kansai B dialect should be mapped to a stem with a long vowel [kaa] throughout the paradigm.

In underived forms, the final state grammar in (53) and (54) correctly predicts lengthening of /ka/ based on the inequality *w*MɪɴWᴅ > *w*IO-Iᴅ-LᴇɴɢᴛH + *w*LᴏɴɢV.

(55) *Underived forms with unattested input /ka/ – restrictive*[12]

	/ka/	MINWD $w=101$	OO-ID-LENGTH $w=100$	IO-ID-LENGTH $w=55$	*LONGV $w=45$	H
i.	☞ kaa			-1	-1	-1(55)+-1(45) = **-100**
ii.	ka	-1				-1(101) = **-101**

The evaluation of derived forms is more problematic, as illustrated in (56) for input /ka+ga/ and base [kaa]. With this grammar, the optimal derived form is actually in flux: *either* correct [kaaga] *or* incorrect [kaga] can be chosen, because the harmony scores of both complex forms sum to -100.

(56) **Variation** *for derived forms with unattested input /ka/ – not fully restrictive*

	/ka+ga/ base: [kaa]	MINWD $w=101$	OO-ID-LENGTH $w=100$	IO-ID-LENGTH $w=55$	*LONGV $w=45$	H
i.	☞ kaaga			-1	-1	-1(55)+-1(45) = **-100**
ii.	☞ kaga		-1			-1(100) = **-100**

The grammar that the Kansai B learner has acquired through error-driven learning is thus insufficiently restrictive. When faced with input/base pairs, the desired restrictive paradigm is chosen for input forms of the type attested in the target language {/kaa/, /kaa+ga/}, but this restrictiveness does not extend to input forms of a type not seen during learning {/ka/, /ka+ga/}.

5.2.3   Solving the Problem: Speeding up M-demotion in Phonotactic Learning

The difficulty for Kansai B arises because, in contrast with Marina's OO-Faith case in section 4.2.1, there is no additional markedness constraint for OO-Faith to gang up with in order to prefer the leveled paradigm; no constraint prefers [kaaga] to [kaga] on markedness grounds. OO-Faith *alone* must thus select the correct derived form. Unlike an OT grammar, where OO-Faith's (biased) high ranking would be sufficient to rule out {[kaa], [kaga]} in a tableau like (56), the HG-GLA system developed here will only reproduce the desired result if the weight of OO-Faith is greater than the summed weight of IO-Faith and the conflicting markedness constraint *LONGV. In the current scenario, the summed weight of IO-Faith and *LONGV is 100 – the same as the unchanged starting weight of OO-Faith. This equality creates the problematic variation.[13]

---

[12]   With added noise, considerable variation between outputs [kaa] and *[ka] is expected to arise in (55). This issue is resolved by the solution advanced in section 5.2.3 to address the [kaaga]~*[kaga] variation problem.

[13]   As discussed in section 4.2.2, Amahl's OO-Faith stage emerges without OO-Faith needing to gang up with any other constraint. The crucial difference is that, unlike in (56), IO-Faith in Amahl's case does not share the same favouring relations as Markedness. Instead, the two constraints conflict. Unlike in the Kansai B situation, then, there is no opportunity in Amahl's case for IO-Faith and Markedness to gang up together to overcome OO-Faith and circumvent paradigm leveling.

By now it may be clear that this equality of weights is not an accident. In the initial state, *LONGV has a value of 100 and IO-ID-VLENGTH has a value of 0; each time that an error like (50) or (51) is made, the two constraints' weights are adjusted equally. Since the constraints' weights are changed at the same rate, a candidate that incurs just one violation of *LONGV and one violation of IO-ID-LENGTH will always receive a harmony score of -100 (see 52a, 55, 56).[14] This results in the situation illustrated in (56), where this summed score of -100 competes with the score of -100 attained by the candidate that violates OO-FAITH alone. If IO-Faith and Markedness are adjusted strictly in tandem they can never reach a summed weight greater than or less than the starting weight of the Output-based constraints (Markedness and OO-Faith). Therefore, when, as in the Kansai B case, there are no errors to trigger the promotion of OO-Faith, no final state OO-Faith restrictiveness effect is possible.

In order to resolve this problem we suggest that constraint weights should **not** all be adjusted at the same rate. We thus propose an amendment to the learning algorithm such that Markedness values move at **twice**[15] the speed of IO-Faithfulness values. To revise the GLA procedure given in (9):

(57)   *GLA procedure, revised from (9)*

    a.   Given an input-output pair from the ambient language, the learner takes the input and feeds it to his grammar (GEN, EVAL) to determine which output candidate his current grammar deems optimal.

    b.   If the output candidate selected by his grammar matches the observed output, the grammar remains unchanged.

    c.   If the output candidate selected by his grammar does not match the observed output, the observed is identified as the *winner* and the output selected by the grammar is identified as the *loser*. The grammar is then adjusted by:
- Increasing the numerical value of winner-favouring IO-Faithfulness constraints by some small amount *x*, and winner-favouring Markedness constraints by *2x*,
- Decreasing the numerical value of loser-favouring IO-Faithfulness constraints by some small amount *x*, and loser-favouring Markedness constraints by *2x*.

With this revision to the GLA, the outcome of phonotactic learning for Kansai B is different than in (53). The initial state error /kaaga/→[kaaga]~*[kaga] now results in *LONGV being demoted *twice as fast* as IO-ID-VLENGTH is promoted. The most recent versions of Praat (beginning with v.4.6.11) provide the option of individually specifying constraints' plasticity, which allows the revised algorithm in (57) to be implemented.

---

[14]   Proof: Assuming that all errors that cause promotion of IO-ID-VLENGTH cause equal demotion of *LONGV, let y be the extent to which each constraint's value has been adjusted. Thus, at any stage, wIO-ID-VLENGTH = $0+y$ and w*LONGV = $100-y$. A candidate violating each constraint once will thus have a harmony score of $H = -1(0+y) + -1(100-y) = -y + -100 + y = -100$.

[15]   The choice to use 2 as the factor by which x is multiplied for Markedness constraints is essentially arbitrary. Any value greater than 1 would suffice to achieve this effect.

Setting the plasticity of the Output-based constraints at 2 and the Input-Output-based constraints at 1 gives us the phonotactic end-state values in (58) below.[16]

(58) *REVISED End state of Kansai B phonotactic learning, given procedure in (57)*

/kaaga/	MINWD w=102	OO-ID- VLENGTH w=100	IO-ID- VLENGTH w=38	*LONGV w=24	H
i. ☞ kaaga				-1	-1(24) = **-24**
ii. kaga			-1		-1(38) = **-38**

With these weights, the Kansai B grammar chooses only restrictive outputs and paradigms once morphological awareness emerges. Unattested input bases like /ka/ will be correctly lengthened to [kaa] (59a), and, crucially, when faced with the input /ka+ga/, the grammar will now only choose the OO-restrictive derived form [kaaga] (59b).

(59) *REVISED Kansai B grammar*
   a. *Restrictive grammar for underived forms given input /ka/*

/ka/	MINWD w=102	OO-ID- LENGTH w=100	IO-ID- LENGTH w=38	*LONGV w=24	H
i. ☞ kaa			-1	-1	-1(38)+-1(24) = **-62**
ii. ka	-1				-1(102) = **-102**

   b. ***Restrictive** grammar for derived forms given input /ka+ga/*

/ka+ga/ base: [kaa]	MINWD w=102	OO-ID- LENGTH w=100	IO-ID- LENGTH w=38	*LONGV w=24	H
i. ☞ kaaga			-1	-1	-1(38)+-1(24) = **-62**
ii. kaga		-1			-1(100) = **-100**

Beyond ensuring that the restrictive grammar of Kansai B and other similar languages is learned, this revision to the GLA also has the appeal of minimizing the weight of unimportant constraints in the grammar. Under this approach Markedness constraints that are regularly violated in the target have relatively lower weights than would otherwise be the case, effectively decreasing the disharmony of candidates that violate them. We leave the effects of this to future research.

In sum, OO-Faithful final states emerge naturally in a HG-GLA system. The required restrictiveness is observed even when the learner receives inputs to which he has never previously been exposed and which are illicit in the target language. The only adjustment necessary is for Markedness constraints to move at a faster pace during phonotactic learning than do IO-Faithfulness constraints.

---

[16] For the reader who (rightly) wishes to be convinced of these values: note that IO-ID-VLENGTH has been promoted by **38** points, *LONGV has been demoted by 100-24=**76** points, and 38x2 = 76.

6.   Discussion

We have argued that with an additive mode of constraint interaction and a slightly revised version of the GLA learning procedure, only one bias is necessary to ensure restrictiveness: Output-based constraints over Input-Output-based constraints.   The desired emergent and final-state effects arise through additive interaction as the constraint values are gradually adjusted based on the available target-language input. In this section we compare the HG-GLA system developed here with other approaches in the literature that aim to account for similar types of restrictiveness in learning.

6.1   Specific IO-Faithfulness

Prince & Tesar (2004; see also Hayes 2004) propose to ensure restrictiveness in ranked OT grammar learning by incorporating persistent biases into the general Constraint Demotion Algorithm (Tesar & Smolensky 1998, 2000).   As Prince & Tesar (2004) recognize, however, this Biased Constraint Demotion approach encounters a number of difficulties with respect to Specific Faithfulness constraints, which must be ranked above their more general counterparts to ensure restrictiveness.

Specific IO-Faith >> General IO-Faith constraint biases cause two primary problems for BCDA-style models. First, general vs. specific relationships can in some cases be language specific (Prince & Tesar 2004). In a language where word-initial syllables are always stressed but non-initial syllables can also bear stress in longer words, for example, positional faithfulness constraints referring to stressed syllables (e.g., IDENT-σ') and to word initial position (e.g., IDENT-INITIAL) in fact stand in a general/specific relationship. The environments in which IDENT-σ' applies are a proper superset of those in which IDENT-INITIAL applies. The general/specific nature of this relationship, however, can only be determined on a language-specific basis, as it is dependent upon the placement of stress. These relationships will thus need to be actively computed by the BCDA learner in some way in order for the bias to be implemented (for such implementation, see Hayes 2004, Tessier 2006a, 2007).

In the HG-GLA system developed here no such calculations of general/specific relationships are necessary. All IO-Faithfulness constraints begin with an initial value of 0 and have their weights gradually increased on the basis of positive evidence from the target language. As a logical necessity, any error that causes the value of a specific faithfulness constraint to increase will cause the value of its general counterpart to do the same. If the target language is a restrictive one, learning will cease when the summed weight of the general and specific IO-Faithfulness constraints is sufficient to overcome markedness pressures. For example, in a target language where initial syllables are a proper subset of stressed syllables and voicing is preserved only in the specific (initial) environment, learning will cease when the summed weights of IDENTVOICE-σ' and IDENTVOICE-INITIAL overcome the weight of the conflicting constraint *VOICE.

(60)　*Target language stresses all initial syllables, preserves voicing only word-initially*

　　　a.　*HG-GLA initial state*
　　　　　w*VOICE (=100) > wIDENTVOICE-σ' (=0) + wIDENTVOICE-INITIAL (=0)

　　　b.　*Errors*
　　　　　/'da.ta.,ta/→*['ta.ta.,ta]　triggers promotion of wIDENTVOICE-σ' and
　　　　　　　　　　　　　　　　　　　　　wIDENTVOICE-INITIAL, demotion of w*VOICE

　　　c.　*Final state – no errors (restrictive)*
　　　　　wIDENTVOICE-σ' + wIDENTVOICE-INITIAL > w*VOICE
　　　　　w*VOICE > wIDENTVOICE-σ'

Restrictive IF stages of the type displayed by Théo in section 4.1 similarly result from the additive effect of a general IO-Faith constraint and its specific counterpart. General/ specific effects emerge as a direct consequence of target-language evidence and additive interaction in the HG-GLA model; no additional computation is necessary.

The second problem that the BCDA faces relates to the modeling of restrictive intermediate IF stages in target General Faith >> Markedness languages.[17] These are cases like Théo's described in section 3, where the target language allows a marked structure in all contexts but the child nonetheless passes through a stage where the marked structure is preserved only in privileged contexts. The problem for the BCDA is simply that no evidence from the target language ever favours a SpecFaith >> Markedness >> GenFaith ranking. On encountering errors involving both privileged and non-privileged positions, the BCDA learner automatically demotes the Markedness constraint to below General IO-Faithfulness, bypassing the IF stage entirely. In contrast, the HG-GLA system is an on-line learner that changes the positions of constraints gradually rather than categorically; together with the weighted mode of evaluation, this ensures that restrictive IF stages will emerge even in the acquisition of languages that show no evidence of such positional effects in the end state.

It is worth emphasizing here that gradual learning alone is not sufficient; gradual approaches without additive interaction (i.e., OT-GLA) also face difficulties in accounting for restrictive specific faithfulness effects. In a target language like French which requires that General Faith >> Markedness, for example, restrictive IF stages are not predicted to occur in an OT-GLA system. The reason for this is quite simple: general faithfulness constraints are implicated in proper superset of the errors in which specific faithfulness constraints are implicated, and so their values increase more quickly, preventing the restrictive stage from ever emerging.

---

[17]　　Prince & Tesar (2004) do not intend for the BCDA to model intermediate stages in language acquisition. It is thus not surprising that this approach encounters difficulties when extended to such data.

(61)   a.   *OT-GLA French initial state*
            *COMPLEX >> MAX, MAX-σ'

       b.   *Errors*
            /CV.'CCV/ →   [CV.'CV]   triggers promotion of MAX and MAX-σ'
            /CCV.'CV / → [CV.'CV]   triggers promotion of MAX

       c.   *French final state - no IF stage emerges*
            MAX >> *COMPLEX >> MAX-σ'

This problem is avoided in the HG-GLA system through the reliance on additive interaction rather than strict ranking. The emergence of an IF stage is guaranteed by the subset-superset relationship that holds between the constraints in question.

The lack of additive interaction is also a problem for OT-GLA when SpecFaith >> M >> GenFaith target languages are considered. In this case, the two faithfulness constraints are adjusted at the same rate during learning, resulting in a final state where the two IO-Faithfulness constraints are both ranked above Markedness.

(62)   a.   *OT-GLA French' initial state (allows clusters only in stressed syllables)*
            *COMPLEX >> MAX, MAX-σ'

       b.   *Errors*
            /CV.'CCV/ →   [CV.'CV]   triggers promotion of MAX and MAX-σ'

       c.   *French' final state - not restrictive*
            MAX, MAX-σ' >> *COMPLEX

Additive interaction allows the HG-GLA model to avoid this problem as well. Errors cease in HG-GLA learning when the individual weights of both IO-Faithfulness constraints are still less than that of the conflicting markedness constraint, but their summed weight is greater than that of markedness. The final state thus only admits clusters when doing so allows both MAX and MAX-σ' to be satisfied.

These problems with the ranked-constraint GLA model could perhaps be solved if a SpecificFaith >> GeneralFaith bias were implemented at least in the initial state. As with the BCDA, however, this would required that general/specific relationships be calculated by the learner for their particular language – a challenge that is particularly great in the case of an on-line algorithm like the GLA where ranking arguments and mark-data pairs are not stored. With the HG version of the GLA this problem is circumvented; the target language patterns directly inform adjustments to constraint values and additive interaction ensures that appropriate restrictiveness is attained.

6.2   OO-Faithfulness

OO-Faith restrictiveness can be ensured in BCDA-style OT grammar learning by incorporating a persistent high OO-Faith ranking bias into the general algorithm (Hayes 2004, McCarthy 1998, Tessier 2006b, 2007). The class of OO-Faith constraints can be identified in a straightforward fashion and, unlike the general/specific relationships of IO-Faithfulness constraints, is not subject to language-particular vagaries. This makes a persistent high OO-Faith bias reasonably simple to implement in OT learning.

Nonetheless, there are interesting differences in predictions between the OT-BCDA approach and the HG-GLA approach advanced here. In particular, the range of OO-Faith intermediate stages that are predicted to be able to emerge in the OT-BCDA system is greater than that predicted to be possible in the HG-GLA system. By way of illustration, consider the hypothetical pattern in (63) where the target is a modified version of English which, unlike actual English, strictly disallows sequences of coronal stops plus laterals – i.e., *TL is strictly obeyed. The child in this case shows an emergent OO-Faith stage where the target [tait~taikli:] paradigm is leveled to [tait~taitli:].

(63) *English' emergent paradigm leveling pattern (hypothetical)*

	Target	Child	
a.	[pʌɡəl]	[pʌɡəl]	⇒ *monomorphemic*
b.	[tait]	[tait]	⇒ *monomorphemic base*
c.	[taikli:]	[taitli:]	⇒ *bimorphemic derived form*

This emergent pattern is easily modeled in an OT ranking approach that imposes a high OO-Faith bias. Indeed, at the end of phonotactic learning when morphological awareness emerges, the expected ranking for the English' learner is OO-FAITH >> *TL >> IO-FAITH. As can be seen in (64) below, this is precisely the constraint ordering necessary for the child pattern in (63) to arise.

(64) *Emergent OO-Faith stage in English'*

	/tait+li:/ base: [tait]	OO-IDENT	*TL	IO-IDENT
i.	☞ taitli:		*	
ii.	taikli:	*!		*

This type of emergent stage cannot be modeled in the HG-GLA system. There, *TL is promoted during the course of phonotactic learning to a value above the starting weight of OO-Ident. At the same time, IO-Ident is regularly violated in the target language and so remains low-valued; with a weight of 0, IO-Ident cannot gang up with OO-Ident to favour the leveled paradigm. Without any additional markedness constraint favouring the leveled paradigm, the hypothetical emergent stage depicted in (63) cannot emerge.

Removing the OO-Faith >> Markedness bias from the HG-GLA system means that in cases where the leveled paradigm is actively disfavoured by a markedness constraint that is unviolated in the target language, like *TL in (63) above, there must be some additional markedness constraint in the grammar with which OO-Faith can gang up. If there is no such markedness pressure, no OO-Faith intermediate stage will emerge.[18] This additional markedness constraint will normally be a general constraint that can be assessed across a range of contexts: the *Ç constraint seen with Marina's case in section 4.2.1 is one example. The HG-GLA system advanced here thus limits the range of possible emergent OO-Faith stages to a greater extent than does a BCDA-based approach with a high OO-Faith bias. These restrictions are supported by the range of emergent OO-Faith stages attested in the literature, though realistically our knowledge of these patterns is still limited and their actual distribution remains an empirical question.

The OO-Faith restrictiveness problem is more acute with OT-GLA systems, where the major issue becomes one of ensuring that the value of OO-Faith stays higher than that of Markedness throughout phonotactic learning. As illustrated in (64), within a ranking system OO-Faith effects emerge when OO-Faith outranks Markedness and Markedness outranks IO-Faith. In a case like that of Marina discussed in section 4.2.1, then, it is necessary for the ranking OO-FAITH >> *XI >> *Ç >> IO-FAITH to hold. As also shown in section 4.2.1, however, during the course of GLA-based phonotactic learning the value of *XI increases while the value of OO-FAITH remains stable. This prevents the necessary ranking from being easily reached. An initial ranking of OO-Faith above Markedness could, of course, be imposed, but particularly within more complex systems it is difficult to determine *how* high the initial value of OO-Faith must be in order for this to be effective. Such emergent stages pose no problem within the HG-GLA system; there, the effects emerge through additive interaction as OO-Faith gangs up with an additional markedness constraint that favours the leveled paradigm (for Marina, *Ç).

Before concluding, one potential problem shared by the HG-GLA and OT-GLA approaches is worth noting. The crucial case comes from final state grammars that rely on OO-Faithfulness to allow marked configurations in derived words – Hayes (2004) and Tessier (2007) provide the distribution of Canadian Raising (Joos 1942) as an example. In underived words, Canadian English restricts the raised diphthongs [ʌj] and [ʌw] to contexts immediately preceding a voiceless obstruent – e.g., *write* [ɹʌjt]; the diphthongs [aj] and [aw] appear in all other environments – e.g., *ride* [ɹajd], *eye* [aj]. In derived words, however, the quality of the diphthong is retained so that raised diphthongs can occur before voiced segments when a raised diphthong appears in the base – e.g., *writer* [ɹʌjɾəɹ]. The learning problem here relates to the timing of the onset of morphological awareness. While the child is still unaware of the complex nature of words like *writer*, he will take these as evidence that the diphthongs [ʌj] and [aj] contrast before voiced segments; this will cause the value of IO-IDENT to increase and the value of *ʌj to decrease. If this state of pre-morphological awareness persists for too long, the value of IO-IDENT may come to surpass that of *ʌj, resulting in a grammar that allows the raised diphthong in all contexts, regardless of morphological complexity. This lack of

---

[18]   In the Kansai B case discussed in section 5.2 the value of OO-Faith alone is sufficient to ensure a final state OO-Faith restrictiveness. In that case, however, there is no unviolated markedness constraint in the target language that actively disfavours the leveled paradigm; MINWORD is neutral with respect to the choice between {[kaa], [kaaga]} and *{[kaa], [kaga]}. Similarly, in Amahl's case discussed in section 4.2.2 there is no unviolated markedness constraint in the target language that disfavours paradigm leveling; *TL is regularly violated in actual English.

restrictiveness is likely undesirable (but cf. Mielke et al. 2003), and suggests that some form of persistent bias preferring grammars where the relative importance of IO-Faith is reduced when OO-Faith becomes active may be necessary (see Tessier 2007 for an implementation within the BCDA framework). We leave further exploration of this issue to future research.

6.3 Summary

This paper has demonstrated that restrictive phonological learning can be modeled using only the single bias in (65) when the mode of constraint interaction is additive as in Harmonic Grammar and learning is gradual as in the GLA. This stands in contrast to OT models where at least three biases are necessary in order to capture the same range of attested effects.

(65) *Single bias required for restrictive learning in HG-GLA*
     wOUTPUT-BASED CONSTRAINTS > wINPUT-OUTPUT-BASED CONSTRAINTS

Restrictiveness effects in HG-GLA emerge primarily through additive interaction. Specific Faithfulness intermediate stages are the result of general and specific IO-Faithfulness constraints ganging up to overcome the weight of a conflicting markedness constraint. Final state Specific Faithfulness grammars are accounted for through the same types of inequalities. This approach avoids the need to compute language-particular general/specific relationships and ensures that final-state grammars will be sufficiently restrictive.

(66) *Inequality responsible for Specific Faith restrictiveness*
     wGENERALFAITH + wSPECIFICFAITH > wMARKEDNESS

OO-Faith restrictiveness effects are more varied in nature, though they too can rely on additive interaction. Emergent OO-Faith stages where a target language process is blocked in the child language depend upon OO-Faith ganging up with a second Markedness constraint. Similar stages where it is a child-specific process that is blocked can rely on OO-Faith alone. Final state OO-Faith restrictiveness is similar to this second type of emergent OO-Faith stage, relying on the continued high weight of OO-Faith and the absence of multiple constraints with which IO-Faith and Markedness can gang up to overcome the inequality.

(67) *Inequalities responsible for OO-Faith restrictiveness*
     a. wOO-FAITH + wGENMARKEDNESS > wSPECMARKEDNESS + wIO-FAITH
     b. wOO-FAITH > wMARKEDNESS + wIO-FAITH (only possible when Markedness
         is violated under pressure from IO-Faith in target underived words)

The HG-GLA system is thus capable of modeling both restrictive intermediate stages and restrictive final states using a learning algorithm that is gradual, on-line and error driven. This is a significant advantage, given the difficulties encountered by the ranked-constraint learners discussed in sections 6.1 and 6.2. Still, there remains much scope for further research into the HG-GLA model. Differences in the speed of weight adjustment between different types of constraints (discussed in section 5.2.3) are of particular interest and should be explored as a means of implementing persistent biases. The range and nature of emergent restrictiveness effects in acquisition is similarly in need of further exploration, with many empirical questions remaining to be answered. Nonetheless, it is clear that a combination of additive constraint interaction with a gradual on-line learning algorithm offers considerable restrictiveness advantages; this is an important result, offering novel support for the Harmonic Grammar model and for constraint weighting more generally.

References

Albright, Adam. 2004. Inflectional paradigms have bases too: arguments from Yiddish. Ms., Cambridge MA: MIT. [http://web.mit.edu/Albright/www/papers/Albright-InflectionalParadigmsHaveBasesToo.pdf]

Albright, Adam. 2005. The morphological basis of paradigm leveling. In *Paradigms in Phonological Theory*, ed. Laura Downing, Tracy Alan Hall & Renate Raffelsiefen. Oxford: Oxford University Press.

Alderete, John D. 1999. *Morphologically-Governed Accent in Optimality Theory.* PhD dissertation. Amherst, MA: University of Massachusetts. [ROA-309].

Barton, David. 1976. *The Role of Perception in the Acquisition of Phonology.* PhD dissertation. Stanford, CA: Stanford University.

Barton, David. 1980. Phonetic perception in children. In *Child Phonology, vol. 2: Perception*, ed. Grace Yeni-Komshian, James Kavanagh & Charles Ferguson, 97-116. New York: Academic Press.

Benua, Laura. 1997. *Transderivational Identity: Phonological Relations Between Words.* PhD dissertation. Amherst, MA: University of Massachusetts.

Berwick, Robert C. 1985. *The Acquisition of Syntactic Knowledge.* Cambridge, MA: MIT Press.

Boersma, Paul. 1998. *Functional Phonology: Formalizing the Interactions Between Articulatory and Perceptual Drives.* PhD dissertation. Amsterdam: University of Amsterdam.

Boersma, Paul. 2006. The acquisition and evolution of faithfulness rankings. Paper presented at the *Manchester Phonology Meeting 14.* May 2006.

Boersma, Paul & Bruce Hayes. 2001. Empirical tests of the Gradual Learning Algorithm. *Linguistic Inquiry* 32: 45-86. [ROA-348].

Boersma, Paul & Clara Levelt. 2000. Gradual constraint-ranking learning algorithm predicts acquisition order. In *Proceedings of the 30th Child Language Research Forum*, ed. E.V. Clark, 229–237. Stanford, CA: CSLI. [ROA-361].

Boersma, Paul & Joe Pater. 2007. Testing gradual learning algorithms. Ms., University of Amsterdam & University of Massachusetts Amherst.

Boersma, Paul & David Weenink. 2007. *PRAAT: Doing Phonetics by Computer.* [www.praat.org].

Broselow, Ellen. 1982. On predicting the interaction of stress and epenthesis. *Glossa* 16: 115-132.

Chambless, Della. 2006. *Asymmetries in Consonant Cluster Acquisition.* PhD dissertation. Amherst, MA: University of Massachusetts.

Demuth, Katherine. 1995. Markedness and the development of prosodic structure. In *Proceedings of NELS 25*, ed. Jill Beckman. Amherst, MA: Graduate Linguistic Student Association. [ROA-50]

Dinnsen, Daniel A. & Laura W. McGarrity. 2004. On the nature of alternations in phonological acquisition. *Studies in Phonetics, Phonology and Morphology* 10: 23-41.

Dinnsen, Daniel A., Kathleen M. O'Connor & Judith A. Gierut. 2001. The puzzle-puddle-pickle problem and the Duke-of-York gambit in acquisition. *Journal of Linguistics* 37: 503-525.

Dresher, Bezalel Elan. 1999. Charting the learning path: cues to parameter setting. *Linguistic Inquiry* 30(1): 27-67.

Dresher, Bezalel Elan & Jonathan D. Kaye. 1990. A computational learning model for metrical phonology. *Cognition* 34: 137-195.

Gnanadesikan, Amalia. 2004. Markedness and faithfulness in child phonology. In *Fixing Priorities: Constraints in Phonological Acquisition*, ed. René Kager, Joe Pater & Wim Zonneveld, 73-108. Cambridge: Cambridge University Press. [ROA-67].

Goad, Heather & Yvan Rose. 2004. Input elaboration, head faithfulness and evidence for representation in the acquisition of left-edge clusters in West Germanic. In *Fixing Priorities: Constraints in Phonological Acquisition*, ed. René Kager, Joe Pater & Wim Zonneveld. Cambridge: Cambridge University Press

Hale, Mark & Charles Reiss. 1998. Formal and empirical arguments concerning phonological acquisition. *Linguistic Inquiry* 29(4): 656-683.

Hayes, Bruce. 2004. Phonological acquisition in Optimality Theory: the early stages. In *Fixing Priorities: Constraints in Phonological Acquisition*, ed. René Kager, Joe Pater & Wim Zonneveld. Cambridge: Cambridge University Press. [ROA-327].

Hayes, Bruce & Zsuzsa Londe. 2006. Stochastic phonological knowledge: the case of Hungarian vowel harmony. *Phonology* 23: 59-104.

Jäger, Gerhard. to appear. Maximum entropy models and stochastic Optimality Theory. In *Architectures, Rules, and Preferences: A Festschrift for Joan Bresnan*, ed. Jane Grimshaw, Joan Maling, Chris Manning, Jane Simpson & Annie Zaenen. CSLI Publications, Stanford.

Jarosz Snover, Gaja. 2006. *Rich Lexicons and Restrictive Grammars – Maximum Likelihood Learning in Optimality Theory.* PhD dissertation. Baltimore, MD: Johns Hopkins University.

Jesney, Karen. 2005. *Chain Shift in Phonological Acquisition.* MA thesis. Calgary, AB: University of Calgary. [http://people.umass.edu/kjesney/Jesney2005MA.pdf].

Jesney, Karen. 2007a. Child chain shifts as faithfulness to input prominence. In *Proceedings of the 2nd Conference on Generative Approaches to Language Acquisition North America (GALANA)*, ed. Alyona Belikova, Luisa Meroni & Mari Umeda, 188-199. Somerville, MA: Cascadilla.

Jesney, Karen. 2007b. The locus of variation in weighted constraint grammars. Poster presented at the *Workshop on Variation, Gradience and Frequency in Phonology.* Stanford, CA: Stanford University. July 2007.

Joos, Martin. 1942. A phonological dilemma in Canadian English. *Language* 18: 141-

144.

Kazazis, Kostas. 1969. Possible evidence for (near-)underlying forms in the speech of a child. In *Papers from the Fifth Regional Meeting of the Chicago Linguistic Society (CLS 5)*, ed. Robert I. Binnick, Alice Davison, Georgia McGreen & Jerry L. Morgan, 382- 388. Chicago, IL: Chicago Linguistic Society.

Kehoe, Margaret & Carol Stoel-Gammon. 1997. Truncation patterns in English-speaking children's word productions. *Journal of Speech, Language, and Hearing Research* 40: 526-541.

Keller, Frank. 2000. *Gradience in Grammar: Experimental and Computational Aspects of Degrees of Grammaticality*. PhD dissertation. Edinburgh: University of Edinburgh.

Keller, Frank. 2006. Linear Optimality Theory as a model of gradience in grammar. In *Gradience in Grammar: Generative Perspectives*, ed. Gisbert Fanselow, Caroline Féry, Ralph Vogel & Matthias Schlesewsky. Oxford: Oxford University Press.

Ladefoged, Peter & Ian Maddieson. 1996. *The Sounds of the World's Languages*. Oxford: Blackwell.

Legendre, Geraldine, Yoshiro Miyata & Paul Smolensky. 1990. Harmonic Grammar – a formal multi-level connectionist theory of linguistic wellformedness: an application. In *Proceedings of the Twelfth Annual Conference of the Cognitive Science Society*, 884–891. Cambridge, MA: Lawrence Erlbaum.

Macken, Marlys A. 1980. The child's lexical representation: the 'puzzle-puddle-pickle' evidence. *Journal of Linguistics* 16: 1-17.

McCarthy, John J. 1998. Morpheme structure constraints and paradigm occultation. In *Papers from the Thirty-second Regional Meeting of the Chicago Linguistic Society (CLS 32), Part 2: The Panels*, ed. M. Catherine Gruber, Derrick Higgins, Kenneth Olsen & Tamra Wysocki, 123-150. Chicago, IL: Chicago Linguistic Society.

McCarthy, John J. 2002. *A Thematic Guide to Optimality Theory*. Cambridge: Cambridge University Press.

McCarthy, John J. 2007. *Hidden Generalizations: Phonological Opacity in Optimality Theory*. London: Equinox.

McCarthy, John J. & Alan Prince. 1993. *Prosodic Morphology I: Constraint Interaction and Satisfaction*. Technical Report #3, Rutgers University Center for Cognitive Science.

McCarthy, John J. & Alan Prince. 1995. Faithfulness and reduplicative identity. *Papers in Optimality Theory: University of Massachusetts Occasional Papers* 18: 249-384.

Mielke, Jeff , Mike Armstrong & Elizabeth Hume. 2003. Looking through opacity. *Theoretical Linguistics* 29(1-2): 123-139.

Pater, Joe. 1997. Minimal violation in phonological development. *Language Acquisition* 6(3): 201-253.

Pater, Joe. 2007. Harmonic Grammar, gradual learning, and phonological gradience. Paper presented at the *Workshop on Variation, Gradience, and Frequency in Phonology*. Stanford, CA: Stanford University. July 2007.

Pater, Joe. to appear. Gradual learning and convergence. *Linguistic Inquiry*. [ROA-917].

Pater, Joe, Karen Jesney & Anne-Michelle Tessier. 2007. Phonological acquisition as weighted constraint interaction. In *Proceedings of the Conference on Generative Approaches to Language Acquisition - North America 2*, ed. Alyona Belikova, Luisa Meroni & Mari Umeda. Somerville, MA: Cascadilla Press.

Pater, Joe, Chris Potts & Rajesh Bhatt. 2007. Linguistic Optimization. Ms., University of Massachusetts Amherst. [ROA-872].

Pater, Joe, Christine Stage & Janet Werker. 2004. The perceptual acquisition of phonological contrasts. *Language* 80(3): 384-402.

Prince, Alan. 1980. A metrical theory for Estonian quantity. *Linguistic Inquiry* 11(3): 511-562.

Prince, Alan. 2002. Anything goes. In *New Century of Phonology and Phonological Theory*, ed. Takeru Honma, Masao Okazaki, Toshiyuki Tabata & Shinichi Tanaka, 66-90. Tokyo: Kaitakusha. [ROA-536].

Prince, Alan & Paul Smolensky. 1993/2004. *Optimality Theory: Constraint Interaction in Generative Grammar*. Technical Report, Rutgers University and University of Colorado at Boulder, 1993. Revised version published by Blackwell, 2004. [ROA-537].

Prince, Alan & Bruce Tesar. 2004. Learning phonotactic distributions. In *Fixing Priorities: Constraints in Phonological Acquisition*, ed. René Kager, Joe Pater & Wim Zonneveld. Cambridge: Cambridge University Press. [ROA-353].

Pulleyblank, Douglas & William J. Turkel. 1998. The logical problem of language acquisition in optimality theory. In *Is the best good enough? Optimality and Competition in Syntax*, ed. Pilar Barbosa, Danny Fox, Paul Hagstrom, Martha McGinnis & David Pesetsky, 399-420. Cambridge, MA: MIT Press.

Revithiadou, A. & Marina Tzakosta. 2004. Markedness hierarchies vs. positional faithfulness and the role of multiple grammars in the acquisition of Greek. In *Proceedings of Generative Approaches to Language Acquisition (GALA)*. Utrecht: LOT Occasional Series.

Rosenblatt, Frank. 1958. The perceptron: a probabilistic model for information storage and organization in the brain. *Psychological Review* 65: 386-408.

Smith, Jennifer L. 2000. Positional faithfulness and learnability in Optimality Theory. In *Proceedings of ESCOL 99*, ed. Rebecca Daly & Anastasia Riehl, 203-214. Ithaca, NY: CLC Publications.

Smith, Neilson V. 1973. *The Acquisition of Phonology: A Case Study*. Cambridge: Cambridge University Press.

Smolensky, Paul. 1996. On the comprehension / production dilemma in child language. *Linguistic Inquiry* 21: 720-731.

Smolensky, Paul & Geraldine Legendre. 2006. *The Harmonic Mind: From Neural Computation to Optimality-Theoretic Grammar*. Cambridge, MA: MIT Press.

Stampe, David. 1973. *A Dissertation in Natural Phonology*. PhD dissertation. Chicago, IL: University of Chicago.

Tesar, Bruce & Paul Smolensky. 1998. Learnability in Optimality Theory. *Linguistic Inquiry* 29(2): 229-268.

Tesar, Bruce & Paul Smolensky. 2000. *Learnability in Optimality Theory*. Cambridge, MA: MIT Press.

Tessier, Anne-Michelle. 2006a. Learning stringency relations and the contexts of faithfulness. Paper presented at the *80th Annual Meeting of the Linguistic Society of America*, Albuquerque, NM. January 2006.

Tessier, Anne-Michelle. 2006b. Testing for OO-Faithfulness in artificial phonological acquisition. In *Proceedings of the 30th Annual Boston University Conference on Language Development*, ed. David Bamman, Tatiana Magnitskaia & Colleen Zaller, 619-639. Somerville, MA: Cascadilla. [ROA-817].

Tessier, Anne-Michelle. 2007. *Biases and Stages in Phonological Acquisition*. PhD dissertation. Amherst, MA: University of Massachusetts. [ROA-883].

Tessier, Anne-Michelle. to appear. Slowly learning to be faithful: frequency of violation and constraint-based learning. *Alberta Working Papers in Linguistics*.

Wilson, Colin. 2000. *Targeted constraints: An approach to contextual neutralization in Optimality Theory*. PhD dissertation. Baltimore, MD: Johns Hopkins University.

Karen Jesney
Department of Linguistics
226 South College
University of Massachusetts
Amherst, MA 01003 USA

kjesney@linguist.umass.edu

Anne-Michelle Tessier
Department of Linguistics
4-22 Assiniboia Hall
University of Alberta
Edmonton, AB T6G 2E7 Canada

amtessier@ualberta.ca

The role of psychoacoustic similarity in Japanese imperfect puns[*]

Shigeto Kawahara[1] and Kazuko Shinohara[2]
[1]University of Georgia and [2]Tokyo University of Agriculture and Technology

Using a corpus of Japanese imperfect puns, this paper shows that the degree of similarity of two consonants positively correlates with their likelihood of making a pun pair. This paper further shows that when Japanese speakers compose imperfect puns, they exploit psychoacoustic similarity—perceived similarity between sounds based on detailed acoustic information. The result supports the hypothesis that speakers possess rich knowledge of psychoacoustic similarity and deploy that knowledge in verbal art patterns (Steriade 2001a, b, 2003).

1. Introduction

Similarity plays a fundamental role in the phonetic and phonological organization of grammar: for example, phonology requires that inputs and outputs to be as similar as possible (Prince and Smolensky 2004; Steriade 2001b); morphologically related words are required to be similar (Benua 1997; Steriade 2000); languages avoid using similar contrastive sounds (Liljencrants and Lindblom 1972; Lindblom 1986); languages avoid pairs of adjacent similar consonants (Frisch, Pierrehumbert and Broe 2004; McCarthy 1986, 1988). Therefore, understanding the nature of speakers' knowledge about similarity is important for current theories of both phonetics and phonology.

Against this background, this paper investigates the knowledge of similarity that Japanese speakers possess by examining patterns of *dajare*, imperfect puns in Japanese. *Dajare* is a language game—or a linguistic joke—in which speakers make a sentence out of two words or phrases that closely resemble each other. An illustrative example is *huton-ga huttonda* 'a futon was blown away' which involves juxtaposition of two similar words: *huton* and *huttonda*. A congruent English example would be something like "Titanic in panic".

It has been known that in many languages, similar sounds tend to form sound pairs in a range of verbal art patterns, including rhymes, alliterations, and imperfect puns (see

---
[*] We are grateful to people who provided imperfect puns for us, and Michael Becker, John Kingston, Kazu Kurisu, Dan Mash, Lisa Shiozaki, and Chiaki Yamada for their comments. Please contact the first author for the database of imperfect puns in an Excel file, Excel functions that calculate O/E ratios, and a perl script which creates a co-occurrence table from a list of consonant pairs.

Michael Becker (ed.): Papers in theoretical and computational phonology. University of Massachusetts Occasional Papers in Linguistics 36, 111-133.
GLSA Amherst.

Kawahara 2007 for a recent overview). The role of similarity in imperfect puns has been explored in English (Fleischhacker 2005; Hempelmann 2005; Lagerquist 1980; Sobkowiak 1991; Zwicky and Zwicky 1986) as well as in Japanese (Cutler and Otake 2002; Otake and Cutler 2001; Shinohara 2004). All of these studies agree that similarity plays a crucial role in the formation of imperfect puns. However, a statistical study of segmental similarity in Japanese imperfect puns has not been undertaken—a gap we wish to fill presently.

We take a statistical approach because we want to discover phonetic/phonological patterns that could easily be covered by non-phonological noise and therefore missed by an impressionistic survey. Noise enters into imperfect pun formations because composers are concerned not only with the sound aspects of two corresponding words but also with the syntactic coherence and semantic humor (Hempelmann 2005). Therefore, a large number of data will help to us to discover phonetic/phonological patterns, and verify whether the discovered patterns are convincingly real.

Based on the compiled corpus, we first show that similarity plays a role in the formation of imperfect puns. Building on that, we argue that composers use psychoacoustic similarity—perceived similarity between sounds based on detailed acoustic information—when they compose imperfect puns. It has been shown previously that Japanese lyrists use psychoacoustic similarity when composing half rhymes (Kawahara 2007), and we replicate this result with imperfect puns. Our conclusion lends support to the P-map hypothesis that speakers possess knowledge of a matrix of psychoacoustic similarity and deploy that knowledge in shaping verbal art patterns (Fleischhacker 2005; Kawahara 2007; Minkova 2003; Steriade 2001b, 2003).

The rest of this paper proceeds as follows. In §2 we provide an overview of Japanese imperfect puns, and describe how we collected and analyzed the data. In §3 we present evidence for the role of similarity in the formation of Japanese imperfect puns. In §4 we make the case that speakers deploy psychoacoustic, rather than featural, similarity when they compose imperfect puns.

2. Method
2.1. An overview of Japanese imperfect puns

Imperfect puns are very common in Japanese, and some speakers create new puns on a daily basis (Mukai 1996; Takizawa 1996). In composing puns, speakers deliberately juxtapose a pair of similar-sounding words or phrases (we explore the precise definition of "similarity" in further depth later in the paper). The two corresponding parts can include identical sound sequences as in *buta-ga butareta* 'a pig was hit', an example of a *perfect pun*, or the two corresponding words can include similar but non-identical sounds, as in (1). The latter is an example of an *imperfect pun* because it includes corresponding pairs of non-identical sounds (indicated in bold letters in (1): [m]-[t], [h]-[b]). We focus on imperfect puns that include mismatched consonant pairs in this paper.[1]

(1)   **man**h**attan**-de su**t**an**b**attan
    Manhattan-LOC   stand-by
    'I stood by at Manhattan'

In (1), *manhattan* and *sutanbattan* are a pair of similar phrases that form an imperfect pun.[2] In this paper, we use the following notations. We mark *corresponding domains* in imperfect puns by underline: we define corresponding domains as sequences of syllables in which corresponding vowels are identical.[3] We use bold letters to indicate non-identical pairs of corresponding consonants, which are the focus of our analysis.

The pun in (1) is an imperfect pun in that it does not involve perfectly identical sequences of sounds. Even though Japanese puns can involve non-identical pairs of consonants, previous studies have noted that imperfect pun pairs tend to involve similar consonants (Cutler and Otake 2002; Otake and Cutler 2001; Shinohara 2004). The importance of

---

[1] Other types of imperfect puns involve metathesis (e.g. *shima*ne *no shinema* 'Cinema at Shimane'), phrasal boundary mismatches (e.g. *wakusee waa, kusee* 'Man, that planet is smelly'), syllable intrusion (e.g. *bundoki bundottoki* 'Just take a protractor away from him'), etc. Analyzing these patterns is beyond the scope of this paper, but it is an interesting topic for future research

[2] Speakers sometimes change the underlying form of one form to achieve better resemblance to the corresponding form, as in (i) (Shinohara 2004; Takizawa 1996):

(i)   Ho**kk**ai**doo**-wa   de**kk**ai   **d**oo
    Hokkaido-TOP   big   PARTICLE
    'Hokkaido is big'

In this example, the sentence-final particle [doo] is pronounced as [zo] in canonical speech, but speakers pronounce /zo/ as [doo] to make the word *dekkaizo* sound similar to *Hokkaidoo*. We also analyzed examples of puns like (i), but found that this type of puns are mainly created by mimicking non-standard speech styles. For example, for the change from /zo/ to [do] in (i), speakers are probably mimicking southern dialects of Japanese in which the particle *zo* is pronounced as [do]. Another common pattern is palatalization, as in (ii):

(ii)   Un**d**oo**j**oo-o   kashite kudasai.   U**n**   **d**oo**j**o
    playground-ACC lend   please   Yes,   please
    'Please let us use your playground. Yes, please'

The second [doojo] is usually pronounced as [doozo]: /z/ is palatalized to mimic *undoojoo*. This sort of palatalization is common in Japanese child speech and motherese (Mester and Itô 1989), and composers may be mimicking these styles of speech. Our database thus does not include examples like (i) and (ii) which involve some changes from underlying forms to surface forms.

[3] In an example like *ha*i*degaa-no zense wa ha*e*dekka?* 'Was Heidegger's previous life a fly?', the corresponding domain could be interpreted as coinciding with word boundaries, including a pair of non-identical vowels ([i]-[e]). However corresponding domains and word boundaries do not necessarily coincide with each other, as in *huton-ga hutonda* 'a futon was blown away'. We therefore define corresponding domains based on sequences of matched vowels rather than on word boundaries. Since examples like *ha*i*degaa-no zense wa ha*e*dekka?* were relatively rare in our corpus, our results below should not depend on the particular definition of the corresponding domain we have chosen.

similarity in imperfect puns can be illustrated by examples like: *aizusan-no aisu* 'ice cream from Aizu' ([z] and [s] are minimally different in voicing) and *okosama-o okosanaide* 'don't wake up the kid' ([m] and [n] are minimally different in place). Drawing on this observation, this paper statistically assesses what kind of "similarity" plays a role in imperfect puns. We conclude that speakers deploy their knowledge about psychoacoustic similarity based on detailed acoustic information. This finding shows that speakers possess knowledge of psychoacoustic similarity and make use of that knowledge to form verbal art patterns (Fleischhacker 2005; Kawahara 2007; Minkova 2003; Steriade 2001b, 2003).

2.2. Data collection

This subsection describes how we compiled the database for this study. In order to investigate how similarity influences the formation of Japanese imperfect puns, we collected examples of imperfect puns from three websites.[4] We also elicited data from native Japanese speakers. In total, we collected 2373 examples of Japanese imperfect puns.

Recall that we define "corresponding domains" in imperfect puns as sequences of syllables in which corresponding vowels are identical. For example, in *okosama-o okosanaide* 'don't wake up the kid', the corresponding domains include the first four syllables. In the domains defined as such, we counted pairs of corresponding consonants between the two words. We ignored identical pairs of consonants, because we are interested in similarity, not identity. Therefore, from the example *okosama-o okosanaide*, for instance, we extracted the [m-n] pair.

A few remarks on our coding convention are in order. We counted only onset consonants, and ignored coda consonants because they place-assimilate to the following consonant (Itô 1986). We also ignored singleton-geminate distinctions because our interest lies in segmental similarity. We compiled the data based on surface forms, following a recent body of work which argues that similarity is based on surface forms rather than phonemic forms (Kang 2003; Kawahara 2006, 2007; Kawahara, Ono and Sudo 2006; Kenstowicz 2003; Kenstowicz and Suchato 2006; Minkova 2003; Steriade 2001b; cf. Jakobson 1960; Kiparsky 1970, 1972, 1981; Malone 1987). For instance, the onset of the syllable [ʃi] is arguably derived from an underlying /s/, but it was counted as [ʃ]. Finally, we excluded pairs which are underlyingly different but are neutralized at the surface because of independent phonological processes (even when the neutralization is optional). For example, the second consonant [dd] in *beddo* 'bed' can optionally devoice in the presence of another voiced obstruent (Kawahara 2006; Nishimura 2003). Thus given an example like *beddo-dai-wa betto itadakimasu* 'please pay for the bed separately', we did not consider the /dd/-/tt/ pair as a pair of non-identical consonants, since the pun-maker could have pronounced /beddo/ as [betto] when s/he composed the pun. Similarly, many puns

---

    [4] http://www.dajarenavi.net/
        http://www.ipc-tokai.or.jp/~y-kamiya/Dajare/
        http://www.geocities.co.jp/Milkyway-Vega/8361/umamoji3.html

included examples of [y] corresponding with Ø in the context of [i _ a], as in *kanariØa-o kauno-wa kanari iya* 'I don't like having a canary'. However, we did not count these cases since /ia/ surfaces as [iya] (Katayama 1998; Kawahara 200?).

2.3. Data analysis: O/E ratios

The general hypothesis tested in this paper is that the more similar two consonants are, the more frequently speakers use them in imperfect puns. Testing the hypothesis requires a measure of combinability between two segments. For this purpose, we use O/E ratios as a measure of the combinability of two elements. O/E ratios are the ratios between how often a pair is actually observed (O-values) with respect to how often it is expected to occur if two elements are combined at random (E-values). Mathematically, the O-value of a sound [A] is how many times [A] occurs in the corpus, and the E-value of a pair [A-B] is $P(A) \times P(B) \times N$ (where $P(X)$ = the probability of the sound [X] to occur in the corpus; N = the total number of consonants). O/E ratios greater than 1 indicate that the given consonant pairs are combined as pun pairs more frequently than expected (overrepresentation), while O/E ratios less than 1 indicate that the given consonant pairs are combined less frequently than expected (underrepresentation) (see Frisch et al. 2004; Kawahara 2007; Trubetzkoy 1969 for related discussion).

3. Results
3.1. The correlation between similarity and combinability

The results of the O/E analysis show that similarity influences the combinability of two consonants in imperfect puns: the more similar two consonants are, the more frequently they make imperfect puns. As a first approximation, we estimated the similarity of consonant pairs in terms of how many feature specifications they share (Bailey and Hahn 2005; Kawahara 2007; Klatt 1968; Shattuck-Hufnagel and Klatt 1977; Stemberger 1991). We discuss an alternative measure of similarity in §4, but start with this simple version of featural similarity in order to statistically establish the correlation between similarity and combinability.[5]

To estimate the numbers of shared feature specifications among the set of distinctive consonants in Japanese, we used eight features: [sonorant], [consonantal], [continuant], [nasal], [strident], [voice], [palatalized], and [place]. [Palatalized] is a secondary place feature, which distinguishes plain consonants from palatalized consonants. According to this system, for example, the [p-b] pair shares seven feature specifications, and hence it is treated as highly similar by this system. On the other hand, a pair like [ʃ-m] agrees only in [cons], and is considered as a highly non-similar pair.

When assigning feature specifications to Japanese sounds, we made the following assumptions. Affricates are specified both as [+cont] and [-cont] (Lombardi 1990; Sagey

---

[5] Another possible measure of similarity can be calculated based on the number of shared natural classes over the number of shared and unshared natural classes (Frisch et al. 2004). We do not perform this analysis because we ultimately reject an analysis based on featural similarity in §4.

1986) and disagree with any other segments in terms of [cont]. We treated [h] as a voiceless fricative, not as an approximant (Jaeger and Ohala 1984; Parker 2002: 64-68). We also assumed that sonorants are specified as [+voice] and agree with voiced obstruents in terms of [voice], although phonologically, voicing in sonorants behaves differently from voicing in obstruents in Japanese phonology (see §4.3 for further discussion). See Appendix I for a complete feature matrix assumed in the analysis.

The general hypothesis that speakers use similarity to compose imperfect puns predicts that similarity, as measured by the number of shared feature specifications, positively correlates with combinability, as measured by O/E ratios. In the calculation of the correlation, we ignored the linear order of consonant pairs. Additionally, we excluded consonants whose O-values are less than 20 because including them resulted in extraordinarily high O/E ratios: combining two rare consonants yields a very low E-value, and any observed pair of that type would have an artificially high O/E ratio (e.g. the O/E ratio of [p^j-b^j] is 1166). For this reason, we excluded [ts], [dʒ], [y], and all non-coronal palatalized consonants. The exclusions left 515 pairs of consonants for the subsequent analysis. See Appendix II for the list of O/E ratios.

The scatterplot in Figure 1 illustrates the general correlation between similarity and combinability of consonant pairs. For each consonant pair, it plots the number of shared feature specifications on the x-axis and plots the natural log-transformed O/E ratios multiplied by 10 ($\text{Log}_e(\text{O/E})*10$) on the y-axis. We use log-transformed values on the y-axis because it allows us to fit all the data points in a reasonably small-sized graph. $\text{Log}_e(\text{zero})$ is negative infinity, so we replaced $\text{Log}_e(\text{zero})$ with zero. However, the log of O/E ratios smaller than e are negative, and hence would be incorrectly treated as values smaller than zero (e.g.; .5 > 0, but $\text{Log}_e(.5) < 0$). Therefore, we multiplied O/E ratios by 10 before log-transformation. The plot excludes pairs in which one member is Ø since it is difficult if not impossible to define Ø in terms of distinctive features; we discuss these pairs in §4.4.

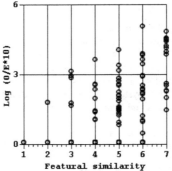

Figure 1: The correlation between the number of shared feature specifications and how likely two consonants make pairs in imperfect puns.

We observe in Figure 1 an upward trend in which the combinability correlates with featural similarity: the more feature specifications a pair shares, the higher the corresponding O/E ratio is. To statistically analyze the linear relationship observed in Figure 1, we calculated a Spearman correlation coefficient r_s, a non-parametric numerical indication of linear correlation. We used a non-parametric measure because we cannot assume a bivariate normal distribution. The result is that r_s is .540 (N=136; p<.001): similarity affects how frequently two consonants are paired to a statistically significant degree.

One implicit assumption in the above analysis is that each feature contributes to similarity by the same amount. This assumption might be too naïve; hence §4.2 re-examines this assumption.

3.2. The effect of place homorganicity

Having established the general role of similarity in imperfect pun formation, we now look at the effect of place homorganicity, which provides further insights about similarity. Table 1 tabulates O/E ratios for consonant pairs according to the place of two corresponding consonants. In the table we classified coronals into two classes, coronal sonorants and coronal obstruents, because in a similar phonological pattern of consonant co-occurrence restrictions, coronal obstruents and sonorants are split into two "identity classes" (Yip 1989). Languages, including Japanese, avoid pairs of adjacent homorganic consonants, but not pairs of coronal sonorants and obstruents—i.e. coronal sonorants and obstruents are not considered as "similar".[6] If similarity underlies both consonant co-occurrence patterns and the formation of imperfect puns, we should observe the same split of coronals into two classes in imperfect puns as well.

Now consider Table 1. The table does not include any pairs of identical consonants or pairs in which one member is Ø. We included the set of rare consonants that are excluded in §3.1 since including them does not yield artificially high O/E ratios in this analysis. As a result, a total N is 526 for this analysis.

---

[6] This pattern holds in many languages including Arabic (Frisch et al. 2004; Greenberg 1950; McCarthy 1988), English (Berkley 1994), Japanese (Kawahara et al. 2005), Javanese (Mester 1986), Russian (Padgett 1992), Tigrinya (Buckley 1997), and Wintu (McGarrity 1999).

	Labial (p, pʲ, b, bʲ, m, Φ, w)	Cor-obs (t, d, ts, s, z, ʃ, ʒ, tʃ, ç)	Cor-son (n, nʲ, r, rʲ, y,)	Dorsal (k, kʲ, g, gʲ)	Pharyngeal (h)
Labial	O=65 O/E=2.72	O=21 O/E=.36	O=12 O/E=1.03	O=14 O/E=.55	O=10 O/E=3.08
Cor-obs	O=7 O/E=.17	O=183 O/E=1.80	O=11 O/E=.54	O=11 O/E=.25	O=2 O/E=.35
Cor-son	O=6 O/E=.57	O=23 O/E=.90	O=18 O/E=3.51	O=7 O/E=.63	O=0 O/E=0
Dorsal	O=8 O/E=.41	O=14 O/E=.29	O=6 O/E=.63	O=70 O/E=3.38	O=2 O/E=.75
Phary	O=17 O/E=2.41	O=9 O/E=.53	O=3 O/E=.88	O=7 O/E=.94	O=0 O/E=0

Table 1: The effect of place homorganicity.

Table 1 shows that pairs of homorganic consonants agreeing in the place of articulation are generally overrepresented: [lab-lab]=2.72; [cor obs-cor obs]=1.80; [cor son-cor son]=3.51; [dors-dors]=3.38. The pairs of pharyngeal consonants are not overrepresented because the only pharyngeal consonant is [h].

We also observe that pairs of coronal obstruents and coronal sonorants are *not* overrepresented (O/E=.56, .92). The split of coronal obstruents and coronal sonorants shows that Japanese pun-makers use the same knowledge of similarity that underlies consonant co-occurrence patterns (see Kawahara 2007 for a similar pattern in Japanese half rhymes).

Aside from homorganic pairs of consonants, the [labial-pharyngeal] pairs are overrepresented (O/E=2.41, 3.08). The overrepresentation may be due to the fact that Japanese pharyngeals are historically—and arguably underlyingly—labial (McCawley 1968; Ueda 1898). For Japanese speakers, these two classes are phonologically related, and their phonological relation may promote similarity between the two classes of sounds (Hume and Johnson 2003; Kawahara 2007; Malone 1987, 1988a, b; Shinohara 2004; Zwicky 1976 cf. Steriade 2003 who doubts this claim).

4. Beyond featural similarity: the role of psychoacoustic similarity

In §3, we used distinctive features to estimate similarity. We argue in this section that measuring similarity in terms of the sum of shared feature specifications does not suffice: Japanese speakers instead use psychoacoustic similarity. By psychoacoustic similarity, we mean perceived similarity between sounds which refers to acoustic details.

One suggestive example that supports the role of psychoacoustic similarity is the [r-d] pair, whose O/E ratio is 3.52. According to the distinctive feature system, the pair agrees in six features (all but [son] and [cont]), but the average O/E ratios of consonant pairs agreeing in six distinctive feature is 1.65 (the 95% confidence interval=.48~2.82). Thus the high O/E ratio of the [r-d] pair is unexpected from featural similarity, but it makes sense from an psychoacoustic perspective. Japanese [r] is a flap which involves a ballistic constriction (Nakamura 2002): both [r] and [d] are similar to each other in that they are voiced consonants with relatively short closures (Price 1981; Steriade 2000).

Below we present four more kinds of arguments that pun composers exploit psychoacoustic similarity rather than featural similarity. First, composers are sensitive to the different perceptual salience of the same feature in different contexts (§4.1.). Second, composers take into consideration the different perceptual salience of different features (§4.2.). Third, composers are sensitive to similarity contributed by a phonologically inert feature (§4.3.). Finally, pun-makers are willing to pair Ø with consonants that are psychoacoustically similar to Ø (§4.4.).

4.1. Sensitivity to context-dependent salience of the same feature

The first piece of evidence that composers use psychoacoustic similarity is the fact that composers are sensitive to different degrees of salience of the same feature in different contexts. Here, we focus on the perceptual salience of [place]. In (2), we list the O/E ratios of minimal pairs of consonants differing in place (a moraic nasal in Japanese, [N], appears only in codas, and is excluded from this study).

(2) O/E ratios of minimal pairs differing in place

[m-n]:	8.43	[b-d]:	1.14	[p-t]:	.92
		[b-g]:	.68	[p-k]:	.93
		[d-g]:	.40	[t-k]:	.91

We observe that the O/E ratio of the [m-n] pair is higher than that of any other minimal pair in (2) (by a non-parametric sign-test, $p<.05$).[7] Recall from §3 that O/E ratios correlate with similarity, thus the data in (2) indicate that composers treat the [m-n] pair as more similar than any minimal pairs of oral consonants: they treat the place distinction in nasal consonants as less salient than in oral consonants.

Evidence from the previous phonetic and psycholinguistic studies supports the lower perceptibility of [place] in nasals than in oral consonants. A similarity judgment experiment by Mohr and Wang (1968) shows that nasal minimal pairs are considered

---

[7] Nasal pairs with different place specifications are also common in English rock lyrics (Zwicky 1976), English and German poetry (Maher 1969, 1972), English imperfect puns (Zwicky and Zwicky 1986), and Japanese rap lyrics (Kawahara 2007).

more similar to each other than oral consonant minimal pairs.[8] Place cues are less salient in nasal consonants than in oral consonants probably because formant transitions into and out of the neighboring vowels are obscured by coarticulatory nasalization (see Boersma 1998; Davis and MacNeilage 2000; Hura, Lindblom and Diehl 1992; Jun 2004; Kurowski and Blumstein 1993; Malécot 1956; Ohala and Ohala 1993; Pols 1983; Steriade 1994 for discussion on the low perceptibility of nasals' [place] and its phonological consequences).

Therefore in measuring similarity due to [place], Japanese speakers take into account the lower perceptibility of [place] in nasal consonants. The lower perceptibility of [place] in nasal has a psychoacoustic root: the blurring of formant transitions caused by coarticulatory nasalization. The data in (2) thus show that speakers use psychoacoustic similarity in composing puns.

On the other hand, if speakers were using featural similarity, then the higher combinability of the nasal pair would remain unexplained. One could postulate that the [place] contributes less to similarity when it is hosted by nasals than when it is hosted by oral consonants. However, introducing such weighting simply restates the observation and has no explanatory power.[9]

4.2. Sensitivity to different saliency of different features

The second argument that composers deploy psychoacoustic rather than featural similarity rests on the fact that they treat some features as more perceptually salient than other features (see Ahmed and Agrawal 1969; Bailey and Hahn 2005; Benkí 2003; Miller and Nicely 1955; Mohr and Wang 1968; Peters 1963; Singh, Woods and Becker 1972; Singh and Black 1966; Walden and Montgomery 1975; Wang and Bilger 1973 for psycholinguistic studies which show non-equivalence of perceptibility of different features).

Here we discuss the perceptibility of [voice]. Some scholars have proposed that among manner features that determine spectral continuity ([cont, nasal, voice]), the [voice] feature only weakly contributes to consonant distinctions. The weaker perceptibility of [voice] obtains support from previous psycholinguistic findings, such as Multi-Dimensional Scaling (Peters 1963; Walden and Montgomery 1975; see also Singh et al. 1972), a similarity judgment task (Bailey and Hahn 2005: 352), and an identification experiment under noise (Wang and Bilger 1973; see also Singh and Black 1966).[10] See

---

[8] Mohr and Wang (1968) also found that voiced obstruent pairs are more similar to each other than voiceless obstruent pairs are, but the difference is not observed in (2)—possibly because the difference is too small to be reflected in our database.

[9] It is impossible to derive the high O/E ratio of the [m-n]-pair from their phonological alternating status, as we proposed for the [labial-pharyngeal] pair. In Japanese phonology, [place] in nasals and [place] in oral consonants do not behave differently: in onset position, neither nasal nor oral consonants alternate with each other; in addition, in codas, both nasal and oral consonants alternate with each other by assimilating to the following consonant (Itô 1986).

[10] A voicing contrast is more robust than other features under white noise (Miller and Nicely 1955). However, its robustness is probably due to the fact that a voicing contrast involves durational cues

also Kenstowicz (2003) and Steriade (2001b) for phonological consequences that might follow from the low perceptibility of [voice].

Given the relatively low perceptibility of [voice], if composers are sensitive to psychoacoustic similarity, we expect that pairs of consonants that are minimally different in [voice] should combine more frequently than minimal pairs that disagree in other manner features. To compare the effect of [cont], [nasal], and [voice], we compare the O/E ratios for the minimal pairs defined by these features, as in (3).

(3)   [cont]   [nasal]   [voice]

[cont]		[nasal]		[voice]	
[p-ɸ]:	5.80	[b-m]:	4.49	[p-t]:	8.84
[t-s]:	.94	[d-n]:	1.16	[t-d]:	8.06
[d-z]:	1.75			[k-g]:	8.22
				[s-z]:	11.7
				[ʃ-ʒ]:	6.29

The O/E ratios of the minimal pairs that differ in [voice] are significantly larger than the O/E ratios of the minimal pairs that differ in [cont] or [nasal] (by a non-parametric Mann-Whitney test; *Wilcoxon W*=15, *z*=2.61, *p*<.01).[11]

In summary, Japanese pun-makers treat minimal pairs that differ only in [voice] as very similar, which indicates that composers unconsciously know that a voicing disagreement contributes less to perceptual dissimilarity than other manner features. In other words, Japanese speakers have an awareness of the varying perceptual salience of different features. A theory that relies on featural similarity cannot explain why [voice] contributes less to similarity than other manner features. One could augment the theory by postulating that [voice] contributes less to similarity, but this analysis simply restates the observation and misses an insight that [voice]'s lesser contribution to similarity has its root in its lower perceptibility.

4.3. Sensitivity to similarity contributed by voicing in sonorants

Third, speakers are sensitive to similarity contributed by a phonologically inert feature—voicing in sonorants—and this fact indicates that speakers deploy psychoacoustic similarity instead of featural similarity. Table 2 shows how often Japanese speakers combine sonorants with voiced obstruents and voiceless obstruents in imperfect puns in our database.

(such as VOT, preceding vowel duration, closure duration, and closure voicing duration: Lisker 1986), and white noise does not cover such durational cues. In fact, under signal-dependent noise, the difference in perceptibility between voicing and other manner features is highly attenuated, if not completely obliterated (Benki 2003).

[11] It has been observed previously that voicing disagreement is common in Japanese imperfect puns (Otake and Cutler 2001; Shinohara 2004), and our study provides statistical support for this observation. Voicing disagreement is also more common than nasality disagreement in English imperfect puns (Lagerquist 1980; Zwicky and Zwicky 1986), as well as in many half rhyme patterns (English: Zwicky 1976; Japanese: Kawahara 2007; Romanian: Steriade 2003; and Slavic: Eekman 1974).

	Voiced obstruent	Voiceless obstruent
[+son]	57 (16.9%)	29 (5.5%)
[-son]	281 (83.1%)	502 (94.5%)
Sum	338	531

Table 2: The probabilities of sonorants corresponding with voiced obstruents and voiceless obstruents.

The probability of voiced obstruents corresponding with sonorants (.17; s.e.=.02) is higher than the probability of voiceless obstruents corresponding with sonorants (.06; s.e.=.01). The difference between these ratios is statistically significant (by approximation to a Gaussian distribution, z=5.04, p<.001). The pattern in Table 2 suggests that composers treat sonorants as being more similar to voiced obstruents than to voiceless obstruents (see Coetzee and Pater 2005; Côté 2004; Frisch et al. 2004; Rose and Walker 2004; Stemberger 1991; Walker 2003 for evidence from other languages that obstruent voicing promotes similarity with sonorants; see Kawahara 2007 for the same pattern in Japanese rhymes).

The thesis that speakers use psychoacoustic similarity when forming puns correctly predicts the effect of sonorant voicing on their similarity with voiced obstruents. First, low frequency energy is present during the consonantal constriction in both sonorants and voiced obstruents but not in voiceless obstruents. Second, Japanese voiced stops are lenited intervocalically, resulting in clear formant continuity (Kawahara 2006), like sonorants. Voiceless stops do not spirantize, resulting in complete formant discontinuity, and thus differ from sonorants. For these reasons, voiced obstruents are acoustically more similar to sonorants than voiceless obstruents are.

On the other hand, if speakers were deploying featural, rather than psychoacoustic similarity, the pattern in Table 2 is not predicted, given the behavior of [+voice] in Japanese sonorants. Phonologically, voicing in Japanese sonorants behaves differently from voicing in obstruents: a well-known phonological restriction in Japanese requires that there be no more than one "voiced segment" within a stem, but only voiced obstruents, not voiced sonorants, count as "voiced segments". Consequently, the previous literature has proposed that either [+voice] in sonorants is underspecified (Itô and Mester 1986; Itô, Mester and Padgett 1995), sonorants do not bear the [voice] feature at all (Mester and Itô 1989), or sonorants and obstruents bear different [voice] features (Rice 1993).[12] Regardless of how we featurally differentiate voicing in sonorants and voicing in obstruents, sonorants and voiced obstruents do not share the same phonological feature

---

[12] One may argue that [+voice] in Japanese nasals is phonologically active. In the native phonology, obstruents are voiced after a nasal, as in /sin+ta/ → [sinda] 'died', which can be regarded as progressive assimilation of [+voice] (Itô et al. 1995). However, we can reanalyze post-nasal voicing as arising from the constraint *NÇ, which prohibits voiceless obstruents after a nasal. This analysis has a broader empirical coverage (Hayes and Stivers 1995; Pater 1999), and obviates the need to assume that [+voice] in nasals is active in Japanese (Hayashi and Iverson 1998; see also Rice 1993).

for voicing. Therefore, if speakers were deploying phonological featural similarity, the pattern in Table 2 is not predicted.

4.4. Sensitivity to consonants' similarity to Ø

Finally, consonants that correspond with Ø are those that are psychoacoustically similar to Ø. In some imperfect puns, consonants in one phrase do not have a corresponding consonant in the other phrase, as in _akagaeru ga wakagaeru_ 'a red frog will become young'. In (4) we list the set of consonants whose O/E ratios with Ø are larger than 1.[13]

(4)   [w]: 5.41 > [h]: 3.86 > [r]: 3.67 > [m]: 2.64 > [n]: 1.55 > [ɰ]: 1.44

The consonants listed in (4) are those that are likely to be psychoacoustically similar to Ø, which supports the claim that speakers use psychoacoustic information when they create imperfect puns.

First, the high frequency of [w] corresponding with Ø makes psychoacoustic sense. Since [w] is a glide, the transition between [w] and the following vowel is blurry, which can make the presence of [w] hard to detect.[14] Myers and Hanssen (2005) demonstrate that given a sequence of two vocoids, listeners misattribute the transitional portion to the second vocoid, effectively lengthening the percept of the second vocoid and shortening the percept of the first vocoid.[15] Thus, due to [w]'s blurry boundaries and consequent misparsing, the presence of [w] is perceptually hard to detect.

Next, the propensity of [h] to correspond with Ø accords with the observation that [h] lacks a superlaryngeal constriction and hence its spectra assimilate to neighboring vowels (Keating 1988), making the presence of [h] difficult to detect: [h] is "a sound with weak perceptual cues" (Mielke 2003: 209). Third, Japanese [r] is a flap, which involves a brief and ballistic constriction in Japanese (Nakamura 2002). The short constriction makes [r] sound similar to Ø.

Fourth, for [m] and [n], we speculate that the edges of these consonants with flanking vowels are blurry due to coarticulatory nasalization, causing them to be interpreted as belonging to the neighboring vowels. Downing (2005) argues that the transitions between vowels and nasals can be misparsed due to their blurry transitions, and that the misparsing effectively lengthens the percept of the vowel. As a result of misparsing, the perceived duration of nasals may become shortened.

---

[13] Shinohara (2004) also found that [h] and [r] are most likely to correspond with Ø in Japanese imperfect puns, although the observation is based on O-values rather than O/E ratios. See also Lagerquist (1980) for a similar pattern in English (cf. Zwicky and Zwicky 1986).

[14] Since the other palatal glide [y] was very rare (O=17), it did not enter the O/E analysis.

[15] The perceived shortening of the first vocoid may be exaggerated by durational contrast by which the percept of one interval gets shortened next to long intervals (Diehl and Walsh 1989; Kluender, Diehl and Wright 1988). However, durational contrast has not been replicated by some later studies (Fowler 1992; van Dommelen 1999).

Finally, [k] is a most "vowel-like" consonant (de Lacy and Kingston 2006) in that it extensively coarticulates with adjacent vowels in terms of tongue backness (Keating 1996; Keating and Lahiri 1993; Liberman, Delattre and Cooper 1952; Sussman, McCaffrey and Matthews 1991). As a result of its extensive coarticulation, [k] fades into its environment and becomes perceptually similar to Ø. Given this explanation, one may wonder why [g] does not behave like [k]. We conjecture that since Japanese [g] is spirantized intervocalically (Kawahara 2006), it stands out from its environment with its frication noise.

To summarize, speakers pair Ø with segments that are psychoacoustically similar to Ø—especially those that fade into their environments—but not with consonants whose presence is highly perceptible. Fricatives, for example, do not correspond with Ø because of their salient long duration and great intensity of the noise spectra (Steriade 2001a; Wright 1996). Also, coronal stops coarticulate least with surrounding vowels (de Lacy and Kingston 2006; Liberman et al. 1952; Sussman et al. 1991) and hence they perceptually stand out from their environments. As a result, they are unlikely to correspond with Ø.

On the other hand, phonological similarity does not offer a straightforward explanation for the set of consonants in (4). The list of consonants in (4) includes sonorant consonants, with the exception of [h] and [k],[16] but there is no sense in which sonorous consonants are similar to Ø phonologically (Kirchner 1998: 33). We should in fact not consider Ø as being sonorous; although languages prefer to have sonorous segments in syllable nuclei (Dell and Elmedlaoui 1985; Prince and Smolensky 2004), no languages prefer to have Ø nuclei.

Rather the list of consonants in (4) includes sonorants because their phonetic properties make them akin to Ø: their edges with flanking vowels are blurry, fading into their environments. This view is supported by the fact that [k] and [h], which like sonorants blend into their environment, are treated as similar to Ø.

Aside from sonority, one could try to characterize Ø in terms of distinctive features, making use of the theory of underspecification. This theory postulates that unmarked feature specifications are underlyingly unspecified (Archangeli 1988; Itô and Mester 1986; Itô et al. 1995; Kiparsky 1982; Mester and Itô 1989; Paradis and Prunet 1991; Steriade 1995). Based on this view, we could postulate that the segment which has the most sparse underlying specifications is closest to Ø. This analysis however does not predict that the list of consonants in (4) are close to Ø. For example, nasal consonants are marked while oral consonants are not, and sonorants are marked while obstruents are not (Chomsky and Halle 1968); therefore, [-nasal] and [-son] should be underspecified. As a result, oral obstruents are predicted to be closest to Ø because they lack underlying specifications for [±nasal] and [±son]. However, the list in (4) includes nasal and

---

[16] Some proposals treat [h] as a voiceless sonorant (Chomsky and Halle 1968), but the [-son] status of [h] is supported by a psycholinguistic experiment (Jaeger and Ohala 1984) as well as by an acoustic experiment (Parker 2002).

sonorant consonants. Moreover, no versions of underspecification postulate that [k] is more sparsely specified than [t]: in fact, some argue for the opposite (see papers in Paradis and Prunet 1991). For these reasons, the theory of underspecification does not account for why the consonants in (4) are treated as close to Ø in Japanese imperfect puns.

4.5. Discussion

Japanese speakers use psychoacoustic similarity when they make imperfect puns. Given that reference to acoustic details is necessary to characterize similarity in imperfect puns, we might dispense entirely with featural similarity in favor of psychoacoustic similarity. A remaining question in making this move, however, is that phonological relation between labials and pharyngeals seems to promote similarity between these two classes of sounds, as shown in §3.2.

Nevertheless, replacing featural similarity with psychoacoustic similarity is worth pursuing. It is possible that the phonological connection between labials and pharyngeals promotes psychoacoustic similarity between these two classes of sounds (Hume and Johnson 2003).[17] Completing this step of analysis however is not within the scope of the present paper: it would require a complete psychoacoustic similarity matrix of Japanese sounds, which must be obtained through psycholinguistic experiments (e.g. identification experiments under noise, similarity judgment tasks). Constructing a psychoacoustic similarity matrix and using it for another analysis of the imperfect pun patterns are interesting topics for future research, but impossible goals for this paper.

5. Conclusion

The combinability of two consonants in imperfect puns in Japanese positively correlates with their similarity. The analysis of imperfect puns has shown that speakers possess rich knowledge of psychoacoustic similarity and deploy it in composing imperfect puns, supporting the tenets of the P-map hypothesis (Fleischhacker 2005; Kawahara 2006, 2007; Steriade 2001a, b, 2003; Zuraw 2005). Featural similarity on the other hand fails to capture the bases of similarity decisions that speakers evidently make.

Finally, in this study Japanese speakers' knowledge of similarity was revealed by "external evidence" (Churma 1979), namely verbal art. We thus conclude that it is fruitful to investigate speakers' grammatical knowledge by examining para-linguistic patterns, which should go in tandem with analyses of more purely phonological data patterns (see references cited above as well as Fabb 1997 for a comprehensive overview).

---

[17] It also remains to be seen whether the split of coronal obstruents and coronal sonorants into two identity classes has a psychoacoustic basis.

Appendix I: Feature matrix used for the analysis in §3.1

	son	cons	cont	nasal	voice	strid	place	pal
p	-	+	-	-	-	-	lab	-
b	-	+	-	-	+	-	lab	-
ɸ	-	+	+	-	-	-	lab	-
m	+	+	-	+	+	-	lab	-
w	+	-	+	-	+	-	lab	-
t	-	+	-	-	-	-	cor	-
d	-	+	-	-	+	-	cor	-
s	-	+	+	-	-	+	cor	-
z	-	+	+	-	+	+	cor	-
ʃ	-	+	+	-	-	+	cor	+
ʒ	-	+	+	-	+	+	cor	+
tʃ	-	+	±	-	-	+	cor	+
n	+	+	-	+	+	-	cor	-
r	+	+	+	-	+	-	cor	-
k	-	+	-	-	-	-	dors	-
g	-	+	-	-	+	-	dors	-
h	-	+	+	-	-	-	phary	-

Appendix II: The O/E chart

	Ø	p	b	ɸ	m	w	t	tʃ	s	ʃ	d	z	ʒ	n	r	k	g	h
Ø	0	.73	.25	.8	2.6	5.4	.67	.47	.37	.39	0	0	0	1.6	3.7	1.4	.48	3.9
p		0	8.8	5.8	0	0	.92	0	1.2	0	0	0	0	0	.38	.93	.25	.80
b			0	1.7	4.5	5.4	.32	0	0	0	1.1	0.4	0	0	0	.26	.68	2.7
ɸ				0	1.2	0	0	0	.84	.87	0	0	0	0	0	2.9	0	4.4
m					0	0	.66	0	.56	0	0	0	0	8.4	2.2	.27	.35	1.7
w						0	0	0	0	0	1.2	0	0	1.6	0	.55	0	3.5
t							0	.59	.94	0	8.1	0	0	.32	.46	.91	.15	.97
tʃ								0	.99	7.7	0	0	14	0	.49	.24	0	0
s									0	4.9	.21	12	0	1.6	.39	.76	0	.81
ʃ										0	0	0	6.3	.56	0	.39	0	.42
d											0	1.8	.41	1.2	3.5	0	.40	.65
z												0	1.3	0	.64	0	0	0
ʒ													0	2.1	.75	0	.97	0
n														0	4.3	.26	1.4	0
r															0	.37	1.2	.4
k																0	8.2	1.8
g																	0	0
h																		0

References

Ahmed, Rais, and Agrawal, S.S. (1969) Significant features in the perception of (Hindi) consonants. *Journal of Acoustical Society of America* 45: 758-773.

Archangeli, Diana (1988) Aspects of underspecification theory. *Phonology* 5: 183-208.

Bailey, Todd, and Hahn, Ulrike (2005) Phoneme similarity and confusability. *Journal of Memory and Language* 52: 339-362.

Benkí, José (2003) Analysis of English nonsense syllable recognition in noise. *Phonetica* 60: 129-157.

Benua, Laura (1997) *Transderivational Identity: Phonological Relations between Words.* Doctoral dissertation, University of Massachusetts, Amherst.

Berkley, Deborah (1994) The OCP and gradient data. *Studies in the Linguistic Sciences* 24: 59-72.

Boersma, Paul (1998) *Functional Phonology: Formalizing the Interaction Between Articulatory and Perceptual Drives.* The Hague: Holland Academic Graphics.

Buckley, Eugene (1997) Tigrinya root consonants and the OCP *UPenn Working Papers in Linguistics* 4: 19-51.

Chomsky, Noam, and Halle, Moris (1968) *The Sound Pattern of English*. New York: Harper & Row.

Churma, Don (1979) *Arguments from External Evidence in Phonology*. Doctoral dissertation, Ohio State University.

Coetzee, Andries, and Pater, Joe (2005) Lexically gradient phonotactics in Muna and Optimality Theory. Ms. University of Massachusetts, Amherst.

Côté, Marie-Hélène (2004) Syntagmatic distinctness in consonant deletion. *Phonology* 21: 1-41.

Cutler, Anne, and Otake, Takashi (2002) Rhythmic categories in spoken-word recognition. *Journal of Memory and Language* 46: 296-322.

Davis, Barbara, and MacNeilage, Peter (2000) An embodiment perspective on the acquisition of speech perception. *Phonetica* 57: 229-241.

de Lacy, Paul, and Kingston, John (2006) Synchronic explanation. Ms. Rutgers University and University of Massachusetts, Amherst.

Dell, François, and Elmedlaoui, Mohamed (1985) Syllabic consonants and syllabification in Imdlawn Tashlhiyt Berber. *Journal of African Languages and Linguistics* 7: 105-130.

Diehl, Randy, and Walsh, Margaret (1989) An auditory basis for the stimulus-length effect in the perception of stops and glides. *Journal of Acoustical Society of America* 85: 2154-2164.

Downing, Laura (2005) On the ambiguous segmental status of nasal in homorganic NC sequences. In *The Internal Organization of Phonological Segments*, eds. M. van Oostendorp and J. M. van der Weijer, 183-216. Berlin: Mouton de Gruyter.

Eekman, Thomas (1974) *The Realm of Rime: A Study of Rime in the Poety of the Slavs*. Amsterdam: Adolf M. Hakkert.

Fabb, Nigel (1997) *Linguistics and Literature: Language in the Verb Arts in the World*. Oxford: Basil Blackwell.

Fleischhacker, Heidi (2005) *Similarity in Phonology: Evidence from Reduplication and Loan Adaptation*. Doctoral dissertation, University of California, Los Angeles.

Fowler, Carol (1992) Vowel duration and closure duration in voiced and unvoiced stops: There are no contrast effects here. *Journal of Phonetics* 20: 143-165.

Frisch, Stephan, Pierrehumbert, Janet, and Broe, Michael (2004) Similarity avoidance and the OCP. *Natural Language and Linguistic Theory* 22: 179-228.

Greenberg, Joseph (1950) The patterning of root morphemes in Semitic. *Word* 6: 162-181.

Hayashi, Emiko, and Iverson, Gregory (1998) The non-assimilatory nature of postnasal voicing in Japanese. *Journal of Humanities and Social Sciences* 38: 27-44.

Hayes, Bruce, and Stivers, Tanya (1995) Postnasal voicing. Ms. University of California, Los Angeles.

Hempelmann, Christian (2005) *Paronomasic Puns: Target Recoverability towards Automatic Generation*. Doctoral dissertation, Purdue University.

Hume, Elizabeth, and Johnson, Keith (2003) The impact of partial phonological contrast on speech perception. *Proceedings of ICPhS 2003*: 2385-2388.

Hura, Susan, Lindblom, Björn , and Diehl, Randy (1992) On the role of perception in shaping phonological assimilation rules. *Language and Speech* 35: 59-72.

Itô, Junko (1986) *Syllable Theory in Prosodic Phonology.* Doctoral dissertation, University of Massachusetts, Amherst.

Itô, Junko, and Mester, Armin (1986) The phonology of voicing in Japanese: Theoretical consequences for morphological accessibility. *Linguistic Inquiry* 17: 49-73.

Itô, Junko, Mester, Armin, and Padgett, Jaye (1995) Licensing and underspecification in Optimality Theory. *Linguistic Inquiry* 26: 571-614.

Jaeger, Jeri, and Ohala, John (1984) On the structure of phonetic categories. In *Proceedings of the Tenth Annual Meeting of the Berkely Linguistics Society*, eds. J. Brugmann et al., 15-26. Berkeley: Berkeley Linguistic Society.

Jakobson, Roman (1960) *Language in Literature.* Cambridge: Harvard University Press.

Jun, Jongho (2004) Place assimilation. In *Phonetically-based Phonology*, eds. B. Hayes, R. Kirchner and D. Steriade, 58-86. Cambridge: Cambridge University Press.

Kang, Yoonjung (2003) Perceptual similarity in loanword adaptation: English postvocalic word-final stops in Korean. *Phonology* 20: 219-273.

Katayama, Motoko (1998) *Optimality Theory and Japanese Loanword Phonology.* Doctoral dissertation, University of California, Santa Cruz

Kawahara, Shigeto (2003) On a certain kind of hiatus resolution in Japanese. *Phonological Studies* 6: 11-20.

Kawahara, Shigeto (2006) A faithfulness ranking projected from a perceptibility scale: The case of voicing in Japanese. *Language* 82: 536-574.

Kawahara, Shigeto (2007) Half-rhymes in Japanese rap lyrics and knowledge of similarity. *Journal of East Asian Linguistics* 16: 113-144.

Kawahara, Shigeto, Ono, Hajime, and Sudo, Kiyoshi (2006) Consonant co-occurrence restrictions in Yamato Japanese. In *Japanese/Korean Linguistics 14*, eds. T. Vance and K. Jones, 27-38. Stanford: CSLI.

Keating, Patricia (1988) Underspecification in phonetics. *Phonology* 5: 275-292.

Keating, Patricia (1996) The phonology-phonetics interface. *UCLA Working Papers in Phonetics* 92: 45-60.

Keating, Patricia, and Lahiri, Aditi (1993) Fronted velars, palatalized velars, and palatals. *Phonetica* 50: 73-101.

Kenstowicz, Michael (2003) Salience and similarity in loanword adaptation: A case study from Fujian. Ms. MIT.

Kenstowicz, Michael, and Suchato, Atiwong (2006) Issues in loanword adaptation: A case study from Thai. *Lingua* 116: 921-949.

Kiparsky, Paul (1970) Metrics and morphophonemics in the Kalevala. In *Linguistics and Literary Style*, ed. D. Freeman, 165-181. Holt: Rinehart and Winston INC.

Kiparsky, Paul (1972) Metrics and morphophonemics in the Rigveda. In *Contributions to Generative Phonology*, ed. M. Brame, 171-200. Austin: University of Texas Press.

Kiparsky, Paul (1981) The role of linguistics in a theory of poetry. In *Essays in Modern Stylistics*, ed. D. Freedman, 9-23. London: Methuen.

Kiparsky, Paul (1982) Lexical phonology and morphology. In *Linguistics in the Morning Calm*, ed. I. S. Yang, 3-91. Seoul: Hanshin.

Kirchner, Robert (1998) *An Effort-Based Approach to Consonant Lenition.* Doctoral dissertation, University of California, Los Angeles.

Klatt, Dennis (1968) Structure of confusions in short-term memory between English consonants. *Journal of the Acoustical Society of America* 59: 1208-1221.

Kluender, Keith, Diehl, Randy, and Wright, Beverly (1988) Vowel-length differences before voiced and voiceless consonants: An auditory explanation. *Journal of Phonetics* 16: 153-169.

Kurowski, Kathleen, and Blumstein, Sheila (1993) Acoustic properties for the perception of nasal consonants. In *Nasals, Nasalization and the Velum*, eds. M. Huffman and R. Krakow, 197-224. New York: Academic Press.

Lagerquist, Linnes (1980) Linguistic evidence from paronomasia. In *Proceedings of Chicago Linguistic Society*, eds. J. Kreiman and A. E. Ojeda, 185-191. Chicago: CLS.

Liberman, Alvin, Delattre, Pierre, and Cooper, F.S. (1952) The role of selected stimulus variables in the perception of unvoiced stop consonants. *American Journal of Psychology* 65: 497-516.

Liljencrants, Johan, and Lindblom, Björn (1972) Numerical simulation of vowel quality systems: The role of perceptual contrast. *Language* 48: 839-862.

Lindblom, Björn (1986) Phonetic universals in vowel systems. In *Experimental Phonology*, eds. J. Ohala and J. Jaeger, 13-44. Orlando: Academic Press.

Lisker, Leigh (1986) "Voicing" in English: A catalog of acoustic features signaling /b/ versus /p/ in trochees. *Language and Speech* 29: 3-11.

Lombardi, Linda (1990) The nonlinear organization of the affricate. *Natural Language and Linguistic Theory* 8: 375-425.

Maher, Peter (1969) English-speakers' awareness of distinctive features. *Language Sciences* 5: 14.

Maher, Peter (1972) Distinctive feature rhyme in German folk versification. *Language Sciences* 16: 19-20.

Malécot, André (1956) Acoustic cues for nasal consonants: An experimental study involving a tape-splicing technique. *Language* 32: 274-284.

Malone, Joseph (1987) Muted euphony and consonant matching in Irish. *Germanic Linguistics* 27: 133-144.

Malone, Joseph (1988a) On the global-phonologic nature of classical Irish alliteration. *Germanic Linguistics* 28: 93-103.

Malone, Joseph (1988b) Underspecification theory and Turkish rhyme. *Phonology* 5: 293-297.

McCarthy, John (1986) OCP Effects: Gemination and antigemination. *Linguistic Inquiry* 17: 207-263.

McCarthy, John (1988) Feature geometry and dependency: A review. *Phonetica* 43: 84-108.

McCawley, James (1968) *The Phonological Component of a Grammar of Japanese*. The Hague: Mouton.

McGarrity, Laura (1999) A sympathy account of multiple opacity in Wintu. In *Indiana University Working Papers in Linguistics*, eds. K. Baertsch and D. Dinnsen, 93-107. Bloomington: IULC Publications.

Mester, Armin (1986) *Studies in Tier Structure*. Doctoral dissertation, University of Massachusetts, Amherst.

Mester, Armin, and Itô, Junko (1989) Feature predictability and underspecification: Palatal prosody in Japanese mimetics. *Language* 65: 258-293.

Mielke, Jeff (2003) The interplay of speech perception and phonology: Experimental evidence from Turkish. *Phonetica* 60: 208-229.

Miller, George, and Nicely, Patricia (1955) An analysis of perceptual confusions among some English consonants. *Journal of Acoustical Society of America* 27: 338-352.

Minkova, Donca (2003) *Alliteration and Sound Change in Early English.* Cambridge: Cambridge University Press.

Mohr, B., and Wang, W.S. (1968) Perceptual distance and the specification of phonological features. *Phonetica* 18: 31-45.

Mukai, Yoshihito (1996) *Kotoba Asobi no Jyugyoo Zukuri*: Meiji Tosho.

Myers, Scott, and Hanssen, Benjamin (2005) The origin of vowel-length neutralization in vocoid sequences. *Phonology* 22: 317-344.

Nakamura, Mitsuhiro (2002) The articulation of the Japanese /r/ and some implications for phonological acquisition. *Phonological Studies* 5: 55-62.

Nishimura, Kohei (2003) Lyman's law in loanwords. Ms. University of Tokyo.

Ohala, John, and Ohala, Manjari (1993) The phonetics of nasal phonology: Theorems and data. In *Nasals, Nasalization, and the Velum*, eds. M. Huffman and R. Krakow, 225-249. New York: Academic Press.

Otake, Takashi, and Cutler, Anne (2001) Recognition of (almost) spoken words: Evidence from word play in Japanese. *Proceedings of European Conference on Speech Communication and Technology.* 7: 464-468.

Padgett, Jaye (1992) OCP subsidiary features. *Proceedings of North East Linguistic Society* 22: 335-346.

Paradis, Carol, and Prunet, Jean-François eds. (1991) *The Special Status of Coronals: Internal and External Evidence.* San Diego: Academic Press.

Parker, Steve (2002) *Quantifying the Sonority Hierarchy.* Doctoral dissertation, University of Massachusetts, Amherst.

Pater, Joe (1999) Austronesian nasal substitution and other NC effects. In *The Prosody-Morphology Interface*, eds. R. Kager, H. van der Hulst and W. Zonneveld, 310-343. Cambridge: Cambridge University Press.

Peters, Robert (1963) Dimensions of perception for consonants. *Journal of the Acoustical Society of America* 35: 1985-1989.

Pols, Louis (1983) Three mode principle component analysis of confusion matrices, based on the identification of Dutch consonants, under various conditions of noise and reverberation. *Speech Communication* 2: 275-293.

Price, Patti (1981) *A Cross-linguistic Study of Flaps in Japanese and in American English.* Doctoral dissertation, University of Pennsylvania.

Prince, Alan, and Smolensky, Paul (2004) *Optimality Theory: Constraint Interaction in Generative Grammar.* Malden and Oxford: Blackwell.

Rice, Keren (1993) A reexamination of the feature [sonorant]: The status of sonorant obstruents. *Language* 69: 308-344.

Rose, Sharon, and Walker, Rachel (2004) A typology of consonant agreement as correspondence. *Language* 80: 475-532.

Sagey, Elizabeth (1986) *The Representation of Features and Relations in Nonlinear Phonology.* Doctoral dissertation, MIT.

Shattuck-Hufnagel, Stefanie, and Klatt, Dennis (1977) The limited use of distinctive
      features and markedness in speech production: Evidence from speech error data.
      Journal of Verbal Learning and Behavior 18: 41-55.
Shinohara, Shigeko (2004) A note on the Japanese pun, dajare: Two sources of
      phonological similarity. Ms. Laboratoire de Psycheologie Experimentale.
Singh, Rajendra, Woods, David, and Becker, Gordon (1972) Perceptual structure of 22
      prevocalic English consonants. *Journal of Acoustical Society of America* 52:
      1698-1713.
Singh, Sadanand, and Black, John (1966) Study of twenty-six intervocalic consonants as
      spoken and recognized by four language groups. *Journal of Acoustical Society of
      America* 39: 372-387.
Sobkowiak, Wlodzimierz (1991) *Metaphonology of English Paronomasic Puns*. Lang:
      Frankfurt.
Stemberger, Joseph (1991) Radical underspecification in language production. *Phonology*
      8: 73-112.
Steriade, Donca (1994) Positional neutralization and the expression of contrast. Ms.
      University of California, Los Angeles [A revised written-up version of the 1993
      NELS handout].
Steriade, Donca (1995) Underspecification and markedness. In *Handbook of
      Phonological Theory*, ed. J. Goldsmith, 114-174. Cambridge, MA: Blackwell.
Steriade, Donca (2000) Paradigm uniformity and the phonetics-phonology boundary. In
      Papers in Laboratory Phonology V: Acquisition and the Lexicon, eds. M. B. Broe
      and J. B. Pierrehumbert, 313-334. Cambridge: Cambridge University Press.
Steriade, Donca (2001a) Directional asymmetries in place assimilation: A perceptual
      account. In *The Role of Speech Perception in Phonology*, eds. E. Hume and K.
      Johnson, 219-250. New York: Academic Press.
Steriade, Donca (2001b) The phonology of perceptibility effect: The P-map and its
      consequences for constraint organization. Ms. University of California, Los
      Angeles.
Steriade, Donca (2003) Knowledge of similarity and narrow lexical override. In
      Proceedings of Berkeley Linguistics Society 29, eds. P. M. Nowak, C. Yoquelet
      and D. Mortensen, 583-598. Berkeley: BLS.
Sussman, Harvey, McCaffrey, Helen, and Matthews, Sandra (1991) An investigation of
      locus equations as a source of relational invariance for stop place categorization.
      Journal of Acoustical Society of America 90: 1309-1325.
Takizawa, Osamu (1996) *Nihongo Syuuzihyougen no Kougakuteki Kenkyuu
      [Technological Study of Japanese Rhetorical Expressions]*. Koganei: Tsuushin
      Sogo Kenkyuusho.
Trubetzkoy, Nikolai (1969) *Principles of Phonology*. Berkeley: University of California
      Press.
Ueda, Kazutoshi (1898) P-Onkoo [On the sound P] *Teikoku Bungaku [National
      Literature]* 4.
van Dommelen, Wim (1999) Auditory accounts of temporal factors in the perception of
      Norwegian disyllables and speech analogs. *Journal of Phonetics* 27: 107-123.

Walden, Brian, and Montgomery, Allen (1975) Dimensions of consonant perception in normal and hearing-impaired listeners. *Journal of Speech and Hearing Research* 18: 445-455.

Walker, Rachel (2003) Nasal and oral consonant similarity in speech errors: Exploring parallels with long-distance nasal agreement. Ms. University of Southern California.

Wang, Marlyn, and Bilger, Robert (1973) Consonant confusions in noise: A study of perceptual identity. *Journal of Acoustical Society of America* 54: 1248-1266.

Wright, Richard (1996) *Consonant Clusters and Cue Preservation in Tsou.* Doctoral dissertation, University of California, Los Angeles.

Yip, Moira (1989) Feature geometry and cooccurrence restrictions. *Phonology* 6: 349-374.

Zuraw, Kie (2005) The role of phonetic knowledge in phonological patterning: Corpus and survey evidence from Tagalog reduplication. Ms. University of California, Los Angeles.

Zwicky, Arnold (1976) This rock-and-roll has got to stop: Juniors head is hard as a rock. In *Proceedings of Chicago Linguistic Society 12*, eds. S.Mufwene, C.Walker and S.Steever, 676-697. Chicago: CLS.

Zwicky, Arnold, and Zwicky, Elizabeth (1986) Imperfect puns, markedness, and phonological similarity: With fronds like these, who needs anemones? *Folia Linguistica* 20: 493-503.

Shigeto Kawahara
Department of English
University of Georgia
Park Hall 254
Athens, GA 30602-6205

kawahara@uga.edu

Kazuko Shinohara
Division of Mathematics and Human Sciences
Institute of Symbiotic Science and Technology
Tokyo University of Agriculture and Technology
2-24-16 Nakacho, Koganei-shi
Tokyo 184-8588

k-shino@cc.tuat.ac.jp

Erculator: A Web Application for Constraint-Based Phonology

Jason Riggle, Max Bane, Edward King, James Kirby, Heather Rivers, Evelyn Rosas, and John Sylak

University of Chicago
Chicago Language Modeling Lab

1 Introduction

Constraint-based phonology is complicated. Simple constraints can interact in fiendishly opaque ways and the accidental omission of even a single relevant candidate can invalidate an entire analysis. To make matters worse, vague constraint definitions make it difficult to compare putatively different analyses of the same phenomenon and often require readers to reverse engineer an author's intended definition from the violations assigned to candidates in tableaux. The fact that an occasional erroneous or omitted violation mark is quite common (even in peer-reviewed publications) can make this task all but impossible. Most of these difficulties are further compounded in models that allow additional complexities, such as probability distributions over rankings or weighted constraints. While analyzing models by hand can certainly be instructive, these problems (and a host of others) make manual analysis infeasible for large numbers of candidates and constraints. We aim to rectify these problems by providing software designed to automate the tedious, repetitive, and computationally intensive aspects of constraint-based analyses.

Erculator (www.erculator.com) is open source software developed by the Chicago Language Modeling Lab (CLML) at the University of Chicago that is designed to help phonologists analyze large amounts of data quickly and accurately, as well as to provide a tool for students learning to work with phonological models. Erculator provides information on winning candidates, constraint rankings, harmonically bounded candidates, and possible language typologies. The intuitive, easy-to-use interface allows linguists of all experience levels to quickly create and work with constraint-based models and tableaux. The software can generate publication-quality tableaux and ranking diagrams in a variety of formats. The web-based implementation is platform-independent, does not require the user to download or install any special programs, and offers a forum for researchers to share data, constraints,

Michael Becker (ed.): Papers in theoretical and computational phonology. University of Massachusetts Occasional Papers in Linguistics 36, 135-150.
GLSA Amherst.

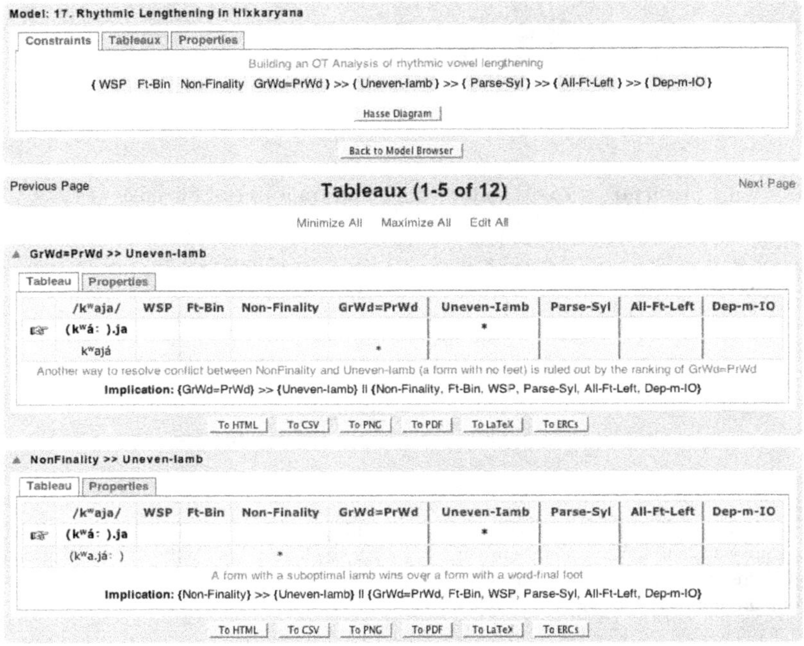

Figure 1: A screenshot of the Erculator GUI.

and analyses. Finally, the software attempts to provide a unified framework for creating and evaluating analyses in a variety of constraint-based models, such as Optimality Theory (Prince & Smolensky, 1993), Stochastic Optimality Theory (Boersma & Hayes, 2001), Harmonic Grammar (Legendre, Miyata, & Smolensky, 1990), and others.

The main components of Erculator are `erculator-cli`, a textual command line interface; `erculator-web`, a web-based graphical user interface (GUI); `erculator-lib`, a library of open source code available for modification by end users; and the cPhon XML file specification, which acts as a platform- and software-independent repository for phonological model data. This technical report provides a brief overview of the core Erculator compoments, a short tutorial, and a description of features in active development.

2 Erculator 1.0

2.1 Overview of features

`Erculator-cli` and `erculator-web` provide the following functionality:

- Creating tableaux that describe the constraint violations incurred by the candidate outputs for some input.

- Generating the Elementary Ranking Conditions (ERCs) implied by a tableau.

- Detecting logical inconsistencies between tableaux (e.g., incompatible winners).

- Identifying harmonically bounded candidates.

- Grouping tableaux over the same constraints into full models of phenomena.

- Specifying possible rankings of a model's constraints, either through a collection of partial ordering statements (e.g., DepC >> MaxV), or as a set of ERCs.

- Determining the possible winning candidates under (possibly partial) constraint rankings.

- Inferring (partial) rankings from hand-chosen winners.

- Generating the resulting typology of languages under all possible constraint rankings.

- Exporting tableaux for use in other programs, such as Word, Excel, and LaTeX.

- Exporting files for analysis with other programs, such as OTSoft (Hayes, Tesar, & Zuraw, 2003) and Praat (Boersma & Weenink, 2007).

With `erculator-lib`, a Python software library containing Erculator's source code, these capabilities may be incorporated into third-party applications.

2.2 Erculator-lib

`Erculator-lib` is a library of source code for the Erculator software. It is written in Python and allows a user to customize the Erculator program however he or she likes by modifying the source code. It also provides a window into the architecture and algorithms that are the 'machinery' of Erculator.

`Erculator-lib` allows linguists interested in modifying the Erculator software to develop algorithms and customizations not only for their own needs, but for the use of the entire Erculator community. This is one of the main benefits of open source software as a whole, and will allow CLML to incorporate future modifications into the main Erculator package. Thus, by offering a library of Erculator's source code, the program remains a dynamic entity which is being constantly improved and extended.

2.3 Erculator-cli

Erculator-cli is a command line interface to Erculator's backend code (offered in erculator-lib). Erculator-cli offers full functionality and clear directions throughout the process of creating an Optimality Theory model. A user navigates erculator-cli through a series of menus in which single letter commands may be entered into a prompt. These commands either execute processes or introduce the user to a new menu. A universal help command is available at all times.

A user can start using erculator-cli simply by typing n for a new model, then naming the new model and specifying some constraints and initial constraint rankings. A tableau can be created by entering an input followed by one or more candidates. After each candidate is entered, the program guides the user through assessing constraint violations and indicating whether a certain candidate is optimal.

After creating a tableau, the user can choose to analyze either the individual tableau or the entire model. A *model* is a collection of tableaux that share common constraints and constraint rankings. From the analysis menu, the user can have erculator-cli calculate possible winners or constraint rankings, minimize ERC sets or the model's ranking arguments, and generate a typology of possible languages. In addition to analyzing the tableaux, users may choose to export tableaux in a variety of forms. The Erculator user manual provides a tutorial for working with erculator-cli, and is available on the Erculator website.

2.4 Erculator-web

Erculator-web is an intuitive, attractive graphical front-end to erculator-cli (see Figure 1). It offers the same capabilities and functionality of erculator-cli with visual navigation and effects. The straightforward navigational interface focuses on a thin bar at the top of the screen and an expandable sidebar on the left. This enhances the visual space available for tableaux and makes them the focus of the user's attention while keeping all necessary tools and model navigation aids in the conveniently-placed, expandable sidebar. In addition, erculator-web can generate Hasse diagrams for inclusion in documents.

Erculator-web also allows users to freely register a username to be associated with a personal account, which allows them to edit models and provides a user page to share models and discuss analyses with other users. A user may view models that other users have made public and copy these models to his or her own account for modification and extension. This design is intended to foster web-based collaboration and allow real-time discussion and analysis of linguistic data. We envision a future in which field researchers are able to upload data directly to the website for instant collaboration with other researchers.

/kʷaja/	WSP	Ft-B	N-Fn	GW=PW	U-Imb	F-Syl	FL	Dp-M
☞ (kʷá:).ja					*			
kʷajá				*				

Figure 2: A publication-quality image of the first tableau from the model in Figure 1 as generated by erculator-web for inclusion in documents. — Linguists should not spend time formatting tables!

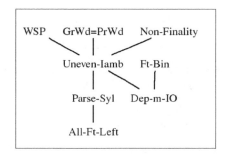

Figure 3: The Hasse diagram for the model in Figure 1 as generated by Erculator. — Linguists should not spend time drawing diagrams!

Erculator-web is fully Unicode compliant, and for users that do not have a convenient way to enter Unicode characters, erculator-web offers an easy-to-use IPA Palette. The palette shows all the IPA symbols and diacritics, which can be used in tableaux by clicking on the desired symbol. Characters generated by the IPA Palette can be used in the text fields specifying constraints, inputs, candidates, and captions, which offers users maximal descriptiveness in their models. These characters will be used in the typeset tableaux produced by Erculator, allowing linguists to use the software to produce tableaux for inclusion in documents (see Figure 2).

Erculator will also generate Hasse diagrams for models. Unlike the stratified hierarchies, which resolve all ambiguously ranked constraints by ranking them as high as possible, the Hasse generation function generates a disjunction of all Hasse diagrams that are consistent with rankings that make the winners in the tableaux optimal. Because the number of disjuncts can be quite high (sometimes in the thousands), Erculator limits diagrams to 30 disjuncts for a single model. Usually, adding tableaux is all that is required to lower the number of disjuncts below this limit. In Figure 3, we present a Hasse diagram generated by Erculator.

2.5   Demonstration

This section presents an example of how to produce an analysis using Erculator. It details what the process of building an analysis consists of and explains what a user should be seeing.

To begin using Erculator, simply go to erculator.com. The initial page provides a description of the Erculator software along with information on how to learn more about Erculator and begin using it. If you wish to use the command line interface (erculator-cli), feel free to follow the link listed on the homepage and consult the manual for a tutorial. If you would like to see a demonstration of the Erculator's graphical user interface (erculator-web), please click on the **gui** link on the top right of the page. The top right of the page also includes links to **log in** and **register** (see Section 2.4 above).

The opening page for the Erculator GUI shows two tabs. The first, leftmost tab shows models in the anonymous account if the user is not logged in, and shows his or her own models if he or she is logged in. The second, rightmost tab allows you to explore other users' models. If you are following this tutorial, we suggest that you create a user account to save your changes, but it is by no means obligatory for using Erculator.

The opening page of the Erculator GUI is called the *Model Browser*. Clicking the Create New Model button causes Erculator to prompt the user for the model's name. After the model has been named, Erculator will show three tabs: Constraints, Tableaux, and Properties. The Constraints tab is highlighted by default and the Edit mode is activated by default.

The next step is to add some constraints. Click on the New Constraint button. When you have clicked the button, erase the text and enter *VV, then click on the New Constraint button again, erase the text, and enter Max-IO(V). When you have finished, click on the Save Changes button, and you will see that right now, the constraints are entered but not ranked.

To add a tableau, click the Tableaux tab and then the Add New Tableau button, and name the tableau when prompted. After the name for the tableau has been added, enter the input form VVC; then click on **New Candidate** link to add a new candidate form. Make the first candidate VC and the second candidate VVC. There are blanks in which to enter the violations that each candidate has incurred. Violations may be entered either as asterisks or as integers. Now, click on the Save and Check button just above the tableau. This will save the changes you have made to your tableau and check for any harmonically bounded candidates. After this, you are free to select the winner. For this demonstration, choose VC as the winning candidate. Erculator will respond by showing the implication that *VV dominates Max-IO(V) in the constraint ranking. Erculator takes this implication into consideration and changes the tableau row where the constraints are displayed in order to reflect this ranking.

At this point, you have created a simple model using Erculator. The tableau may be exported in the format of your choice by clicking on one of the To ... buttons, where the ellipsis stands for the format or word processor to which Erculator will export the tableau (e.g., Word, PNG, etc.).

3 Theory

3.1 Elementary Ranking Conditions

The name Erculator comes from the acronym ERC for Elementary Ranking Condition (Prince, 2002). Most of the major functions of the software, such as detecting inconsistencies across tableaux, detecting harmonically bounded candidates, and generating Hasse diagrams for models, are implemented using ERCs "under the hood" to encode and manipulate information about candidates and tableaux. This section provides a brief description of the logic of Elementary Ranking Conditions, but see Prince (2000, 2002), Riggle (2004, 2006), and Prince & Brasoveanu (2005) for more detailed discussions.

A constraint $\mathbb{C}_i$ is a function from $(input, candidate)$ mappings to natural numbers. The number that $\mathbb{C}_i$ assigns to an input-candidate mapping indicates the number of times that that mapping violates the constraint. In standard Optimality Theory (Prince & Smolensky, 1993), optimality is defined as in (1).

(1) a. An input-candidate mapping (i,c) is more *harmonic* than (i,c'), written $(i,c) \succ (i,c')$, if (i,c) is assigned fewer violations by the highest ranking constraint that assigns (i,c) and (i,c') different numbers of violations.

    b. (i,c) is *optimal* according to ranking R iff no (i,c') is more harmonic than (i,c).

Elementary Ranking Conditions encode statements about constraint rankings. They can be derived from pairs of candidates in OT tableaux and make it possible to represent and store information about optimal candidates without storing the candidates themselves. ERCs are vectors that use the symbols e, L, and W to encode disjunctions of partial orderings of constraints. Each constraint is arbitrarily given a numeric index, and in each ERC α, the ith coordinate α_i refers to the constraint with the ith index, $\mathbb{C}_i$. The meaning of an ERC is that at least one constraint whose coordinate contains a W outranks all of the constraints whose coordinates are filled with L's. This is illustrated in (2).

(2) $\langle$L, e, W, $e\rangle$ – means that constraint $\mathbb{C}_3$ outranks constraint $\mathbb{C}_1$

    $\langle$W, L, W, $e\rangle$ – means that either $\mathbb{C}_3$ or $\mathbb{C}_1$ outranks constraint $\mathbb{C}_2$

    $\langle$W, W, L, L$\rangle$ – means that $\mathbb{C}_1$ or $\mathbb{C}_2$ each outrank either $\mathbb{C}_3$ and $\mathbb{C}_4$

For two mappings with the same input (i,c) and (i,c'), $erc(c \succ c')$ yields a single ERC α that encodes the rankings under which $(i,c) \succ (i,c')$ where $\alpha_i =$ W if (i,c) has fewer violations of $\mathbb{C}_i$, $\alpha_i = \text{L}$ if (i, c') has fewer violations of $\mathbb{C}_i$, and $\alpha_i = e$ otherwise.

(3)

input	$\mathbb{C}_1$	$\mathbb{C}_2$	$\mathbb{C}_3$	$\mathbb{C}_4$	
☞ cand. A		*	*	**	*winner*
cand. B		*	**	*	$erc(A \succ B) = \langle e, e, \text{W}, \text{L} \rangle$
cand. C	*	**		*	$erc(A \succ C) = \langle \text{W}, \text{W}, \text{L}, \text{L} \rangle$
cand. D	*			**	$erc(A \succ D) = \langle \text{W}, \text{L}, \text{L}, e \rangle$

For candidate A to beat B, constraint $\mathbb{C}_3$ must outrank $\mathbb{C}_4$. (The violations of $\mathbb{C}_2$ are irrelevant because both violate it equally.) For A to beat C, either $\mathbb{C}_1$ or $\mathbb{C}_2$ must outrank both $\mathbb{C}_3$ and $\mathbb{C}_4$, and for A to beat D, $\mathbb{C}_1$ must outrank both $\mathbb{C}_2$ and $\mathbb{C}_3$.

ERCs are useful in many ways – they collapse various quantitative differences among candidates' violations to conditions on constraint dominance, their logical structure can be used to draw inferences from sets of ranking conditions, they can easily be turned into familiar representations like stratified hierarchies, and they make it possible to represent ranking conditions drawn from distinct tableaux as a single set of conditions.

Whenever a tableau is saved in Erculator, an ERC set is generated for each candidate. The ERC set at the right in (3) encodes the rankings that make candidate A optimal. A simple recursive *consistency check* based on Tesar's Recursive Constraint Demotion algorithm (Tesar & Smolensky, 1993) can then be performed on the ERC set to check whether the candidate it corresponds to can be optimal under any ranking of the constraints. If not, then the candidate is marked as harmonically bounded.

If a model contains several tableaux, an ERC set for the whole model can be derived by taking the union of the ERCs for the candidates that are marked as winners. A simple consistency check on the union of the ERCs for two winners in different tableaux reveals whether they are compatible (i.e. there is at least one ranking under which both are optimal). Furthermore, because each candidate in each tableau is annotated with the ERCs that make it optimal, it is possible to show how the field of possibly optimal candidates in one tableau is narrowed by the selection of winners in another tableau. In this case, we mark incompatible winners with bombs.

Taking the union of ERC sets for candidates and checking for consistency provides an extremely simple (albeit computationally intensive) method for generating typologies. Given a constraint set CON and a set of tableaux, the typology generated by CON over the candidates in the tableaux can be obtained by taking the cross-product of the candidates in each tableau and eliminating any combination with incompatible ERCs. Erculator-web does not currently allow the generation of factorial typologies due to the strain this would place on the server. However, typology generation is highly parallelizable, which leaves open the possibility for adding this functionality to `erculator-web` as our computational infrastructure grows. We are also currently developing a stand-alone application that users can download to generate factorial typologies from cPhon XML files produced by `erculator-web`.

3.2   Optimality Broadly Defined

Optimality can be defined in such a way as to include ranked, weighted, and hard (inviolable) constraints. Models that use only one of these categories of constraints represent special cases of this broader definition. Stochastic models of ranking (or weighting) are compatible with the definitions here; they simply involve probability distributions on the grammar that are resolved to specific rankings (or weightings, or whatever) before optimization is carried out. (But see Riggle & Wilson (2005) for models in which rankings can change intra-derivationally.)

Given a constraint set CON, a grammar is a triple $(\text{CON}, R_{\text{CON}}, W_{\text{CON}})$, where R_{CON} is a partial ordering of the constraints in CON and W_{CON} is a weighting of the constraints. In standard Optimality Theory, R_{CON} is restricted to the case of a total ordering (which renders the weights irrelevant), and in strictly weighted models the constraints are unordered (only the weights are relevant). Hard constraints can be implemented as constraints that are ranked at the top of the hierarchy and given infinite weights. However, to ensure that the computation always produces some result, models that use them should include at least one candidate in each derivation that does not violate any of the hard constraints (possibly a special output of NULL or INEFFABLE).

The language generated by $(\text{CON}, R_{\text{CON}}, W_{\text{CON}})$ is the set of *(input, candidate)* mappings that are *optimal* as defined in (4).

(4)   a. A group of constraints with the same rank in R_{CON} is a *block* of constraints.

      b. The *weight* of an input-candidate mapping (i,c) at block b_i is the sum, for each $\mathbb{C}_i \in b_i$, of the violations that $\mathbb{C}_i$ assigns to (i,c) times the weight of $\mathbb{C}_i$ given by W_{CON}.

      c. Mapping (i,c) is more *harmonic* than (i,c'), written $(i,c) \succ (i,c')$, if (i,c) has a lower weight at the highest ranked block of constraints for which (i,c) and (i,c') have different weights.

      d. (i,c) is *optimal* according to R_{CON} iff no (i,c') is more harmonic than (i,c).

Currently, all of the computations in Erculator are based on standard Optimality Theory. In the next section, we describe extensions to include stochastic models and weighted constraints. Once these are implemented, it will be possible to create "hybrid models" of the sort outlined here.

4   Upcoming Features

Future versions of Erculator will include new features that will focus on lessening the amount of input required by the user, integrating alternative ranking hypotheses, and enhancing usability.

4.1   Automatic Violation Assessment and Candidate Generation

At present, Erculator requires that the user manually input each violation for each constraint. In future versions, it will be possible to include constraints that are represented as regular expressions in the program's back-end code to automatically fill in the violations that each candidate incurs for each constraint. The first version of this feature will allow users to select constraints from a list of constraints that have been computationally implemented. Later versions of the software (Erculator 2.0) will provide an interface for users to build their own computational implementations of constraints.

Automatic violation completion will significantly decrease the time it takes to produce a model by lessening the workload for the end user. It will also be essential for improving the accuracy of each tableau because it will eliminate human error in violation assessment. We are currently developing a constraint wiki to collect commonly used constraints and provide a forum for discussion of their ramifications and where they are observed. The wiki will also serve as a repository for computational implementations of the constraints. Future versions of Erculator will allow users to import constraints from the wiki to their constraint-based models.

By having Erculator reformulate each constraint as a regular expression in its code, constraints will have to be expressed in an explicit way. This will significantly ameliorate the problem of figuring out how a constraint assesses violations. Often, phonologists must reverse engineer constraints using the description the author gives and by careful examination of the violations each candidate incurs. Erculator will amend this problem by making the application of constraints transparent and explicit.

Not all constraints can be represented as regular expressions, and so Erculator will allow models that involve mixtures of constraints with manually and automatically marked violations. Though correspondence theoretic constraints cannot in the general case be represented as regular expressions,[1] It remains possible to automatically determine the violations of candidates whose correspondence relations have been marked manually.

---

[1]   This is because the index set is not a finite alphabet. This necessitates the use of push-down automata in the machine implementation of the constraints, rather than the finite state automata used for regular constraints. Push-down automata can efficiently assign violations to manually generated candidates, but significantly complicate the process of automatically generating candidates.

Similarly to automatically assessing violations, Erculator will be able to automatically generate candidates when all of the constraints in the model are represented as regular expressions. In this case, Erculator can generate the entire set of *contenders* — the candidates that are not harmonically bounded in a tableau (Riggle, 2004). The use of contender sets in a tableau guarantees that the researcher cannot fail to consider a relevant candidate. A ranking that makes a candidate more harmonic than all of the contenders makes the candidate globally optimal.

4.2 Representing Other Constraint-based Grammar Models

In future versions, Erculator will support alternative constraint-based grammar models, such as those utilizing weighted constraints, stochastic constraint rankings, and models combining standard rankings with weighted and stochastic ranking systems (such as maximum entropy models). The ability to integrate these capabilities seamlessly with Erculator's present state will be handled by the Chicago Language Modeling Lab, but much of the architecture of the models themselves will be contributed by collaborators at other institutions. See Section 5 for further details. This open-ended system will be well poised to accommodate new developments in constraint-based phonology and make it possible to directly compare analyses across frameworks.

4.3 Enhancing Usability

Erculator was developed to simplify the creation and analysis of phonological models for both research and pedagogical purposes. Usability features are a core part of the simplicity of Erculator, and future versions of Erculator will respond to the changing needs and requests of its users. The Chicago Language Modeling Lab is already planning a variety of usability features. Examples of such updates include allowing users to customize the look of Erculator by dragging and dropping entities (e.g., the IPA Palette), allowing users to edit a field and have Erculator check the resulting tableau simply by clicking on the field, and adding a user settings page for each user to customize certain aspects of Erculator's behavior.

In addition to the high-level usability enhancements described above, Erculator will soon feature specific resources for teachers and students. These will include the ability to create example models and partially completed models for students to work on or modify. Instructors will also be able to create specific profile pages designed for students which can function as problem sets or homework assignments. Erculator's export features will help students easily include tableaux in their work.

5 Collaboration on Developing Erculator

Erculator is meant to serve researchers and students in linguistics by bringing as many computational approaches together as possible. Thus, collaborative development is essential to ensure that the software serves the needs of a wide variety of users and stays abreast of cutting-edge developments in phonological theory. In that spirit, CLML has developed an XML scheme to store model data called *cPhon*. This cPhon file specification allows Erculator to integrate alternative constraint-based models of grammar.

5.1 The cPhon XML File

The cPhon XML file provides researchers with a human-readable grammar specification markup language with all the advantages of the XML language. Storing data in the cPhon format provides several additional benefits for phonologists:

- cPhon functions as a common markup language for phonological models, Optimality Theoretic and otherwise.

- The common cPhon file format facilitates collaboration on software development.

- Stored phonological data can be used on any operating system with a variety of software.

The cPhon XML scheme is an important tool for storing data generated by Erculator and for facilitating collaboration among scholars. It is able to store the data encoded by files specific to both OTSoft (Hayes, Tesar, & Zuraw, 2003) and Praat (Boersma & Weenink, 2007) in addition to Erculator. The cPhon file, then, could be used as a common file format to encode the same set of data to be analyzed using each program. This would allow linguists to take advantage of a wider range of software in addition to Erculator. It should be possible to adapt the format to accommodate HaLP (Potts, Becker, Bhatt, & Pater, 2007) and CCamelOT (Becker, 2005).

5.2 Collaborators

Some scholars collaborating on Erculator include Bruce Hayes and Colin Wilson at UCLA, Jeff Heinz at the University of Delaware, Alan Prince at Rutgers, and Joe Pater, Christopher Potts, Rajesh Bhatt, and Michael Becker at UMass Amherst. These collaborative efforts are described below.

5.2.1 Stochastic OT and the Gradual Learning Algorithm (GLA)

The Gradual Learning Algorithm (GLA) can accommodate distinctions of *optionality* and obligation that influence constraint rankings. These distinctions arise when a learner notices stochastic distributions of instances of usage between one form or another, for example, between an assimilated nasal and a non-assimilated nasal (Boersma, 1997). Work done by Paul Boersma in this area is based upon earlier work by Bruce Tesar (Tesar, 1995, 1997, 1998) and Paul Smolensky, especially with regard to their Constraint Demotion Algorithm (Tesar & Smolensky, 1993), which provided much of the initial impetus for researching learnability in Optimality Theory (Boersma & Hayes, 2001).[2]

---

[2]   See Tesar & Smolensky (2000) for more information on learnability in OT.

We are currently collaborating with Bruce Hayes on the implementation of a version of the GLA for inclusion in Erculator. Furthermore, we are committed to working together on protocols and standards for storing information in constraint based models (see the cPhon specification) that should allow users to seamlessly transport data from Erculator to existing programs like OTSoft (Hayes, Tesar, & Zuraw, 2003). Paul Boersma also has an implementation of the GLA in the Praat software package (Boersma & Weenink, 2007), and we are currently working on a function that will reformat cPhon files into versions that are readable by Praat.

5.2.2 ERC manipulation and the Fusional Reduction (FRed)

Alan Prince and Adrian Brasoveanu have developed an algorithm, the Fusional Reduction Algorithm (FRed), designed to reduce sets of Elementary Ranking Conditions to smaller sets that encode the same information. They call this reduced version of an ERC set a Maximally Informative Basis, or MIB (Prince & Brasoveanu, 2005). We at CLML are currently working to code up FRed as an option in Erculator We have also built an ERC-set minimizer (Riggle, Bane, Kirby, & O'Brien, 2007) based on ideas in Riggle (2004). These algorithms are designed to do the same thing, but they work in different ways. Because every data point in our models is represented with an ERC set and these sets frequently need to be unioned and checked for consistency, it could be quite a boon to have a more efficient representation of the sets.

While it is possible to compute worst-case complexity results for both algorithms, what is more important is the average-case complexity. Until now, the idea of an average-case has only been approximable through odd and artificial assumptions (e.g., a uniform probability distribution over possible ERC sets). However, as we collect more phonological models in Erculator, it will become possible to actually begin to construct a notion of what an average case looks like. It could be the case that one of these minimization algorithms is more efficient than the other, or it could be the case that each is best for certain types of data. With both implemented in a common platform, it will be possible to test these algorithms (and any that are developed in the future) head-to-head on the same range of data.

5.2.3 Harmonic Grammar (HG)

Joe Pater, Christopher Potts, Rajesh Bhatt, and Michael Becker have been working on computational implementations of Harmonic Grammar (Legendre, Miyata, & Smolensky, 1990; Pater, Potts, & Bhatt, 2006). Their efforts (presented in the HaLP program) can be seen online (Potts, Becker, Bhatt, & Pater, 2007). In Harmonic Grammar, constraints are assigned weights rather than rankings, and the candidate that is assigned the lowest weight at the end of the evaluation is the optimal candidate. Pater, Potts, and Bhatt have developed a method of describing weight-based Harmonic Grammars as linear systems. This allows them to employ the Simplex Algorithm (originally developed in 1947 by George Dantzig) to efficiently solve these linear systems (Pater, Potts, & Bhatt, 2006). We have begun collaborative work with Pater *et al.* to include this functionality in Erculator.

Because HG and OT use much of the same architecture in terms of candidate sets and violations, we will be able to create a single system for analyzing linguistic phenomena under these disparate models. We should also be able to create a sort of hybrid model (see Section 3.2) that incorporates aspects of both systems.

5.2.4 Maximum Entropy Grammars

Bruce Hayes and Colin Wilson have been working on another constraint based phonological model with weighted constraints (Hayes & Wilson, 2007). In this system the constraints and their weightings are learned via information theoretic strategies involving expectation maximization. Goldsmith & Riggle (2007) have also recently been working on models for discovering and weighting constraints. Ideally, much of the infrastructure needed for representing the weighted constraints of Harmonic Grammar will be portable to Maximum Entropy (Maxent) models.

6 Conclusion

Erculator provides researchers and students in linguistics with an accessible yet full-featured means of harnessing the computational resources demanded by the complexity of current phonological models. CLML is always seeking feedback from users in order to increase the usability of Erculator and augment its feature set. Collaborative development of Erculator is also encouraged since Erculator is meant to be a tool that makes computational resources more accessible to all working phonologists and their students. As researchers contribute constraints to the constraint wiki, post (possibly in-progress) analyses of linguistic phenomena to the user pages, and contribute data sets (of both the real-world and pedagogical types), we hope that Erculator and the CLML website will become a nexus for online collaboration and linguistic research.

References

Becker, Michael. 2005. "CCamelOT." *Software Package* URL http://wwwx.oit.umass.edu/~linguist/CCamelOT.

Boersma, Paul. 1997. "How We Learn Variation, Optionality, and Probability." *Proceedings of the Institute of Phonetic Sciences, Amsterdam* 21: 43–58.

Boersma, Paul. 1998. *Functional Phonology: Formalizing the Interactions Between Articulatory and Perceptual Drives*. Ph.D. thesis. The Hague: Holland Academic Graphics.

Boersma, Paul & Bruce Hayes. 2001. "Empirical Tests of the Gradual Learning Algorithm." *Linguistic Inquiry* 32: 45–86.

Boersma, Paul & David Weenink. 2007. "Praat." *Software Package* URL http://www.praat.org/.

Goldsmith, John & Jason Riggle. 2007. "Information Theoretic Approaches to Phonological Structure: The Case of Vowel Harmony." Ms., University of Chicago.

Hayes, Bruce, Bruce Tesar, & Kie Zuraw. 2003. "OTSoft 2.1." *Software Package* URL http://www.linguistics.ucla.edu/people/hayes/otsoft/.

Hayes, Bruce & Colin Wilson. 2007. "A Maximum Entropy Model of Phonotactics and Phonotactic Learning." UCLA. [To Appear: *Linguistic Inquiry*]

Legendre, Geraldine, Yoshiro Miyata, & Paul Smolensky. 1990. "Harmonic Grammar – A Formal Multi-Level Connectionist Theory of Linguistic Well-Formedness: Theoretical Foundations." *Proceedings of the Twelfth Annual Conference of the Cognitive Science Society* pp. 388–395.

Pater, Joe, Christopher Potts, & Rajesh Bhatt. 2006. "Harmonic Grammar with Linear Programming."

Potts, Christopher, Michael Becker, Rajesh Bhatt, & Joe Pater. 2007. "HaLP: Harmonic Grammar with Linear Programming." *Software Package* URL http://web.linguist.umass.edu/~halp/.

Prince, Alan. 2000. "Comparative Tableaux." Ms., Rutgers University, New Brunswick. ROA-376.

Prince, Alan. 2002. "Entailed Ranking Arguments." *Rutgers Optimality Archive* ROA-500. roa.rutgers.edu.

Prince, Alan & Adrian Brasoveanu. 2005. "Ranking and Necessity." *Rutgers Optimality Theory Archive* (ROA) 794-1205. roa.rutgers.edu.

Prince, Alan & Paul Smolensky. 1993. "Optimality Theory: Constraint Interaction in Generative Grammar." Ms., Rutgers University, New Brunswick, and University of Colorado, Boulder. RuCCS-TR-2.

Riggle, Jason. 2004. *Generation, Recognition, and Learning in Finite State Optimality Theory*. Ph.D. thesis, University of California, Los Angeles.

Riggle, Jason. 2006. "Using Entropy to Learn OT Grammars from Surface Forms Alone." *Proceedings of the 25th West Coast Conference on Formal Linguistics* .

Riggle, Jason, Max Bane, James Kirby, & Jeremy O'Brien. 2007. "Efficiently Computing OT Typologies." Linguistic Society of America 2007 Annual Conference in Anaheim, CA. http://clml.uchicago.edu/erculator.

Riggle, Jason & Colin Wilson. 2005. "Local Optionality." *Proceedings of the 35th Annual Meeting of the North Eastern Linguistic Society* .

Tesar, Bruce. 1995. *Computational Optimality Theory*. Ph.D. thesis, University of Colorado.

Tesar, Bruce. 1997. "Multi-Recursive Constraint Demotion." Ms. Rutgers University.

Tesar, Bruce. 1998. "Error-driven Learning in Optimality Theory via the Efficient Computation of Optimal Forms." Ms.

Tesar, Bruce & Paul Smolensky. 1993. "The Learnability of Optimality Theory: an Algorithm and Some Basic Complexity Results." Ms., Department of Computer Science & Institute of Cognitive Science, University of Colorado, Boulder.

Tesar, Bruce & Paul Smolensky. 2000. *Learnability in Optimality Theory*. MIT Press.

Chicago Language Modeling Lab
Department of Linguistics
1010 E. 59th St.
Chicago, IL 60637
clml.uchicago.edu
clml@listhost.uchicago.edu

What constraint connectives should be permitted in OT?[*]

Matthew Wolf

University of Massachusetts Amherst

1. Introduction

In Optimality Theory (Prince & Smolensky 2004 [1993]), the surface form of a given linguistic input is selected by determining which member of a set of candidate surface forms best satisfies a language-particular ranking of the universal constraint-set CON. Much (and quite possibly most) research within OT is concerned with what constraints are to be found in CON; that is, with the question of what constraints must be assumed to exist in order to properly account for language typology.

A related but distinct question is where the constraints in CON come from. Clearly at least some must be supplied by some mechanism outside of the linguistic system itself: constraints may be innate, or their existence may be inferred by the language learner from universal experiences that occur during acquisition, e.g. observing one's expenditures of articulatory effort during babbling (Hayes 1999) or one's errors in perceptually classifying speech sounds (Flack 2007a,b). Constraints that are supplied by the extra-grammatical world, either by the learner's genes or via the learner's inferences from observation of phonetic facts, can be referred to as *primitive*. It is obvious that any version of OT must assume the existence of primitive constraints. However, it is not necessarily the case that *all* constraints available in OT grammars are primitive. It might be the case that learners also can create new constraints based upon two (or more) pre-existing constraints. Constraints which are constructed from other constraints can be referred to as *complex*.

The first and by far most widely used proposal for a device that creates complex constraints is Local Conjunction (or LC: Smolensky 1993, 1995, 1997). A locally

---

[*] A portion of this work was previously circulated on the Rutgers Optimality Archive as 'A note on the construction of complex OT constraints by material implication'. Thanks are due to John McCarthy and Michael Becker for helpful feedback on several versions of this paper. All errors should be attributed to me.
[1] 'Primitive' is used here in a different sense than it is in Eisner (1999), which argues that CON is structured in such a way that all constraints are instantiations of one of two basic ('primitive') constraint schemas.

Michael Becker (ed.): Papers in theoretical and computational phonology. University of Massachusetts Occasional Papers in Linguistics 36, 151-179.
GLSA Amherst.

conjoined constraint [A&B]$_D$ is violated if and only if constraint A and constraint B are both violated within some domain D. LC has come to enjoy wide (though certainly not universal) acceptance among practitioners of OT, but relatively little attention has been paid to the possibility that other logical connectives with different semantics might be made available by the human language faculty.

Several connectives besides LC are proposed by Hewitt & Crowhurst (1996), Crowhurst & Hewitt (1997), Archangeli, Moll, & Ohno (1998), Crowhurst (1998), Downing (1998, 2000), and Balarí, Marin & Vallverdú (2000). However, these works do not exhaust the space of conceivable constraint connectives. Indeed, there are sixteen possible connectives which would take two constraints as arguments and yield a third constraint whose satisfaction or violation depended on the satisfaction or violation of the arguments. This is because, for any two constraints P and Q, there are four distinct situations in which a complex constraint P•Q formed by some connective • will be satisfied or violated:

(1)   a. P is satisfied and Q is satisfied
        b. P is satisfied and Q is violated
        c. P is violated and Q is satisfied
        d. P is violated and Q is violated

The complex constraint P•Q can have one of two values—violated or satisfied—in each of the four situations in (1). In the case of LC, the constraint [P&Q] is violated in situation (1)d, but satisfied in the other three. In principle, however, nothing prevents us from imagining (say) a constraint that was satisfied in situation (1)a, but violated otherwise, or which was violated in situations (1)b-c, and satisfied otherwise. The full space of imaginable constraint connectives is formed by letting P•Q take on each possible combination of being violated or satisfied in each of (1)a-d. Given these four situations and the two possible values that P•Q can have in each of them, there are $2^4 = 16$ possible constraint connectives.

Out of these sixteen options, LC has received by far the greatest amount of empirical attention, both pro and con, in the OT literature to date. Is this skew of attention justified? Is there a principled reason to suspect that Universal Grammar might make only LC, and no other connectives, available to natural languages? This paper will show that the following criterion comes very close to doing so:

(2)   A logical connective • is available in natural-language OT grammars if and only if, for any two constraints A and B (each of which is either a markedness or a faithfulness constraint) A•B is either a markedness or a faithfulness constraint.

I will demonstrate that there are only four analytically interesting connectives that satisfy criterion (2), and that two of these cease to possess linguistic interest given assumptions about the locality of constraint coordination which are independently motivated by the need to restrain the typological predictions of LC itself (Łubowicz 2005). Of the remaining two connectives, one is LC, and the other is a connective which will create, from any two constraints, an instance of the economy constraint *STRUC (Prince & Smolensky 2004 [1993], Zoll 1993, 1996). *STRUC is itself controversial and may need to be excluded in principle from OT grammars (Gouskova 2003): if such a move were made, then LC would be left as the only connective standing.

The remainder of this paper is organized as follows: Section 2 lays out the empirical motivation for maintaining the null hypothesis that there are only markedness and faithfulness constraints, namely the fact that it correctly predicts the absence of circular or infinite chain shifts in natural-language grammars (Moreton 1999). Section 3 demonstrates the stakes involved in positing novel constraint connectives by showing an example of one proposed non-LC connective which is able to give rise to circular chain shifts. Section 4 then applies criterion (2) to the space of possible constraint connectives, showing that there are only five (out of a possible sixteen) which meet it, one of which is clearly analytically uninteresting because the complex constraints it creates never assign violation-marks to any candidate. Section 5 motivates the locality convention which strips two of the remaining four connectives of typological utility, and shows that the third will give rise to the independently-banned *STRUC, leaving LC as the only permitted connective. Section 6 concludes.

2.   Reasons to think that there are only markedness and faithfulness constraints

Most work in OT adheres, explicitly or implicitly, to a null hypothesis that CON contains only two general types of constraints: markedness constraints and faithfulness constraints. These two constraint types may be formally defined in a manner proposed by Moreton (1999):

(3)   a. A constraint C is a markedness constraint if, for any given candidate surface form [X], C always assigns the same number of violation-marks to [X], regardless of what the underlying form is.

b. A constraint C is a faithfulness constraint if it always assigns zero violation-marks to a candidate surface form that is identical to the underlying form.

Markedness constraints are responsible for disallowing marked structure in surface forms. The standard hypothesis about markedness constraints, as expressed in definition (3)a, is that they 'don't care' about the input. For example, a markedness constraint *RoundVowel will assign a single violation mark to a candidate surface form like [kop], irrespective of whether the [o] derives from an underlying round vowel, derives from an underlying non-round vowel, or is epenthetic.

Faithfulness constraints, on the other hand, demand that the surface form of some linguistic expression retain certain properties of the underlying form. This means, as expressed in definition (3)b, that a faithfulness constraint will never penalize a candidate surface form which retains *all* of the properties of the underlying form. Of course, not every faithfulness constraint will penalize a given unfaithful mapping. For instance, the anti-deletion constraint MAX will be entirely indifferent between a candidate where underlying /pat/ surfaces faithfully as [pat], and a candidate [pa.tə] which adds an epenthetic vowel. Crucially, though, there will be no faithfulness constraint which prefers [pa.tə] over [pat] as the realization of underlying /pat/. This is guaranteed if every faithfulness constraint always assigns zero marks to a fully-faithful candidate like /pat/ → [pat].

The null hypothesis that every constraint in CON is either markedness or faithfulness makes an empirical prediction about the kinds of input-output mappings that can be generated by an OT grammar. Specifically, Moreton (1999) gives a formal proof that an OT grammar with only markedness and faithfulness constraints cannot model circular or infinite chain shifts. The proof of the impossibility of circular chain shifts can be informally summarized as follows: faithfulness constraints will only be violated if doing so improves performance on some higher-ranked markedness constraint. This means that if underlying /X/ maps to surface [Y], [Y] must be less marked than its losing faithful competitor *[X] given the constraint hierarchy of the language. If this is so, then there is no rationale for underlying /Y/ to map unfaithfully to *[X], since this output will be both more marked *and* less faithful than [Y].

With respect to infinite chain shifts, the argument is similar. Suppose that underlying $/X_1/ \rightarrow [X_2]$, $/X_2/ \rightarrow [X_3]$, and so on *ad infinitum*. Since no faithfulness constraint can favor mapping an underlying form $/X_n/$ onto anything other than $[X_n]$, each of the unfaithful mappings in the infinite chain shift would have to improve performance on the markedness constraints. That is, every $[X_n]$ would have to be less marked than $[X_{n-1}]$ with respect to the ranking of the markedness constraints which prevailed in the language in question. But this could not go on forever, since there is a lower bound on how marked a candidate can be, namely to receive no violation-marks from any markedness constraint. Psychological plausibility demands that there be only finitely many constraints and that candidates be of finite (even if unbounded) size. This means that every candidate surface form $[X_n]$ receives a finite number of markedness violations: $[X_n]$ contains only a finite number of structures, and there is only a finite number of markedness constraints that could potentially penalize each of those structures.[2] Every $[X_n]$ is therefore worse than the immaculate surface form, with no markedness violations, by only a finite number of steps. As such, an OT grammar with only markedness and faithfulness constraints cannot model an infinitely long chain shift, since such a chain shift would involve an infinite number of markedness-reducing steps.[3]

This result is important, insofar as it is independent of any particular hypothesis about exactly what the markedness and faithfulness constraints in the universal constraint-set CON *are*. The exclusion of circular and infinite chain shifts is a formal

---

[2] This argument also involves the assumption that no markedness constraint assigns an infinite number of violation-marks to a single violating structure. This assumption is, needless to say, quite standard, and indeed it has been argued that OT constraints only ever assign one violation-mark to each structure that violates them (McCarthy 2003b).
[3] The role of the finitude of CON in ruling out unconditional augmentation is pointed out by McCarthy (2002: 186, fn. 24).

universal predicted by OT's theory of constraint interaction, coupled with the assumption that all of the relevant constraints are either markedness or faithfulness.

This prediction is also almost certainly correct. There are a few reported examples of circular chain shifts that arise in morpheme realization, most famously in the Nilotic language DhoLuo, which is claimed to mark the plural and genitive (in part) by reversing the [voice] specification of the last consonant in the noun stem (Gergersen 1972, Okoth-Okombo 1982). However, a number of empirical doubts have been raised about whether the [voice] alternations in DhoLuo nouns are accurately described as an exchange process (Trommer 2005, Bye 2006, Pulleyblank 2006, Baerman 2007). Additionally, it is significant that the alleged DhoLuo exchange rule is a morphological mutation process. If a morpheme like the DhoLuo genitive has two listed allomorphs, one with a floating feature [+voice] and and one with a floating feature [-voice], then the selection of the allomorph that will produce a visible change when docked onto a stem segment can be achieved using only markedness and faithfulness constraints (de Lacy 2002, Wolf 2007). Nearly all other plausible cases of exchange rules arise in this same kind of morpheme-realization context (see Anderson & Browne 1973, McCawley 1974, Alderete 1999, Moreton 1999, Wolf 2007 for relevant discussion), and so would presumably be amenable to an analysis along the same lines.

The one other situation which supplies plausible examples of circular chain shifts is tone sandhi, with the most famous example being the four-step 'tone circle' in Taiwanese. For that language, it has been argued that the tone alternations are simply lexicalized listed allomorphy (Tsay & Myers 1996, Myers 2006). This conclusion is supported by an abundant body of experimental work which shows that at least some of the alternations making up the tone circle are not productive processes in the synchronic phonology of Taiwanese (Hsieh 1970, 1975, 1976, Lin 1988, Tseng 1995, Wang 1995, Peng 1998, Myers & Tsay 2002, Zhang, Lai & Turnbull-Sailor 2006).[4]

The evidence for infinite chain shifts in natural languages is even sparser than that for circular shifts. The only case I know of that has been characterized as possibly constituting one involves high tone spread in the Bantu language Chilungu; this process is the subject of a reanalysis (relying on only markedness and faithfulness) by Key & Bickmore (in prep.).

Because the exclusion of circular and infinite chain shifts is an empirically desirable result, we should be attentive to potential sources of novel constraint types— neither markedness nor faithfulness—which would subvert the assumption about CON which underlies Moreton's (1999) proof. In the most obvious cases, this possibility arises when a linguist explicitly proposes some new constraint type. For example, McCarthy's (2003a) Comparative Markedness constraints, and Łubowicz's (2003) Preserve-Contrast

---

[4] See Yue-Hashimoto (1986) for a survey of reported circular shifts in the tone sandhi systems of other Chinese languages. A three-step tone circle is also reported in Choapan Zapotec (Lyman & Lyman 1977), and two-step circles are reported in certain Hmongic languages (Mortensen 2004).

constraints are capable of generating circular chainshifts in input-output mappings.[5] (For Preserve-Contrast constraints, see Barrie 2006 for a demonstration of this). The other possible source of neither-markedness-nor-faithfulness constraints lies in the various novel logical connectives that have been proposed for combining two OT constraints into a larger complex constraint. The next section demonstrates how one proposed connective does just this.

3.   Case study: Material implication

The constraint connective to be focused on in this section is independently proposed by Archangeli, Moll, & Ohno (1998) and Balari, Marín, and Vallverdú (2000), who view it as corresponding to the logical operator of material implication ($\rightarrow$). To understand the connection with material implication, a small about of background discussion will be required. Crowhurst & Hewitt (1997) observe that, if constraint violation is viewed as corresponding to logical falsity and constraint satisfaction as corresponding to logical truth, then the semantics of LC are parallel to those of disjunction in classical propositional logic. A locally-conjoined constraint [A&B]$_D$ is violated iff both of its arguments are violated in the domain D, but is not violated if one (but not both) of A or B is violated in D. Similarly, the disjunction EvF of two propositions E and F is false iff E and F are both false; if one is false and the other true, EvF is true.

Having observed this parallel, Crowhurst and Hewitt (1997) proceed to investigate whether other operators of propositional logic would be useful in OT. They argue that logical *conjunction* ($\wedge$) and material implication ($\rightarrow$) are needed. The classical semantics for material implication are given in the truth table below, together with the semantics of a complex constraint constructed by material implication, under the assumption that violation is equivalent to falsehood and satisfaction to truth:

(4)

P	Q	P→Q		P	Q	P→Q
0	0	1		*	*	✓
1	0	0		✓	*	*
0	1	1		*	✓	✓
1	1	1		✓	✓	✓

*(0 = falsity, 1 = truth; * = constraint violation, ✓ = constraint satisfaction)*

As shown, the material implication P→Q is false iff P is true and Q is false. Importantly, though, if P is false, P→Q is true regardless of whether Q is true or false. Likewise, a constraint P→Q will be violated only just in case constraint P is satisfied and constraint Q is violated. If constraint P is violated, P→Q will be satisfied irrespective of whether Q is violated or not.

---

[5] Transderivational antifaithfulness (Alderete 1999, 2001) and REALIZE-MORPHEME (Kurisu 2001) can also model circular and infinite chain shifts, but only ones which occur for the sake of marking a morphological category (like the alleged DhoLuo exchange rule). An input-output antifaithfulness constraint, which in principle could generate infinite chain shifts, is proposed in Baković (1996).

The semantics of Crowhurst & Hewitt's (1997) proposed material implication connective for OT in fact differ from this—they treat the constraint [A→B] as satisfied iff A and B are both satisfied. However, classical material implication as a tool for building complex constraints is proposed by Balari, Marín, & Vallverdú (2000), in reply to Crowhurst & Hewitt (1997); an apparently identical connective is also used by Archangeli, Moll, & Ohno (1998).[6] For these authors, a constraint [A→B] is always satisfied by a given candidate if that candidate violates constraint A, since a material implication, as mentioned, is always true if its antecedent is false.

If we augment OT with a constraint connective that has these semantics, circular chainshifts can be modeled by creating a constraint [A→B] in which A is a faithfulness constraint and B is a markedness constraint. To illustrate, suppose that we have the following constraint ranking:

(5)
IDENT[+round] » [IDENT[-tense] → *[+round]] » *[+tense] » IDENT[-tense], *[+round]

Constraint definitions:
IDENT[+round]: Assign a violation-mark if an input [+round] segment corresponds to an output [-round] segment.
IDENT[-tense]: Assign a violation-mark if an input [-tense] segment corresponds to an output [+tense] segment.
*[+tense]: Assign a violation-mark for every [+tense] segment in the output.
*[+round]: Assign a violation-mark for every [+round] segment in the output.

Given the ranking in (5), consider what happens to an input segment that is [+round, +tense][7]:

(6)

/y/	IDENT [+round]	[IDENT[-tense]→ *[+round]]	*[+tense]	IDENT [-tense]	*[+round]
a. [y]		*	*!		*
b. → [Y]		*			*
c. [i]	*!		*		
d. [ɪ]	*!				

The undominated constraint IDENT[+round] rules out all candidates that change the input's [+round] to [-round]. This leaves [y] and [Y] as contenders. The complex

<hr/>
[6] A connective with the semantics of classical conjunction is also argued for in Hewitt & Crowhurst (1996) and Downing (1998, 2000). Łubowicz (2005) argues that material implication has a role to play in the semantics of LC, for the purpose of preventing LC from generating so-called markedness reversals (Ito & Mester 1998).
[7] In the following examples, [y] is [+tense, +round]; [Y] is [-tense, +round]; [ ] is [+tense, -round], and [ɪ] is [-tense, -round].

constraint [IDENT[-tense] → *[+round]] will not distinguish between these two candidates: first, since the input does not contain a feature specification [-tense], the antecedent IDENT[-tense] is vacuously satisfied by all candidates; and second, both of the remaining contenders are [+round], and therefore violate the consequent of the conditional. Hence, both of the remaining contenders equally violate [IDENT[-tense]→ *[+round]], by virtue of satisfying the antecedent while violating the consequent. The choice is then passed down to the markedness constraint *[+tense], which chooses lax [Y] over tense [y].

Now consider what happens when the input is /Y/:

(7)

/Y/	IDENT [+round]	[IDENT[-tense]→ *[+round]]	*[+tense]	IDENT [-tense]	*[+round]
a. → [y]			*	*	*
b. [Y]		*!			*
c. [i]	*!		*	*	
d. [ɪ]	*!				

As before, the undominated status of IDENT[+round] immediately reduces the set of contenders to [y] and [Y]. Moving down to the next highest-ranked constraint, we now encounter [IDENT[-tense] → *[+round]]. Unlike before, the input now contains a [-tense] specification, so it is no longer the case that all candidates vacuously satisfy the antecedent of the conditional.

   The faithful candidate [Y] satisfies the antecedent (IDENT[-tense]) by virtue of preserving the input's [-tense] specification, but it violates the consequent (*[+round]) by virtue of having a [+round] specification. Because it satisfies the antecedent but violates the consequent, this candidate violates the material implication. By contrast, the unfaithful candidate [y] also violates the consequent *[+round], as it too has an output [+round] specification, but it differs from the faithful candidate in violating the antecedent constraint IDENT[-tense]. Because it violates the antecedent, [y] satisfies the material implication, and thus wins.

   Building complex constraints by material implication thus allows us to model circular chain shifts in OT. In our example, input /y/ surfaces as [Y], while input /Y/ surfaces as [y]. The reason for this has to do with the fact that our complex constraint [IDENT[-tense] → *[+round]] has a faithfulness constraint as its antecedent and a markedness constraint as its consequent. Such a constraint rewards unfaithfulness, as can be seen in (7): [y] violates the antecedent by being unfaithful, and by so doing it is exempted from having to satisfy the consequent, whereas the faithful candidate [Y] satisfies the antecedent, and therefore would have to satisfy the consequent (which it doesn't) in order to satisfy the material implication. So, even though, for input /Y/, faithful [Y] and unfaithful [y] both violate *[+round], only the faithful candidate violates the material implication [IDENT[-tense] → *[+round]].

As mentioned, Moreton's (1999) proof that circular chain shifts cannot be modeled in OT rests on the assumption that OT grammars contain only markedness and faithfulness constraints. Inspection of tableaux (6)-(7) quickly reveals that [IDENT[-tense] → *[+round]] is neither a markedness constraint nor a faithfulness constraint, under the definitions employed by Moreton (1999) and presented in (3). It isn't a markedness constraint, since the candidate surface form [y] gets a violation from the complex constraint when the input is /y/, as in (6), but does not get a violation when the input is /Y/, as in (7). Nor is [IDENT[-tense] → *[+round]] a faithfulness constraint, since the fully-faithful candidates (6)a and (7)b both incur violations from it. Instead, given the appropriate circumstances in (7), [IDENT[-tense] → *[+round]] can serve as an input-output *anti*faithfulness constraint: it prefers an unfaithful candidate over a faithful one, because being unfaithful (violating the antecedent) exempts a candidate from a pressure to be unmarked (i.e., to obey the consequent).

This example prompts the very limited conclusion that proposals for a material-implication connective are probably best eschewed. More broadly, it poses the question of which possible connectives should be allowed in OT, and which should be excluded by virtue of violating criterion (2). In the next section, I show which five possible connectives pass that criterion.

4.   Which connectives will yield only markedness and faithfulness?
4.1   Introduction

As described earlier in (1) with respect to OT constraints, if we have two propositions P and Q and a logical operator •, there are four situations in which P•Q can be either true or false:

(8)   a. P is true and Q is true
        b. P is true and Q is false
        c. P is false and Q is true
        d. P is false and Q is false

Because P•Q can be either true or false in each of these situations, there are $2^4 = 16$ possible two-place logical operators in a two-valued zeroth-order logic. With respect to the construction of complex OT constraints, the two relevant logical values at issue are constraint violation and constraint satisfaction (rather than truth and falsehood); in what follows I will use the symbols '*' and '✓', respectively, to denote violation and satisfaction.

The discussion in the following subsections will be based on a truth table (or, as we may call it, a 'violation table') of the following form:

(9)

C_1	✓	✓	*	*
C_2	✓	*	✓	*
$C_1 \bullet C_2$	1st	2nd	3rd	4th

When I speak of $C_1 \bullet C_2$ having a * or a ✓ in one of its 'positions', what I mean is that it is either violated or satisfied in each of the four combinations of violation or satisfaction of Constraint$_1$ and Constraint$_2$, which I number in ascending order from left to right, as in (9).

In order to determine which logical operators • could create a complex constraint $C_1 \bullet C_2$ that is neither markedness nor faithfulness, there are four situations that we have to consider with respect to the identities of C_1 and C_2: when C_1 is a markedness constraint and C_2 a faithfulness constraint; when C_1 is a faithfulness constraint and C_2 is a markedness constraint; when both are faithfulness constraints; and when both are markedness constraints. I now proceed to examine each of these in turn.

4.2   M•F

To begin, we look at the case where the first argument of • is a markedness constraint and the second a faithfulness constraint—that is, the case where we have the following violation table:

(10)

M	✓	✓	*	*
F	✓	*	✓	*
M•F	1st	2nd	3rd	4th

The following must hold in order for M•F to be either a markedness or a faithfulness constraint:

(11)   a. In order to be a faithfulness constraint, M•F must not be violated when F is satisfied, since otherwise it would assign a violation-mark to the fully-faithful candidate. In the violation table used here, • must not have a * in the first or third positions.

b. In order to be a markedness constraint, whether or not M•F is violated must never depend on whether or not F is violated, since otherwise M•F would be sensitive to the input. In the notation used here, • must be identical in the first and second positions, and in the third and fourth positions.

As such, the operators that will yield a faithfulness constraint and those that will yield a markedness constraint when their first argument is markedness and their second faithfulness are those represented in the following violation tables:

(12)   *Operators • for which M•F is faithfulness or markedness*

Faithfulness:

M	✓	✓	*	*
F	✓	*	✓	*
M•F	✓	✓	✓	✓

M	✓	✓	*	*
F	✓	*	✓	*
M•F	✓	*	✓	*

M	✓	✓	*	*
F	✓	*	✓	*
M•F	✓	✓	✓	*

M	✓	✓	*	*
F	✓	*	✓	*
M•F	✓	*	✓	✓

Markedness:

M	✓	✓	*	*
F	✓	*	✓	*
M•F	✓	✓	*	*

M	✓	✓	*	*
F	✓	*	✓	*
M•F	✓	✓	✓	✓

M	✓	✓	*	*
F	✓	*	✓	*
M•F	*	*	✓	✓

M	✓	✓	*	*
F	✓	*	✓	*
M•F	*	*	*	*

4.3   F•M

We now turn to identifying the class of operators • for which F•M will be either markedness or faithfulness. In this case, the violation table is as in (13):

(13)

F	✓	✓	*	*
M	✓	*	✓	*
F•M	1st	2nd	3rd	4th

In this case, the operators that satisfy (2) will have the following properties:

(14)   a. In order for to be a faithfulness constraint, F•M must not be violated when F is satisfied, since otherwise F•M would assign a violation to the fully-faithful candidate. In terms of the violation table above, • must not have a * in either of the first two positions.

b. In order to be a markedness constraint, whether or not F•M is violated must never depend on whether or not F is violated, since otherwise F•M would be sensitive to the input. In the notation used here, • must be identical in the first and third positions, and also in the second and fourth positions.

The operators that satisfy one or the other of these criteria are:

(15)   *Operators • for which F•M is faithfulness or markedness*

Faithfulness: *Markedness*:

F	✓	✓	*	*
M	✓	*	✓	*
F•M	✓	✓	*	*

F	✓	✓	*	*
M	✓	*	✓	*
F•M	✓	*	✓	*

F	✓	✓	*	*
M	✓	*	✓	*
F•M	✓	✓	✓	*

F	✓	✓	*	*
M	✓	*	✓	*
F•M	✓	✓	✓	✓

F	✓	✓	*	*
M	✓	*	✓	*
F•M	✓	✓	*	✓

F	✓	✓	*	*
M	✓	*	✓	*
F•M	*	*	*	*

F	✓	✓	*	*
M	✓	*	✓	*
F•M	✓	✓	✓	✓

F	✓	✓	*	*
M	✓	*	✓	*
F•M	*	✓	*	✓

4.4   F•F

We now consider which operators will pass (2) when both of their arguments are faithfulness constraints. The violation table here is:

(16)

F_1	✓	✓	*	*
F_2	✓	*	✓	*
$F_1•F_2$	1st	2nd	3rd	4th

These are the conditions under which $F_1•F_2$ will yield a faithfulness or a markedness constraint:

(17)   a. In order to be a faithfulness constraint, $F_1•F_2$ must not be violated when F_1 and F_2 are both satisfied, since otherwise $F_1•F_2$ would assign a violation-mark to the fully-faithful candidate. In terms of the notation used here, • must not have a * in the first position.

b. In order to be a markedness constraint, whether $F_1•F_2$ is violated must not depend on whether *either* argument is violated, since otherwise $F_1•F_2$ would be sensitive to the nature of the input. Notationally, this means that • must be identical in all four positions.

The operators that satisfy one or the other of these criteria are:

(18) *Operators • for which $F_1•F_2$ is either faithfulness or markedness*

Faithfulness:

F_1	✓	✓	*	*
F_2	✓	*	✓	*
$F_1•F_2$	✓	*	*	*

F_1	✓	✓	*	*
F_2	✓	*	✓	*
$F_1•F_2$	✓	✓	✓	*

F_1	✓	✓	*	*
F_2	✓	*	✓	*
$F_1•F_2$	✓	✓	*	*

F_1	✓	✓	*	*
F_2	✓	*	✓	*
$F_1•F_2$	✓	✓	*	✓

F_1	✓	✓	*	*
F_2	✓	*	✓	*
$F_1•F_2$	✓	*	✓	✓

F_1	✓	✓	*	*
F_2	✓	*	✓	*
$F_1•F_2$	✓	*	✓	✓

F_1	✓	✓	*	*
F_2	✓	*	✓	*
$F_1•F_2$	✓	*	*	✓

F_1	✓	✓	*	*
F_2	✓	*	✓	*
$F_1•F_2$	✓	✓	✓	✓

Markedness:

F_1	✓	✓	*	*
F_2	✓	*	✓	*
$F_1•F_2$	✓	✓	✓	✓

F_1	✓	✓	*	*
F_2	✓	*	✓	*
$F_1•F_2$	*	*	*	*

4.5   M•M

Lastly, we consider the operators that will pass (2) when both of their arguments are markedness constraints. Here, the relevant violation table is:

(19)

M_1	✓	✓	*	*
M_2	✓	*	✓	*
$M_1•M_2$	1st	2nd	3rd	4th

These are the conditions under which $M_1•M_2$ will yield a faithfulness or a markedness constraint:

(20) a. In order to be a faithfulness constraint, $M_1•M_2$ must never assign a violation-mark to a fully faithful candidate. Since, depending on the input, a fully-faithful candidate could satisfy or violate any markedness constraint, this is only guaranteed when $M_1•M_2$ is never violated, i.e. when • has a ✓ in every position.

b. In order to be a markedness constraint, there are no restrictions on •, since the assignment of violations by both of its arguments are insensitive to the properties of the input.

The operators that satisfy one or the other of these criteria are:

(21)   *Operators • for which M_1•M_2 is either faithfulness or markedness*

Faithfulness:

M_1	✓	✓	*	*
M_2	✓	*	✓	*
M_1•M_2	✓	✓	✓	✓

Markedness: Anything

4.6   Summary

In order for an operator to be fully general and pass criterion (2), it must yield either a faithfulness or a markedness constraint regardless of whether each of its two arguments is faithfulness or markedness. That is, it must appear in the lists of potentially-valid operators adduced in each of the subsections 4.2-4.5. Inspection reveals that the following five operators are the only ones that appear in all four lists:

(22)   *Operators which always yield markedness or faithfulness*

a.

C_1	✓	✓	*	*
C_2	✓	*	✓	*
C_1•C_2	*	*	*	*

b.

C_1	✓	✓	*	*
C_2	✓	*	✓	*
C_1•C_2	✓	✓	✓	✓

c.

C_1	✓	✓	*	*
C_2	✓	*	✓	*
C_1•C_2	✓	✓	*	*

d.

C_1	✓	✓	*	*
C_2	✓	*	✓	*
C_1•C_2	✓	*	✓	*

e.

C_1	✓	✓	*	*
C_2	✓	*	✓	*
C_1•C_2	✓	✓	✓	*

     One of these operators, (22)e, is LC—it produces a complex constraint that is violated if and only if both of its arguments are violated. Of the remaining four, (22)b is clearly of no linguistic interest. Because the complex constraints that it produces are always satisfied, they always assign zero violation-marks to every candidate. These constraints therefore can never exert a preference between any two candidates, making them (and operator (22)b) completely inert with respect to linguistic typology. This leaves us with three further connectives to consider: (22)a and (22)c-d. Their status is not as immediately obvious, and will be explored in the next section.

5.   Bingeing, locality, and *STRUC
5.1   The bingeing problem

Superficially, it may seem obvious that the operators (22)c-d are analytically uninteresting. (The same goes for (22)a, discussion of which will be deferred until the next subsection.) Operator (22)c simply returns a constraint $C_1 \bullet C_2$ that is violated or satisfied exactly when C_1 is violated or satisfied; likewise, (22)d returns a constraint $C_1 \bullet C_2$ that is violated or satisfied exactly when C_2 is violated or satisfied. One may therefore be tempted to think that these operators will simply yield up a constraint that is identical to either C_1 or C_2, and that they therefore can have no effect on linguistic typology, since they do nothing but produce a clone of an existing constraint.

However, it is not necessarily the case that the complex constraint returned by (22)c-d will be entirely identical to one or the other of its arguments. The point of difference arises if we consider cases where one of the constraints that serves as an argument of the connective is violated more than once. To illustrate, let's consider (22)c, and use the symbol ☆ to represent that logical connective; (22)d will behave in a parallel fashion. Suppose that we have a complex constraint $[\text{ONSET}☆X]_{\text{PWd}}$, where X is any constraint. As can be seen in (22)c, the violation or satisfaction of a complex constraint produced using ☆ is sensitive only to the violation or satisfaction of its first argument, so we can omit X from the violation table for $[\text{ONSET}☆X]_{\text{PWd}}$—it simply isn't relevant.

Given this constraint, let's now consider a candidate surface form like [ta.e.o], which contains more than one onsetless syllable. The domain of constraint coordination in $[\text{ONSET}☆X]_{\text{PWd}}$ is the prosodic word, so the logical computation in $[\text{ONSET}☆X]_{\text{PWd}}$'s violation table will be performed a single time for the entire PWd. The candidate word [ta.e.o] violates ONSET—twice in fact—but $[\text{ONSET}☆X]_{\text{PWd}}$ is violated only *once* by that candidate:

(23)

ONSET	✓	✓	**	**
X	✓	*	✓	*
ONSET☆X	✓	✓	*	*

The problem is that our constraint connectives know only two logical values: constraint violation and constraint satisfaction. (Making every numerical degree of violation a separate logical value is clearly absurd, since the logic of constraint coordination would then have infinitely many values.) The complex constraint $[\text{ONSET}☆X]_{\text{PWd}}$ simply says: 'if ONSET is violated somewhere in the prosodic word, assign a violation mark.' It doesn't matter whether a candidate prosodic word contains one, two, or a million onsetless syllables—$[\text{ONSET}☆X]_{\text{PWd}}$ will never assign more than one violation mark per prosodic word. [8]

---

[8] It is a standard assumption of the constraint-connective literature that things can work this way. In Hewitt & Crowhurst (1996) and Crowhurst & Hewitt (1997), the argument for a classical-conjunction operator

The problem with such a constraint is that it can produce implausible effects of a variety which we can refer to as *bingeing*.[9] Suppose that a language has the ranking [ONSET☆X]$_{PWd}$ » DEP. This language will employ epenthesis to achieve a state in which each prosodic word contains zero onsetless syllables, since that is the only circumstance in which [ONSET☆X]$_{PWd}$ is satisfied:

(24)

/taeo/	[ONSET☆X]$_{PWd}$	DEP
→ a. [ta.ʔe.ʔo]		**
b. [ta.ʔe.o]	*!	*
c. [ta.e.ʔo]	*!	*
d. [ta.e.o]	*!	

The fully-faithful candidate (24)d has two onsetless syllables, so it incurs one violation-mark from [ONSET☆X]$_{PWd}$. Candidates (24)b-c do no better on that constraint, since they each have one onsetless syllable per word. The winner, therefore, is (24)a, which has no onsetless syllables and therefore no violation of [ONSET☆X]$_{PWd}$.

This much is typologically innocuous. The problem comes in if some higher-ranked constraint forces just one of the syllables to be onsetless. Consider now what happens if we have a ranking of ANCHOR-LEFT » [ONSET☆X]$_{PWd}$ » DEP, and an input /aeo/:

(25)

/aeo/	ANCHOR-LEFT	[ONSET☆X]$_{PWd}$	DEP
a. [ʔa.ʔe.ʔo]	*!		***
b. [a.ʔe.o]		*	*!
c. [a.ʔe.ʔo]		*	*!*
→ d. [a.e.o]		*	

The constraint ANCHOR-LEFT (McCarthty & Prince 1995) forbids, among other things, epenthesis at the left edge of the word. It therefore penalizes a candidate like (25)a which epenthesizes a consonant at the beginning of the word so as to prevent the syllable headed by [a] from lacking an onset. If ANCHOR-LEFT is top-ranked, it will rule out candidate (25)a, which is the only candidate that satisfies [ONSET☆X]$_{PWd}$, since it is the only candidate that has no onsetless syllables in its PWd.

The elimination of candidate (25)a means that all remaining viable candidates will contain at least one onsetless syllable (the initial one), and consequently will all get a

---

rests, in part, on its ability to collapse the distinction between candidates that have different degrees of violation of some gradient constraint which serves as one of the arguments of the complex constraint.
[9] Credit for this terminology is due to John McCarthy.

single violation-mark from [ONSET☆X]$_{PWd}$, regardless of whether just one, both, or neither of the non-initial syllables are onsetless (as in (25)b-d respectively). Since [ONSET☆X]$_{PWd}$ is indifferent with respect to remaining candidates, the choice is passed down to DEP, which results in (25)d, with no epenthesis, emerging as the winner. Because [ONSET☆X]$_{PWd}$ can't distinguish between having three, two, or one onsetless syllables per PWd, in a situation like (25) where a higher-ranked constraint forces *one* of the syllables to be onsetless, the language will no longer use epenthesis to force *any* of the remaining syllables to have onsets. To speak metaphorically, if the language is compelled to have one onsetless syllable, it will lose all inhibitions and binge on onsetless syllables.

To my knowledge, no language exhibits a bingeing scenario like the one portrayed in (24)-(25). This means that the constraint connectives (22)b-c are not typologically inert, and in fact make *incorrect* predictions—provided that we allow the domain of constraint coordination to operate in the manner assumed in the discussion above. As it turns out, related domain issues arise with respect to LC, and an independently-motivated proposal about how to ensure the 'localness' of local conjunction will also serve to prevent bingeing scenarios, and render (22)b-c typologically inert. This proposal is the topic of the next subsection.

5.2   The solution: Locus-by-locus evaluation

The matter of the domain of conjunction poses overgeneration problems for LC as well (see McCarthy 1999, 2003a,b, Kawahara 2006 for discussion of this point). Consider, for example, a locally-conjoined constraint [*[nasal] & *VCDOBS]$_{PWd}$. This constraint will assign a violation-mark if a single PWd contains both a nasal segment and a voiced obstruent (which need not be one and the same segment). However, it will not assign a violation-mark if the PWd contains nasal segments, but no voiced obstruents; nor will it assign a violaton-mark if voiced obstruents, but no nasals, are to be found in the PWd. The constraint therefore is capable of giving rise to unattested situations like the following:

(26)   *Overgeneration by local conjunction in the domain of the PWd*

   a. *Underlying nasals surface faithfully, if there are no voiced obstruents*:

/na/	[*[nasal] & VCDOBS]$_{PWd}$	MAX	*[nasal]	VCDOBS
→ a. [na]			*	
b. [a]		*!		

   b. *Voiced obstruents surface faithfully, if there are no nasals*:

/de/	[*[nasal] & VCDOBS]$_{PWd}$	MAX	*[nasal]	VCDOBS
→ a. [de]				*
b. [e]		*!		

c. With equal numbers of voiced obstruents and nasals in the input, the nasals are deleted...

/mod/	[*[nasal] & VCDOBS]_{PWd}	MAX	*[nasal]	VCDOBS
a. [mod]	*!		*	*
→ b. [od]		*		*
c. [mo]		*	*!	

d. ...and if there is more of one than of the other, the least numerous type is eliminated:

/bamon/	[*[nasal] & VCDOBS]_{PWd}	MAX	*[nasal]	VCDOBS
a. [bamon]	*!		**	*
b. [ba.o]		**!		*
→ c. [a.mon]		*	**	

The conjoined constraint [*[nasal] & VCDOBS]_{PWd} states that nasals and voiced obstruents cannot co-occur within a single PWd. Even if the conjoined constraint is ranked above faithfulness, words will be able to have nasals *or* voiced obstruents, provided that the markedness constraints against these types of segments are ranked below faithfulness, as seen in (26)a-b. However, a word cannot contain segments of both types, as seen in (26)c. More bizarrely yet, *which* of the two prohibited-from-co-occurring categories (nasals or voiced obstruents) is eliminated can depend on which one there is more of in the input, as seen in the contrast between (26)c and (26)d.

Certainly there is no attested language which allows nasals and voiced obstruents, but does not allow them to co-occur within a single word. The fact that LC is capable of banning the co-occurrence of any two given unrelated types of marked structure within any given prosodic domain suggests that there is something wrong with the original conception of local conjunction. The problem, intuitively, is that the structures that violate each half of the conjoined constraint do not have to have anything to do with one another, if we let the domain of conjunction be wide enough. Some locality restriction needs to be placed on LC in order to eliminate scenarios like the one depicted in (26), which might bring with it the elimination of the free variable of the domain of conjunction in the definition of a conjoined constraint.

One proposal of this sort is advanced by Łubowicz (2005). She proposes to constrain LC using the notion of *locus of violation* (McCarthy 2003a,b). The loci of violation of a constraint are simply the places in the output where it is violated. For markedness constraints, this notion is fairly easy to formalize. If every markedness constraint M has the form "For all output structures having property X, assign a violation-mark" (McCarthy 2003b), then the loci of violation of M are simply all of the pieces of structure[10] in the output satisfying description X. For faithfulness constraints, defining the locus of violation is a bit trickier, but we can intuitively think of the loci of

---

[10] By 'piece of structure' I mean the primitive representational units posited in whatever theory of representations might be assumed in a given analysis—features, root nodes, prosodic constituents like syllables and feet, etc.

violation of a faithfulness constraint F as being all of the pieces cf structure in the output which differ from their input correspondents in the way forbidden by F; the reader is referred to Łubowicz (2005) for a more explicit formalization.

The notion of locus of violation provides us with coherent means to speak of a constraint being violated 'at' a particular piece of structure in the output. It also means that we can speak of a constraint being satisfied 'at' a specific piece of structure. A given piece of structure can be said to be a locus of satisfaction of a constraint C iff it is not a locus of violation of C. Thinking in these terms, we are equipped to generalize Łubowicz's (2005) proposal about locality in LC to apply to complex constraints created using an arbitrary logical operator:

(27) *Locality convention for interpretation of complex constraints*
Given a complex constraint A•B:
For every piece of structure S in the output:
    i. Let a be the logical value (violation or satisfaction) of A at S.
    ii. Let b be the logical value (violation or satisfaction) of B at S.
    iii. Compute a•b using the violation table for •.
    iv. If a•b = *, A•B assigns a violation-mark.

Let's now examine how this convention solves the locality problem for LC. A conjoined constraint [*[nasal] & *VcDObs] will no longer be able to penalize a candidate surface form like [mod], as in (26)c, because there is no locus at which both of the conjuncts are violated. If we ignore autosegmental and prosodic structure (for the sake of simplifying the example), then the only three structural loci in [mod] are the three segments [m], [o], and [d]. The following table shows the logical value of each of the arguments of [*[nasal] & *VcDObs] at each of those three loci:

(28) *Loci of violation and satisfaction in [mod]*

constraint	m	o	d
*[nasal]	*	✓	✓
*VcDObs	✓	✓	*
[*[nasal] & *VcDObs]	✓	✓	✓

As can be seen in (28), because the logical value of the conjoined constraint [*[nasal] & *VcDObs] is computed independently at every locus in the output, it will not assign the logical value 'violated' to any locus in the candidate [mod]. This is because [mod] does not contain any locus at which *both* of the arguments *[nasal] and *VcDObs have the logical value 'violated'. By only assigning marks where both of its conjuncts are violated at the same locus, convention (27)—which is a generalization of the proposal in Łubowicz (2005)—prevents LC from producing unattested long-distance co-occurrence restrictions on unrelated marked structures like those depicted in (26). What this means is that, even if we consider just LC, the notion 'domain of conjunction' makes incorrect predictions, furnishing a motivation to discard this element of LC and impose a locality convention like (27) on the interpretation of the logical operator.

We can now proceed to show that eliminating the domain of conjunction in favor of (27) also prevents (22)c-d from generating bingeing effects, and thereby strips (22)c-d of the ability to affect language typology. The bingeing problem, recall, arises from the fact that a constraint like [Onset☆X]$_{PWd}$, where ☆ is (22)c, makes no distinction between a candidate like [a.ʔe.ʔo], with one onsetless syllable, and a candidate like [a.e.o], with three onsetless syllables. This was illustrated in tableau (25), which is repeated below as (29):

(29)

/aeo/	Anchor-Left	[Onset☆X]$_{PWd}$	Dep
a. [ʔa.ʔe.ʔo]	*!		***
b. [a.ʔe.o]		*	*!
c. [a.ʔe.ʔo]		*	*!*
→ d. [a.e.o]		*	

Suppose now that we discarded the notion of 'domain of conjunction' from the interpretation of complex constraints, and instead assumed that convention (27) is at work. Doing so will now ensure that [Onset☆X] will always assign one violation-mark for every onsetless syllable in the word—thus behaving no differently from Onset in its distribution of marks. Assuming that the loci at which Onset is potentially violated are syllables, then the locus-by-locus assignment of violation marks by [Onset☆X] will be as in (30):

(30)

constraint	a	e	o
Onset	*	*	*
X	?	?	?
[Onset☆X]	*	*	*

constraint	a	ʔe	ʔo
Onset	*	✓	✓
X	?	?	?
[Onset☆X]	*	✓	✓

Since the violation or satisfaction of X is irrelevant to the violation or satisfaction of [Onset☆X], its value at each locus can be ignored, and hence is given as a question mark. At each syllable in the output, [Onset☆X] will be either violated or satisfied depending on whether Onset is violated or satisfied. As can be seen in (30), this means that in [a.e.o], there are three loci at which [Onset☆X] is violated, whereas in [a.ʔe.ʔo] there is only one locus where [Onset☆X] is violated. Consequently, [a.e.o] gets three violation-marks from [Onset☆X], and [a.ʔe.ʔo] gets only one violation mark. Because it distinguishes between these candidates, [Onset☆X] can no longer produce the bingeing effect.

More generally, if the violation or satisfaction of [Y☆X] is independently computed for every locus in the output, [Y☆X] is guaranteed to exactly match the number of marks assigned by Y, provided that Y assigns only a single violation-mark per locus. That is to say, [Y☆X] will always assign to a given candidate exactly the same number of marks that Y does, provided that Y is *categorical* rather than *gradient*.

In OT, a constraint is said to evaluate *gradiently* if a single marked structure or unfaithful mapping can receive more than one violation-mark from the constraint. For instance, with respect to a candidate [pa.ta.(ra.ki)$_{Ft}$]$_{PWd}$, a gradient alignment constraint like ALIGN(foot, left, PWd, left)—for which see McCarthy & Prince (1993)—will assign two violation-marks, because the lone foot is two syllables away from the left edge of the prosodic word. The locus at which this constraint is violated is the candidate's lone foot, and two marks are assigned to this single locus.

McCarthy (2003b) has argued that gradient evaluation is both unnecessary and empirically undesirable. If we embrace this conclusion, then no constraint will assign more than one violation mark per locus. This means that [Y☆X] will always exactly reproduce the number of marks assigned by Y to every candidate, and that therefore [Y☆X] will have no effect on linguistic typology, since its preferences among candidates will be indistinguishable from those of Y.

To summarize, then: adopting criterion (2) means that only the five logical operators shown in (22) are available in natural-language OT grammars. Of these, (22)b is clearly analytically uninteresting. Operator (22)e is LC, and in order to restrain LC's typological predictions, a locality convention like (27) can be argued for. Convention (27), coupled with the (also independently-motivated) assumption that gradient evaluation is banned from OT, means that (22)c-d will produce constraints which are simply clones of one or the other of their arguments, leaving these operators as well without interest in the modeling of linguistic typology. This leaves us with one final operator to consider: (22)a.

5.3 Locus-by-locus evaluation and *STRUC

The violation table for operator (22)a is reproduced below:

(31)

C_1	✓	✓	*	*
C_2	✓	*	✓	*
$C_1 \bullet C_2$	*	*	*	*

Regardless of whether either of its arguments is violated or satisfied, a constraint produced using this operator is invariably violated. This does not mean, however, that such a constraint will be unable to distinguish between different members of the candidate set, since not all candidates will get the same number of violations from it. (For ease of illustration in what follows, I will employ the symbol ◈ for this connective.)

If we assume that the evaluation of candidates by complex constraints is governed by convention (27), then the violation or satisfaction of a complex constraint [A◈B] will be separately computed at every piece of structure in the output. Since the value of [A◈B] will always come out as 'violated', this means that [A◈B] will assign one violation-mark for every piece of structure in the output. Consequently, for any two constraints A and B, [A◈B] is equivalent to the following constraint introduced by Zoll (1993, 1996) and Prince & Smolensky (2004 [1993]):

(32)   *STRUC
       The output contains no structure.

Versions of *STRUC, both in the fully general form given in (32), and in specific subversions like *STRUC(σ), 'the output contains no syllables' (Zoll 1993, 1996) are posited to account for economy-of-structure effects. Because it prohibits *tout court* segments, syllables, feet, and any other type of structure, *STRUC ensures that such structures will emerge in the output only to the least extent required to satisfy higher-ranked constraints.

Unfortunately, positing the existence of *STRUC also leads to a number of highly implausible typological predictions, as extensively argued by Gouskova (2003). For just one example, a language with no consonants can be generated using the ranking shown in the following tableau:

(33)

/keta/	MAX-V	*STRUC(segment)	MAX-C	ONSET
a. [ke.ta]		***!*		
→ b. [e.a]		**	**	**
c. ∅	*!*		**	

The unattestedness of this and similar effects predicted by *STRUC suggests that this constraint—together with the connective ◈, which can create *STRUC from any pair of pre-existing constraints—does not exist. Moreover, *STRUC constraints arguably are not necessary. With suitable assumptions, attested economy effects can be derived from the interaction of ordinary markedness constraints which lack *STRUC's nihilistic character, meaning that economy-of-structure does not need to be posited as a grammatical principle in its own right. This is argued for Grimshaw (2003) for economy effects in syntax and by Gouskova (2003, to appear) for phonology; Trommer (2001) and Wolf (to appear) make similar points regarding morphology.

Where does this leave the theory of constraint connectives? By combining two independently-motivated assumptions—namely that only markedness and faithfulness constraints are allowed, and that the interpretation of complex constraints is subject to locality condition (27)—we can produce a situation in which OT grammars have only two analytically interesting constraint connectives at their disposal: local conjunction, and ◈, which creates *STRUC. Since LC and *STRUC are widely employed in OT analyses, this is a fortuitous situation, insofar as general principles are able to rule out 'exotic' constraint connectives like material implication in favor of those that are familiar. Still, familiarity is not to be confused with validity. As was argued above, there are convincing reasons to judge that *STRUC constraints are both superfluous and undesirable, and so we might find ourselves in a situation where we wanted to retain LC while dispensing with ◈. What might we add to criterion (2) to do this?

By way of a parallel with (2), one straightforward option would be to assume the additional criterion below:

(34)   A constraint connective • is available in a natural-language OT grammar if and only if, for any two constraints A and B which are not * STRUC constraints, A•B is not a *STRUC constraint.

Clearly, this criterion will rule out ◈. The question that must then be asked is, will it also rule out LC?

To answer this question, we need to be explicit about what will count as a *STRUC constraint. More or less following Gouskova (2003), we may assume the following:

(35)   A constraint C is a *STRUC constraint iff there is some markedness scale $M = a_n > a_{n+1} > \ldots a_{m-1} > a_m$ such that C assigns a violation-mark to every non-$\varnothing$ member of M.

What this means is that in any universal scale of phonological elements, there must always be at least one non-zero member that is fully unmarked with respect to some markedness constraint, in order for that constraint not to count as a *STRUC constraint.

Suppose now that there were some locally-conjoined constraint [A&B] which was a *STRUC constraint in the sense of (35). This would mean that there was some markedness scale M such that every non-null element in M violated [A&B]. Given the definition of LC, this would only obtain if every non-null element in M violated both constraint A and constraint B individually. That would mean that both A and B were themselves *STRUC constraints. Thus, LC cannot create *STRUC constraints in the sense of (35) unless it already has pre-existing *STRUC constraints available to serve as the arguments of the conjunction. If *STRUC constraints are banned in principle from the set of primitive markedness constraints in CON (Gouskova 2003), LC will never be able on its own to create a *STRUC constraint. LC passes criterion (34), while ◈ does not.

Lastly, we can note that the argument for LC's surviving criterion (34) holds even if the definition of *STRUC constraints in (35) should prove incorrect. So long as a constraint would qualify as a *STRUC constraint by virtue of assigning a violation mark to some surface structure X, a locally-conjoined constraint would only be a *STRUC constraint if both of its conjuncts were also *STRUC constraints, since the conjoined constraint cannot penalize X unless both of its conjuncts independently penalize X.

6.   Conclusion

Since the inception of OT, LC has been given vastly more empirical attention than other possible constraint connectives. The results that I have argued for in this paper mean that this skew of attention has been correct. The fifteen possible two-place connectives besides LC are either banned or rendered typologically inert by the following three assumptions:

(36)   a. A logical connective is not allowed if it could produce a constraint that is neither markedness nor faithfulness, given arguments that are both either markedness or faithfulness. (=(2))

b. A logical connective is not allowed if it could produce a *STRUC constraint using arguments that are not * STRUC constraints. (=(34))

c. The violation or satisfaction of a complex constraint is separately computed at every structural locus in the output, with one violation-mark being assigned for every locus at which the complex constraint is violated. (=(27))

Each of these assumptions has an independent motivation involving language typology. Assumption (36)a is motivated by the need to exclude circular and infinite chain shifts, (36)b by the need to exclude the unattested predictions of *STRUC constraints, and (36)c by concerns about LC itself, namely the problematic effects of conjoining in overly-broad domains.

Together, the three assumptions in (36) provide a collective rationalization for assuming that LC is the only typologically-interesting logical operator available to natural-language OT grammars. The existence of a non-arbitrary motivation for excluding everything but LC does not, of course, entail that LC itself should be allowed. Even if the difficulties presented in (26) regarding the domain of conjunction are overcome by adopting a locality convention like (27), there remain a number of empirical objections that can be raised both against LC in general and against LC's usefulness for the various analytic purposes for which it has been employed.[11] One notable problem is LC's ability to create 'markedness reversals' (Ito & Mester 1998): a locally-conjoined constraint [IDENT(voice) & NOCODA] will be violated just in case a coda segment undergoes a change in its input voicing specification, making possible unattested languages which have a voicing contrast in codas but not in onsets. (For a proposed solution to this problem, see Łubowicz 2005). Regardless of the fate of LC, however, there do seem to be rational grounds for concluding that there are not any other logical connectives which OT analysts of natural languages need to consider.

---

[11] To give just two representative examples, the application of LC to counterfeeding opacity (Kirchner 1996) is subject to objections raised by, among others, McCarthy (1999, 2003a, 2007), Padgett (2002), and Jesney (2005); the use of [M&F] conjunction to model derived environment effects (Łubowicz 2002, Kurisu 2006) is critiqued by Inkelas (2000), Blaho (2003), Blumenfeld (2003), McCarthy (2003a), Bradley (2007) and Anttila (to appear).

References

Alderete, John D. (1999). *Morphologically Governed Accent in Optimality Theory*. Ph.D. dissertation, University of Massachusetts, Amherst. [ROA-309]

Alderete, John D. (2001). Dominance effects as trans-derivational anti-faithfulness. *Phonology* **18**, pp. 201-253.

Anderson, Stephen R., and Wayles Browne (1973). On keeping exchange rules in Czech. *Papers in Linguistics* **6**, pp. 445-482.

Anttila, Arto (to appear). Derived environment effects in colloquial Helsinki Finnish. In Kristin Hanson and Sharon Inkelas (eds.), *The Nature of the Word: Essays in Honor of Paul Kiparsky*. Cambridge, MA: MIT Press.

Archangeli, Diana, Laura Moll, and Kazutoshi Ohno (1998). Why not *NÇ. In M. Catherine Guber, Derrick Higgins, Kenneth S. Olson, and Tamara Wysocki (eds.), *CLS 34, Part 1: The Main Session*. Chicago: CLS, pp. 1-26.

Baerman, Matthew (2007). Morphological reversals. *Journal of Linguistics* **43**, pp. 33-61.

Baković, Eric (1996). Foot harmony and quantitative adjustments. Ms., Rutgers University, New Brunswick, NJ. [ROA-168]

Balari, Sergio, Rafael Marín, and Teresa Vallverdú (2000). Implicational constraints, defaults, and markedness. GGT Report de Recerca GGT-00-8, Universitat Autònoma de Barcelona. [ROA-396]

Barrie, Michael (2006). Tone circles and contrast preservation. *Linguistic Inquiry* **37**, pp. 131-141.

Blaho, Sylvia (2003). Derived environment effects in Optimality Theory: The case of pre-sonorant voicing in Slovak. In Wayles Browne, Ji-yung Kim, Barbara H. Partee, and Robert A. Rothstein (eds.), *Annual Workshop on Formal Approaches to Slavic Linguistics: The Amherst Meeting 2002*. Ann Arbor: Michigan Slavic Publications, pp. 103-120.

Blumenfeld, Lev (2003). Russian palatalization and stratal OT: Morphology and [back]. In Wayles Browne, Ji-yung Kim, Barbara H. Partee, and Robert A. Rothstein (eds.), *Annual Workshop on Formal Approaches to Slavic Linguistics: The Amherst Meeting 2002*. Ann Arbor: Michigan Slavic Publications, pp. 141-158.

Bradley, Travis (2007). Morphological derived-environment effects in gestural coordination: A case study of Norwegian clusters. *Lingua* **117**, pp. 950-985. [ROA-834]

Bye, Patrik (2006). Eliminating exchange rules in Dholuo. Ms., Universitetet i Tromsø. [Available online at http://www.hum.uit.no/a/bye/Papers/dholuo-squib.pdf]

Crowhurst, Megan (1998). Conflicting directionality and tonal association in Carib of Surinam. Paper presented at 17th West Coast Conference on Formal Linguistics, University of British Columbia, Vancouver.

Crowhurst, Megan, and Mark Hewitt (1997). Boolean operations and constraint interactions in Optimality Theory. Ms., University of North Carolina, Chapel Hill, and Brandeis University, Waltham, MA. [ROA-229]

de Lacy, Paul (2002). Morpheme distinctiveness and feature exchange in DhoLuo. Talk presented at Phonology Group, University College London, 20 November.

Downing, Laura J. (1998). On the prosodic misalignment of onsetless syllables. *Natural Language and Linguistic Theory* **16**, pp. 1-52.

Downing, Laura J. (2000). Morphological and prosodic constraints on Kinande verbal reduplication. *Phonology* **17**, pp. 1-38.

Eisner, Jason (1999). Doing OT in a straitjacket. Colloquium presented at University of California, Los Angeles, June 14. [Handout available online at http://www.cs.jhu.edu/~jason/papers/eisner.ucla99.handout.large.pdf]

Flack, Kathryn (2007a). *The Sources of Phonological Markedness*. Ph.D. dissertation, University of Massachusetts Amherst.

Flack, Kathryn (2007b). Inducing functionally grounded constraints. Ms., University of Massachusetts Amherst. [ROA-920]

Gouskova, Maria (2003). *Deriving Economy: Syncope in Optimality Theory*. Ph.D. dissertation, University of Massachusetts Amherst. [ROA-610]

Gouskova, Maria (to appear). DEP: Beyond epenthesis. *Linguistic Inquiry* **38**.

Gregersen, Edgar (1972). Consonant polarity in Nilotic. In Erhard Voeltz (ed.), *Proceedings of the Third Annual Conference on African Linguistics*. Bloomington: Indiana University Press, pp. 105-109.

Grimshaw, Jane (2003). Economy of structure in OT. In Angela C. Carpenter, Paul de Lacy, and Andries W. Coetzee (eds.), *University of Massachusetts Occasional Papers in Linguistics* **26**: *Papers in Optimality Theory II*. Amherst: GLSA, pp. 81-120. [ROA-434]

Hayes, Bruce (1999). Phonetically driven phonology: The role of Optimality Theory and inductive grounding. In Michael Darnell, Frederick J. Newmeyer, Michael Noonan, Edith Moravcsik, and Kathleen Wheatley (eds.), *Functionalism and Formalism in Linguistics: Volume 1: General Papers*. Amsterdam: John Benjamins, pp. 243-285. [ROA-158]

Hewitt, Mark S., and Megan J. Crowhurst (1996). Conjunctive constraints and templates in Optimality Theory. In Kiyomi Kusumoto (ed.), *Proceedings of the North East Linguistic Society* **26**. Amherst: GLSA, pp. 101-116.

Hsieh, Hsin-I (1970). The psychological reality of tone sandhi rules in Taiwanese. In *Papers from the Sixth Regional Meeting, Chicago Linguistic Society*. Chicago: CLS, pp. 489-503.

Hsieh, Hsin-I (1975). How generative is phonology? In E.F.K. Koerner (ed.), *The Transformational-Generative Paradigm and Modern Linguistic Theory*. Amsterdam: John Benjamins, pp. 109-144.

Hsieh, Hsin-I (1976). On the unreality of some phonological rules. *Lingua* **38**, pp 1-19.

Inkelas, Sharon (2000). Phonotactic blocking through structural immunity. In Barbara Stiebels and Dieter Wunderlich (eds.), *Lexicon in Focus*. Berlin: Akademie Verlag, pp. 7-40. [ROA-366]

Ito, Junko, and Armin Mester (1998). Markedness and word structure: OCP effects in Japanese. Ms., University of California, Santa Cruz. [ROA-255]

Jesney, Karen (2005). *Chain Shift in Phonological Acquisition*. MA thesis, University of Calgary.

Kawahara, Shigeto (2006). A faithfulness ranking projected from a perceptibility scale: The case of [+voice] in Japanese. *Language* **82**, pp. 536-574.

Key, Michael, and Lee Bickmore (in prep.). Span binarity and overlap. Ms., University of Massachusetts Amherst and State University of New York. Albany.

Kirchner, Robert (1996). Synchronic chain shifts in Optimality Theory. *Linguistic Inquiry* **27**, pp. 341-350.

Kurisu, Kazutaka (2001). *The Phonology of Morpheme Realization*. Ph.D. dissertation, University of California, Santa Cruz. [ROA-490]

Kurisu, Kazutaka (2006). Weak derived environment effect. Paper presented at NELS 37, University of Illinois, Urbana-Champaign.

Lin, Hwei-Bing (1988). *Contextual Stability of Taiwanese Tones*. Ph.D. dissertation, University of Connecticut, Storrs.

Łubowicz, Anna (2002). Derived environment effects in Optimality Theory. *Lingua* **112**, pp. 243-280. [ROA-765]

Łubowicz, Anna (2003). *Contrast Preservation in Phonological Mappings*. Ph.D. dissertation, University of Massachusetts Amherst. [ROA-554]

Łubowicz, Anna (2005). Locality of conjunction. In John Alderete, Chung-hye Han, and Alexei Kochetov (eds), *Proceedings of the Twenty-Fourth West Coast Conference on Formal Linguistics*. Somerville, MA: Cascadilla Proceedings Project, pp. 254-262. [Lingref #1230; ROA-764]

Lyman, Larry, and Rosemary Lyman (1977). Choapan Zapotec phonology. In William R. Merrifield (ed.), *Studies in Otomanguean Phonology*. Dallas: Summer Institute of Linguistics/University of Texas at Austin, pp. 137-162.

McCarthy, John J. (1999). Sympathy and phonological opacity. *Phonology* **16**, pp. 331-399.

McCarthy, John J. (2002). *A Thematic Guide to Optimality Theory*. Cambridge: Cambridge University Press.

McCarthy, John J. (2003a). Comparative Markedness. *Theoretical Linguistics* **29**, pp. 1-51.

McCarthy, John J. (2003b). OT constraints are categorical. *Phonology* **20**, pp. 75-138.

McCarthy, John J. (2007). *Hidden Generalizations: Phonological Opacity in Optimality Theory*. London: Equinox.

McCarthy, John J., and Alan Prince (1993). Generalized Alignment. In Geert Booij and Jaap van Marle (eds.), *Yearbook of Morphology 1993*. Dordrecht: Kluwer, pp. 79-153. [ROA-7]

McCarthy, John J. and Alan Prince (1995). Faithfulness and reduplicative identity. In Jill N. Beckman, Laura Walsh Dickey, and Suzanne Urbanczyk (eds.), *University of Massachusetts Occasional Papers in Linguistics* **18**: *Papers in Optimality Theory*. Amherst: GLSA, pp. 249-384. [ROA-103]

McCawley, James D. (1974). [Review of *The Sound Pattern of English*]. *International Journal of American Linguistics* **40**, pp. 50-88.

Moreton, Elliot (1999). Non-computable functions in Optimality Theory. Ms., University of Massachusetts, Amherst. [ROA-364]

Mortensen, David (2004). Abstract scales in phonology. Ms., University of California, Berkeley. [ROA-667]

Myers, James (2006). Tone circles and chance. Ms., National Chung Cheng University, Min-Hsiung, Chia-Yi, Taiwan. [ROA-843]

Myers, James, and Jane Tsay (2002). Neutralization in Taiwanese tone sandhi. Ms.,
     National Chung Cheng University, Min-Hsiung, Chia-Yi, Taiwan.
Okoth-Okombo, Duncan (1982). *DhoLuo Morphophonemics in a Generative
     Framework*. Berlin: Dietrich Reimer.
Padgett, Jaye (2002). Constraint conjunction versus grounded constraint subhierarchies in
     Optimality Theory. Ms., University of California, Santa Cruz. [ROA-530]
Peng, Shu-hui (1998). Evidence for a UR-free account of tone sandhi in Taiwanese.
     Poster presented at the Sixth Conference of Laboratory Phonology, University of
     York.
Prince, Alan, and Paul Smolensky (2004 [1993]). *Optimality Theory: Constraint
     Interaction in Generative Grammar*. Oxford: Blackwell. [ROA-537]
Pulleyblank, Douglas (2006). Minimizing UG: Constraints upon constraints. In Donald
     Baumer, David Montero, and Michael Scanlon (eds.), *Proceedings of the 25th
     West Coast Conference on Formal Linguistics*. Somerville, MA: Cascadilla
     Proceedings Project, pp. 15-39. [Lingref #1430]
Smolensky, Paul (1993). Harmony, markedness, and phonological activity. Talk
     presented at Rutgers Optimality Workshop I, New Brunswick, NJ. [Handout
     available as ROA-87]
Smolensky, Paul (1995). On the structure of the constraint component CON of UG.
     Talk presented at University of California, Los Angeles. [Handout available as
     ROA-86]
Smolensky, Paul (1997). Constraint interaction in generative grammar II: Local
     conjunction, or random rules in Universal Grammar. Talk presented at Hopkins
     Optimality Theory Workshop/Maryland Mayfest, Baltimore.
Trommer, Jochen (2001). *Distributed Optimality*. Doctoral dissertation, Universität
     Potsdam.
Trommer, Jochen (2005). Against antifaithfulness in Luo. Paper presented at 3rd Old
     World Conference in Phonology, Budapest. [Abstract available online at
     http://www.uni-leipzig.de/~jtrommer/05.pdf]
Tsay, Jane, and James Myers (1996). Taiwanese tone sandhi as allomorph selection. In
     Jan Johnson, Matthew L. Judge, and Jeri L. Moxley (eds.), *Proceedings of the
     22nd Annual Meeting of the Berkeley Linguistics Society*. Berkeley: BLS, pp. 394-
     405.
Tseng, Chin-Chin (1995). *Taiwanese Prosody: An Integrated Analysis of Acoustic and
     Perceptual Data*. Ph.D. dissertation, University of Hawai'i, Mānoa.
Wang, Samuel Hsu (1995). *Experimental Studies in Taiwanese Phonology*. Taipei:
     Crane.
Wolf, Matthew (2007). For an autosegmental theory of mutation. In Leah Bateman,
     Adam Werle, Michael O'Keefe, and Ehren Reilly (eds.), *University of
     Massachusetts Occasional Papers in Linguistics 32: Papers in Optimality Theory
     III*. Amherst: GLSA, pp. 315-404. [ROA-754]
Wolf, Matthew (to appear). Lexical insertion occurs in the phonological component. In
     Bernard Tranel (ed.), *Understanding Allomorphy: Perspectives from Optimality
     Theory*. London: Equinox. [ROA-912]
Yue-Hashiomoto, Anne O. (1986). Tonal flip-flop in Chinese dialects. *Journal of
     Chinese Linguistics* 14, pp. 161-182.

Zhang, Jie, Yuwen Lai, and Craig Turnbull-Sailor (2006). Wug-testing the "tone circle" in Taiwanese. In Donald Baumer, David Montero, and Michael Scanlon (eds.), *Proceedings of the 25th West Coast Conference on Formal Linguistics.* Somerville, MA: Cascadilla Proceedings Project, pp. 453-461. [Lingref #1479]

Zoll, Cheryl (1993). Directionless syllabification and ghosts in Yɛwelmani. Ms., University of California, Berkeley. [ROA-28]

Zoll, Cheryl (1996). *Parsing Below the Segment in a Constraint-Based Framework.* Ph.D. dissertation, University of California, Berkeley. [ROA-143]

Department of Linguistics
University of Massachusetts Amherst
South College, Room 226
150 Hicks Way
Amherst, MA 01003 USA

mwolf@linguist.umass.edu

www.ingramcontent.com/pod-product-compliance
Lightning Source LLC
Chambersburg PA
CBHW052145070326
40689CB00050B/2109